Ed Gallagher traces important theological themes from the book of Exodus to reveal how they relate prominently to teachings developed by New Testament writers. These well-known but difficult themes are often misunderstood by many in our Restoration heritage. Gallagher provides clarity and fresh insight into their meaning and reflects on their implications for Christians today. This is a delightful and informative read. The church needs more of these kinds of resources written by scholars like Gallagher.

— DAVE BLAND, Professor of Homiletics and Co-Director of the Doctor of Ministry Program, Harding School of Theology

Gallagher crafts a tightly woven tapestry connecting the threads of the Book of Exodus to New Testament Christianity and to Christ himself. He includes an abundance of specialized knowledge to enrich and inform the reader. . . . fresh, insightful, and challenging. . . . gives the reader a broader perspective of the history of ancient Israel.

—DEBBIE DUPUY, author of *It's a Red-Letter Day!*

Dr. Gallagher has produced a splendid and impressive work. In exploring the biblical narrative from the book of Exodus, Gallagher has mined rich resources from heavy theological hitters while asking relevant questions for today. It is rare to find a practical, devotional-level work that is rooted in the text of scripture, engages thoughtfully with the history of Christian theology, and provides refreshing application for everyday life. This is a welcome resource for plumbing the depths of scripture to grow ever closer to the beautiful heart of God.

—NATHAN GUY, President of Mars Hill Bible School, Florence, Alabama

Gallagher's newest book is an excellent study of Exodus. It brings the ancient text into conversation with both ancient Jewish and modern Christian readers. It tackles problems of linguistics, theology, and hermeneutics, but does not neglect practical applications to a life of faith. Gallagher is at home in the refined world of scholarship, but also references resources accessible to any reader. This is the rare book to which Bible students can return time and again as they grow in education and knowledge, picking up deeper nuggets of insight with each new encounter.
—JUSTIN ROGERS, Associate Professor of Biblical Studies and Director of the Graduate School of Theology, Freed-Hardeman University

Offering far more than a close look at Exodus, this book is akin to a theological field guide for the biblical terrain: exceedingly helpful for discerning Exodus's prominent features, and for proceeding to draw faith-enriching connections across Old and New Testaments. Gallagher here makes a welcome addition to the body of literature that not only brings together biblical and theological scholarship, but also renders their concepts accessible to a wide readership.
—LAUREN SMELSER WHITE, Assistant Professor of Theology, Lipscomb University

THE BOOK OF EXODUS

Explorations in Christian Theology

Ed Gallagher

THE BOOK OF EXODUS: EXPLORATIONS IN CHRISTIAN THEOLOGY
Cypress Bible Study Series
Published by Heritage Christian University Press

Copyright © 2020 by Ed Gallagher

Manufactured in the United States of America

Cataloging-in-Publication Data
Gallagher, Ed (Edmon Louis), 1979–
The Book of Exodus: Explorations in Christian Theology / by Ed Gallagher
p. cm. — (Cypress Bible Study Series)
Includes bibliographic references (p.) and indexes.
ISBN 978-1-7320483-6-2 (pbk.)
1. Bible. Exodus—Criticism, interpretation, etc. 2. Theology, Doctrinal.
I. Author. II. Title. III. Series
BS1245.2 .G35 2019   222.1206—DC20
Library of Congress Control Number: 2019947455

Cover design by Brittany McGuire and Brad McKinnon
Interior design by Brad McKinnon
Image: Huqoq synagogue mosaic panel of Pharaoh's soldiers drowning in the Red Sea: detail showing Pharaoh's soldier being swallowed by a fish.
Reproduction permission: Jodi Magness
Photo credit: Jim Haberman

All rights reserved. No part of this publication may be reproduced, distributed, stored in a retrieval system, or transmitted in any form or by any means without the prior written permission of the publisher, except in the case of brief quotations embodied in critical reviews and certain other noncommercial uses permitted by copyright law.

For information:
Heritage Christian University Press
3625 Helton Drive
PO Box HCU
Florence, AL 35630
www.hcu.edu

*For Tim and Judy Gallagher,
my parents,
with much love and appreciation*

Contents

Preface		ix
1.	Moses through the Lens of the New Testament	3
2.	God's Name	23
3.	Pharaoh's Hard Heart	49
4.	Passover	83
5.	Bread from Heaven	103
6.	Water from a Rock	121
7.	Kingdom of Priests	139
8.	The Law at Sinai	161
9.	Blood of the Covenant	195
10.	God's Dwelling Place	213
11.	Ark of the Covenant	233
12.	Moses' Shining Face	257
13.	The Divine Cloud	277
Appendix: Questions for Reflection		301
Glossary		311
Bibliography		315
Subject Index		329
Scripture Index		335

Preface

The book of Exodus is foundational for Christian theology. It's not necessarily unique in that regard. The book of Genesis is also foundational for Christian theology, as is the book of Isaiah, and the Psalms, and the list could go on. Or should we be saying that Jesus is foundational for Christian theology? Yes, of course, but then again, we know about Jesus mostly from the New Testament, so maybe the New Testament should be considered as the foundation? It would be hard to argue with any of these suggestions, but let me point out that the Old Testament precedes the New Testament (chronologically), and preceded the earthly existence of Jesus, and the Old Testament was taken as foundational by both Jesus and the writers of the New Testament (cf., e.g., Matt 5:17; Luke 24:27; Rom 15:4). The New Testament writers established the identity of Jesus by quoting the Old Testament (cf. Matt 1:23), and Jesus established his own identity in the same way (cf. Luke 4:21). C. H. Dodd was right: the Old Testament is "the substructure of New Testament theology."[1]

If the entire Old Testament is, then, foundational to Christian theology—well, I guess we could try to rank the most important Old Testament books to try to figure out which parts are the *most* foundational. Without going through that exercise, we can safely say that the book of Exodus would rank near the top. Certainly it is one of the most important books in the Hebrew Bible, the book containing the revelation of God's name to Moses (3:14–15), the revelation of God's character to Moses (34:6–7), the definitive display of divine grace in the Old Testament through the rescue of God's enslaved people (the exodus, from which the book derives its name), the giving of the Law (starting in ch. 20), and the construction of God's dwelling place (the tabernacle) in the midst of his people (chs. 25–40). Those themes alone would make the book of Exodus important in any theology arising from the Bible, but even beyond that, these same themes and others appear frequently and prominently in the New Testament so that no account of Christian theology can avoid the book of Exodus.

You are not holding a commentary but a series of studies on selected themes and passages in the book of Exodus. I chose these particular themes and passages based on their prominence in the New Testament. Not everything in Exodus makes an appearance in the New Testament; a lot of Exodus does, but even some important parts of Exodus,

---

1. See the subtitle of C. H. Dodd, *According to the Scriptures: The Substructure of New Testament Theology* (New York: Scribner, 1953).

such as the Golden Calf episode (Exod 32), receive hardly any attention in the New Testament, nor in this book. But even some material from Exodus that comes up quite a bit in the New Testament receives relatively little attention here, such as the Ten Commandments, which occupies us in this book only as part of the chapter on the Law (Chapter 8). I think this book will help you understand Exodus, but my aim in writing these chapters was less in explaining Exodus than in investigating how the New Testament uses themes from Exodus. Here we are exploring Christian theology, using Exodus as a launching pad.

This is a book for the church. It was written for one specific church, the Sherrod Avenue Church of Christ in Florence, Alabama. I did not teach this material; I wrote it week-by-week for others to teach. I'd like to take this opportunity to thank the three men that worked with this material in its trial-run during the Spring of 2019: Don Harriman, Justin Pannell, and Don Snodgrass. There are thirteen chapters here because these men taught the material over the course of a thirteen-week quarter. They would read the lessons in preparation for each Sunday, and the students would receive weekly ahead of class time the five relevant "discussion questions" now collected in the appendix. The material in each chapter is, of course, far too much to cover in a typical Bible class period; I wanted my teachers to feel comfortable that they knew something about the biblical text and how it had been received.

You will notice that there is a great deal of emphasis in this book on what is now called "Reception History" of the Bible, i.e., the history of interpretation. In some ways this path was determined by my choice to focus on Exodus *in the New Testament*, which is already a reception kind of study. But also I have a particular interest in the history of biblical interpretation. That's the area in which I got my doctorate. The study of how people have interpreted Scripture throughout the centuries interests me deeply, I guess because these ancient (or more modern) readers of the Bible see things that I have never seen before; they have questions and concerns that do not occur to me. But also I think this kind of approach to biblical study—looking at how it has been received—is very helpful to Christians, because we want to know not only what the text might have meant two or three thousand years ago, but how it has led to the Christian doctrines and practices that we take for granted today. In our study of the history of interpretation of Exodus, we'll encounter some people that you may never have heard of before; Wikipedia will almost always know who they are, so look there first. But let me go ahead and introduce you to some of them here.

Broadly we're concerned here with three avenues of biblical interpretation: ancient Jewish interpretation, Christian interpretation (not just ancient), and modern scholarly interpretation. Since modern scholarship typically appears in books and other forms of published material that are familiar to us, I'll not introduce you to it here; you should be able to find it through the footnotes. But the other avenues of interpretation will probably be a little unfamiliar to many modern readers, so I'll mention briefly what they are and how to get a hold of them. The Christian interpretation that concerns us here may be ancient or medieval or early modern, or even later. The ancient Christian literature is often available in English translation in one of several series of such translations.[2] But often this literature can be found in a decent English translation online. I would highly encourage you to read directly the author and work I'm citing, and don't just take my word for what the person says. I recommend you do this partly because reading important Christian interpretations by John Calvin or Origen or Thomas Aquinas is fun, partly because it's educational, and partly because it's interesting and helpful to see exactly how these ancient or medieval (or whatever) authors say something. Since the literature is available at your fingertips these days, just go ahead and read at least some of it. Same thing for the ancient Jewish literature. We've got all kinds of ancient Jewish literature, and I cite a lot of it in this book, but probably Philo and Josephus more than the other stuff. Let me tell you about them: They both wrote in Greek, and lived in the first century AD, but Philo lived in the early first century and in Egypt, while Josephus lived in the late first century and in Palestine and later Rome. Philo was a philosopher and biblical interpreter; most of his writings deal with Genesis and Exodus. Josephus was a historian, who wrote four different books, but the one that concerns us here is the *Antiquities of the Jews*, in twenty volumes, the first half of which narrates the history of the Bible. Aside from these two first-century Greek Jewish sources, we also have the Dead

---

2. Such as the Fathers of the Church series published now by The Catholic University of America Press; the Ancient Christian Writers series published by Paulist; and the Popular Patristics series published by St. Vladimir's Seminary Press.

Sea Scrolls, the Septuagint, Apocrypha, Pseudepigrapha, and Rabbinic Literature. All of these things are briefly explained in the Glossary at the end of this book.

Since this is a book for the church, I have not thought it beneficial to enter into many of the questions that scholars often concern themselves with in regard to the history of the text. Here I have focused solely on the form of the text as it is usually read in churches, with, of course, some attention to the Hebrew text underlying our major English translations. That is not to say that I have not benefited from scholarship in various ways, and readers will notice that this book has many more footnotes than a typical book of Sunday school lessons. In addition to documenting my own indebtedness to the works of others, I hope these footnotes will serve as a guide for interested readers to find further information on a topic. But for those who want at hand a full-scale critical commentary, the best available currently is the two-volume commentary by William Propp in the Anchor Bible series. Another good commentary, one that (unlike Propp) is explicitly interested in Christian theology, is the older commentary by Brevard Childs. For a brief introduction to Exodus for beginners, see Tremper Longman's little book. The bibliography gives full publication information for these volumes, and many more, besides.

No single Bible version serves as the basis for the quotations in this book. I have used mostly (probably) the New Revised Standard Version and the Christian Standard Bible, but even these I have freely altered when I wanted the quotation to match the original language more closely or for some other reason. Typically whatever point I am trying to make is not based on any particular English translation. If I were you, I would use a standard translation as the basis for study, and make frequent comparison to another standard translation. If you come across a difference in translation that seems pretty significant, you should check the NET Bible (available freely online), which has some great textual notes.

The second chapter of this book concerns God's name. Readers will find there that the name of God can be represented by the four capitalized English letters YHWH. I have used this form of God's name throughout the book, often inserting it into quotations of Scripture where published translations have instead "the Lord." I follow this practice to make it clear where the biblical text uses the particular name of Israel's God. I'm sure it will take you some getting used to, but I hope it won't prove too distracting. By the way, whenever I see these four English letters YHWH, the word I say in my head is Adonai. Chapter 2 will explain why.

The footnotes are littered with references to websites, particularly Wikipedia, Google Maps, and YouTube. I acknowledge that you should not trust everything you read on Wikipedia—but, really, what resource can you not say that about? (*Don't trust everything you read in this book, either! I'm sure some of it is wrong.) If you have been distrustful of Wikipedia, I recommend you go to YouTube and watch the 15-min. video called Crash Course: Using Wikipedia; it'll tell you about the pitfalls but also about the wonders of this online encyclopedia. I'll just say that I find Wikipedia essential for Bible study. Same for Google Maps. (I don't find YouTube essential, just fun.) Let me encourage you to make constant use of Google Maps when you study the Bible. When Genesis says Abraham went some place, look up where that place is, and get "directions" to it from where Abraham had last been, and see how far Abraham walked, and think of how long it might have taken him to walk that far. Do the same for Moses, and Jesus, and Paul.

—

Brad McKinnon, Jamie Cox, and Brittany McGuire provided invaluable service in putting these studies into book form. Much of what is useful (the index and bibliography) and beautiful (the layout and cover) about this book is due entirely to them. Thank you. And to the Sherrod Ave. Church of Christ, thank you for enduring these lessons and for employing me in a capacity that would force me to study and write. As I wrote these chapters in the spring of 2019, I spent too many evenings at the computer banging at the keyboard rather than watching *The Andy Griffith Show* with my family. I hope someday you'll read this book, Miriam, and Evelyn, and Josiah, and Jasmine, and Marvin (and now Jada, too, though you weren't with us yet while I was writing it)—if for no other reason than to see what I was up to that spring. And Jodi, thanks for loving me, thanks for being patient with me, and thanks for letting me live with you.

—

The chapters that follow are explorations in Christian theology. Explorers often get things wrong, and I'm sure that's true here as well. I don't know which parts are wrong, else I would change them. But I have every confidence that some of what I say here is wrong. Let me assure you that in some of the discussions that follow (I think especially about Chapter 3 and Chapter 8), I am out of my depth. In fact, I sent Chapter 3 on Pharaoh's hard heart to several people to get their thoughts. Some agreed with my interpretation, others didn't. Two of the ones to whom I sent the chapter are experts in sixteenth-century theology, and I sent it to them to see what they thought about my take on Calvinism and Arminianism. Neither one of them mentioned anything about what I wrote in that regard, but both of them told me my biblical interpretation was off base. They're probably right and I'm probably wrong, but I can't quite see my way there, yet. So, like Pilate, what I have written I have written—because it makes the most sense to me right now. But I'll keep thinking about the issues, and I hope the chapters—all these chapters—help you, dear reader, think about the issues, too.

Let's start exploring.

THE BOOK OF EXODUS

I

Moses Through the Lens of the New Testament

Americans love their Founding Fathers. I guess that's true of all nations. As I write, there is a play, a musical, about the life of Alexander Hamilton that has reignited interest not only in this particular Founding Father but really in the whole period of the American founding. The Fathers have such authority that if you can trace an idea back to James Madison or Thomas Jefferson or John Adams, that idea automatically gains authority, just by virtue of the fact that these Founding Fathers expressed it. People on the left and the right exert enormous amounts of energy interpreting the wording of documents written by Founding Fathers, sometimes even their letters or journals or other personal writings. Since we trace ourselves as a people back to them, we feel like they have significant authority to tell us how our nation ought to operate. Even on an issue like slavery, an issue that was (shall we say?) problematic for that founding generation, an issue on which most of us would want to distance ourselves from their ideas and compromises—still even on this issue we care very deeply about what they thought and said, as if—because we attribute to these men such authority on other matters like the separation of powers and the freedom of expression—we mourn that we have to depart from them so radically on this issue.

Moses was the Founding Father of the Israelite nation. (Yes, I know, God was the "Father" of Israel [cf. Exod 4:22; Hos 11:1], but we're talking about human founders.) But he was more than the Israelite equivalent of any individual American Founding Father—Moses was more than the Israelite George Washington, or Thomas Jefferson, or James Madison. He was like all of those fathers rolled into one. Moses was the national hero who rescued Israel from foreign oppression (Washington), he was the sage who contemplated the deep things of the universe (Jefferson), and he was the great lawgiver promulgating the Israelite Constitution (Madison). But he was still more than a supersized Founding Father combining the traits of Washington, Jefferson, and Madison, because Moses communed with God like no human could ever hope for (cf. Num 12:5-8; Exod 33:11). Moses was called by God (Exod 3) and spoke the words of God, so that the authority Moses carried was beyond any authority enjoyed by even the best of humans.

The New Testament affirms the authority of Moses and seeks to represent the doctrine proclaimed by Jesus as in harmony with the doctrine proclaimed by Moses. Indeed, Jesus himself said, "If you believed Moses, you would believe me, because he wrote about me" (John 5:46). Moses' name appears in the New Testament more times (80x) than the name of any other Old Testament character, including Abraham (72x). Not only are his words considered authoritative in the New Testament, but his life serves as an example of faith for followers of Jesus.

MOSES IN THE NEW TESTAMENT

The name Moses appears in the New Testament 80 times, about half of them in the Gospels (38x).[1] Almost always these references simply regard his writings, the Law: "Moses said," or "Moses commanded," or some such. Nobody in the New Testament ever disagrees with Moses; nobody ever says, "Moses said such-and-such, but he was wrong" or "we should ignore what Moses said." Aside from references to what Moses said, there are a few references to what he did. Once Jesus mentioned that Moses lifted up a snake in the wilderness (John 3:14; cf. Num 21:9), and once he made it clear that Moses was not responsible for the miraculous gift of manna (John 6:32). And Moses made a cameo appearance with Elijah on the mount of Transfiguration (Matt 17:3; Mark 9:4–5; Luke 9:30, 33). In the rest of the New Testament,[2] it's the same: Moses is mentioned almost always as a writer or lawgiver, more rarely as a character who performs

---

1. Matthew (7x) 8:4; 17:3–4; 19:7–8; 22:24; 23:2; Mark (8x) 1:44; 7:10; 9:4–5; 10:3–4; 12:19, 26; Luke (10x) 2:22; 5:14; 9:30, 33; 16:29, 31; 20:28, 37; 24:27, 44; John (13x) 1:17, 45; 3:14; 5:45–46; 6:32; 7:19, 22–23; 8:5; 9:28–29.

2. Acts (19x), 3:22; 6:11, 14; 7:20, 22, 29, 31–32, 35, 37, 40, 44; 13:29; 15:1, 5, 21; 21:21; 26:22; 28:23; Romans (4x) 5:14; 9:15; 10:5, 19; 1 Corinthians (2x) 9:9; 10:2; 2 Corinthians (3x) 3:7, 13, 15; 2 Timothy 3:8; Hebrews (11x) 3:2–3, 5, 16; 7:14; 8:5: 9:19; 10:28; 11:23–24; 12:21; Jude 9; Rev 15:3.

actions. There are some exceptions: Paul develops a theological point from the fact that Moses used to veil his face when he approached God in the Tent of Meeting (2 Cor 3:7–18; cf. Exod 34:29–35); Paul mentions Moses opposing the Egyptian magicians (2 Tim 3:8)[3]; and he makes the assertion that the Israelites were "baptized into Moses" (1 Cor 10:2) in reference to the crossing of the Red Sea.

There are two New Testament passages that give a more extensive treatment of Moses as a character: Stephen's speech in Acts 7 and the briefer account in the "Hall of Faith" chapter, Hebrews 11. Let's start with Hebrews 11.[4]

Moses as an Example of Faith: Hebrews 11

Moses is not the main character of Hebrews 11; he's not the greatest Old Testament example of faith, or the person who receives the most attention for his faith. That would be Abraham, who merits twelve verses here. The preeminence of Abraham in a chapter on faith should occasion no surprise, since Paul has the same focus in Rom 4 and Gal 3. But the writer of Hebrews dedicates seven verses to Moses' faith (vv. 23–29), the second most in the chapter. All of the material that Heb 11 mentions regarding Moses derives from the

---

3. The magicians are unnamed in Exodus, but Paul calls them Jannes and Jambres, in accordance with Jewish tradition. See https://en.wikipedia.org/wiki/Jannes_and_Jambres.

4. Moses was the most famous character from the Bible in the world at large in antiquity; for accounts of Moses among pagan authors, see John G. Gager, *Moses in Greco-Roman Paganism* (Nashville: Abingdon, 1972), 25–72.

Book of Exodus, actually the first half the Book of Exodus, and most of it comes from the second chapter of Exodus.

The first thing Heb 11 mentions about Moses is really not about his faith at all, but about the faith of his parents, Amram and Jochebed (cf. Exod 6:20). They are commended for their bravery in the face of the Egyptian king's command to drown all newborn Israelite boys (cf. Exod 1:22). Instead of obeying the Pharaoh, Amram and Jochebed hid Moses for three months (Heb 11:23; cf. Exod 2:2).[5] This act of defiance against the governmental authority demonstrated bravery motivated by faith.[6]

When the writer of Hebrews starts talking about actions performed by Moses himself, he presents an interesting take on Exodus 2. According to Exodus, when Moses became an adult, he went out to his brothers, the Israelites (2:11).[7] Exodus does not tell us why Moses wanted to visit them or even

---

5. Hebrews also notices that the account in Exodus highlights the child's "beauty" (Exod 2:2), which was translated in the Greek Septuagint with the word *asteios*. This word appears in the New Testament only twice, both times in descriptions of the beautiful baby Moses (Acts 7:20; Heb 11:23). Josephus (*Antiquities of the Jews* 2.231) also stress the great beauty of Moses: "And it happened that many people who happened to meet him as he was borne along the road turned back at the sight of the child and left aside their serious affairs and used their time to view him."

6. When Amram and Jochebed finally did place their son in the Nile, Philo says that they reproached themselves (*Life of Moses* 1.11).

7. Exodus never tells us how old Moses is at this point in his life, though it does tell us later that he was 80 years old when the exodus happened (7:7), which makes sense because Moses was 120 at his death (Deut 34:7), and he led the Israelites in the wilderness for 40 years. Stephen says that Moses was 40 years old when he visited his brothers (Acts 7:23).

how he knew that he himself was not an Egyptian but an Israelite. I suppose we should imagine that Pharaoh's daughter, who raised Moses and even named him (2:10), made no attempt to disguise Moses' ancestry or the way she found him.[8] Moreover, Moses' own mother, Jochebed, raised him for at least a few years—until he was weaned at perhaps age 3.[9] On the other hand, most movie versions that

---

8. Ancient interpreters proposed several names for this daughter of Pharaoh. See the Wikipedia entry "Pharaoh's Daughter (Exodus)." Josephus calls her Thermouthis (*Antiquities of the Jews* 2.224). For other ancient proposals, see Louis H. Feldman, *Flavius Josephus: Judean Antiquities 1–4* (Leiden: Brill, 2000), 195n625. Josephus (2.232) reports that Thermouthis had no other children, and she intended Moses to be the heir of the Egyptian kingdom (i.e., the future Pharaoh, 2.232). Philo basically agrees, though he does not name the princess (*Life of Moses* 1.13, 32). On Josephus' portrayal of Moses, see Louis H. Feldman, *Josephus' Interpretation of the Bible* (Berkeley: University of California Press, 1998), ch. 10. On Philo, see Louis H. Feldman, *Philo's Portrayal of Moses in the Context of Ancient Judaism* (Notre Dame, IN: University of Notre Dame Press, 2007). The 1956 movie *The Ten Commandments* calls the princess "Bithiah," in accordance with another ancient Jewish tradition.

9. Rabbinic literature assumes that a child is weaned at about 24 months; see Jordan Rosenblum, "Blessings of the Breasts: Breastfeeding in Rabbinic Literature," *Hebrew Union College Annual* 87 (2016): 145–77, at 162n73. Some translations make it seem that Moses lived with Jochebed much more than just three years: the CEB says: "After the child had grown up, she [Jochebed] brought him back to Pharaoh's daughter, who adopted him as her son" (Exod 2:10). This is a possible translation of the Hebrew, but most translations say something like, "When the child grew older...," which makes more sense in terms of the story. But the ancient Jewish writing *Jubilees* 47 says that Moses lived with Jochebed for 21 years! But Philo says that Moses was weaned ahead of schedule (*Life of Moses* 1.18).

I've seen make this issue a major plot point, and usually the story goes like this: Moses is ignorant of his true origins; he thinks he's an Egyptian prince; his Egyptian "mother" attempts to convince him that he is her biological son; and the moment when he learns the truth is a life-changing event. That's the way it goes in the classic *The Ten Commandments* (1956), and in the animated *Prince of Egypt* (1998), and in Christian Bale's *Exodus: Gods and Kings* (2014). But both Philo and Josephus indicate that Moses was raised in the palace with the knowledge that he was a Hebrew, and he was nevertheless supposed to be the next Pharaoh.[10] There are different ways of looking at the question how Moses knew that the Hebrew slaves were his brothers.

The writer of Hebrews does not raise the question, but it does answer the question as to why Moses visited his brothers.

> He refused to be called the son of Pharaoh's daughter and chose to suffer with the people of God rather than to enjoy the fleeting pleasure of sin. For he considered the reproach of Christ to be greater wealth than the treasures of Egypt, since he was looking ahead to the reward. (Heb 11:24–25)

---

10. For this view in Josephus, see his account of Moses in *Antiquities of the Jews*, book 2. Philo's view is a little more complicated. At first, he indicates that Pharaoh's daughter pretends that Moses is her biological child (*Life of Moses* 1.19), and she is concerned about his fate if his true identity is known (§ 15), but later Moses seems to have no illusions about his identity (§ 32).

Wow! That's an unexpected reading, at least to my mind. When I read Exodus 2, it does not occur to me to think that Moses went out to visit the Israelites because he didn't like sin and he wanted to bear the reproach of Christ. I don't mean to say that the writer of Hebrews is wrong, or he's making stuff up. On the contrary, this account of Moses' choices helps us to read Exodus with eyes of faith.

Using the lens provided by Hebrews and the ambiguity of the Exodus narrative, we can imagine that Moses was disconcerted (to say the least) about his own position within the royal household in view of that royal household's oppression of the Israelites, whom he knew to be his own people, as the text of Exodus tells us (2:11). Thinking about Moses' life in those terms, we've seen this story before. We've seen the child grow up to turn against the principles his or her family stood for, especially when this young adult perceives these family principles to be oppressive or greedy or some such. It's not hard to imagine Moses being uncomfortable with his opulent lifestyle (= the fleeting pleasure of sin) when outside the door his own family suffered.[11] The book of Exodus doesn't exactly tell us why Moses visited his people, but the idea that he had decided to identify with them rather than their rich oppressors certainly makes sense, even if it meant "refusing to be called the son of Pharaoh's daughter" and instead enduring suffering with these oppressed people (Heb 11:24–25).

---

11. Philo reads the story somewhat similarly to Hebrews at this point (*Life of Moses* 1.32–33), according to whom it was the Pharaoh's decision to enslave the Israelites that prompted Moses to visit the Hebrews (§ 40).

The interpretation of Philo, a first-century Jewish philosopher living in Egypt, is pretty close to that of Hebrews. Philo says that Moses

> gave up the lordship of Egypt, which he held as son to the daughter of the then reigning king, because the sight of the iniquities committed in the land and his own nobility of soul and magnanimity of spirit and inborn hatred of evil led him to renounce completely his expected inheritance from the kinsfolk of his adoption. (*Life of Moses* 1.149)

So, the writer of Hebrews stands in good company in reading the choice of Moses the way he does.

But even so, what about this business of the "reproach of Christ" (Heb 11:26)? How can we say that Moses gave any thought to Christ, since Jesus wouldn't be born for 1500 years? Here I think we need to avoid pressing the phrase "reproach of Christ" too far. We might think about it in terms of the same sort of reproach that Christ suffered. Moses chose to identify with his oppressed people, a decision that engendered reproach, so that in this way Moses became a type of Christ, suffering the same reproach, typologically. Moses knew from the stories Jochebed had told him about the promises God had made (Gen 12:1–3, 7; 15:13–16; etc.), and he looked forward to the fulfillment of those promises, greater than all the treasures of Egypt.

And so Moses left Egypt "not being afraid of the king's anger" (Heb 11:27). What anger? The writer of Hebrews assumes his readers know the story: Moses killed an Egyptian in defense of an Israelite (Exod 2:11–12). But Exodus goes on to say, "When Pharaoh heard about this, he tried to kill Moses, but Moses fled from Pharaoh and went to live in the land of Midian" (2:15). It sort of sounds like Moses was afraid of the king's anger. But not according to Hebrews, and if you look closely at Exod 2:15, you notice that it doesn't actually say that Moses fled Egypt because of his fear at the king's anger. (It does say in Exod 2:14 that Moses was fearful that what he had done would be found out.) Maybe that's the obvious way of reading the story, but the wording in Exodus leaves open the possibility of a different reading, and Hebrews takes up that challenge. In this telling, it's not that Moses was afraid, but rather—like his parents before him (v. 23)—his faith motivated him to leave Egypt to preserve his life (v. 27). In other words, it wasn't fear that took Moses away from Egypt, it was faith, faith that God had something better in store.

The next two things mentioned by Hebrews take us further into Exodus. Faith led Moses to institute the Passover (Exod 12), to protect the Israelites from the destroyer of the firstborn (Exod 12:23). And Moses led the Israelites through the Red Sea on dry ground because they had faith (Exod 14:21–22).

The main point in all of this is that Moses—like Abraham and Noah and Rahab and others—provides an example of faith, which shows itself through the action of turning away from sin, of enduring the reproach of Christ, of seeking out God and obeying his will. Moses had such great faith because he looked to the one who is unseen (v. 27). We might think that this characteristic sets Moses apart from us, since he spoke to God face-to-face (Exod 33:11; cf. v. 20) and he was privileged to see God's back (33:23). But Moses is an example even in this looking at the unseen one, since Hebrews encourages us also to keep our eyes on Jesus, the author and finisher of our faith (12:2).

The Customs of Moses: Stephen's Speech

Stephen was one of the seven who had been appointed by the early Jerusalem church to serve food to widows in order to free the apostles from this worry (Acts 6). We have often thought of these seven as the first deacons. We don't know much about Prochorus, Nicanor, Timon, Parmenas, or Nicolaus—really, only their names (6:5). But Stephen and Philip both distinguished themselves as preachers and evangelists more than as (what we would normally think of as) deacons. Philip evangelized Samaria and the Ethiopian eunuch (Acts 8) before settling in Caesarea (21:8), about 70 miles northwest of Jerusalem. And Stephen was the first Christian martyr.

I wish we had more of Stephen's preaching than just his last sermon. Stephen quickly made enemies, especially among the so-called Synagogue of the Freedmen (6:9), who concocted a series of charges against Stephen, namely, that Stephen had blasphemed Moses and God (v. 11), had spoken against the temple and the law (= Torah, v. 13), and had threatened that Jesus would destroy the temple and change the customs of Moses (v. 14). All of these charges basically amount to speech against the temple (which is probably what the blasphemy against God in v. 11 means) and against the Torah.

Luke explicitly says that the people accusing Stephen of these things were "false witnesses" (v. 13), but I'm willing to bet that these specific accusations were not invented out of thin air. I do not believe that Stephen had been blaspheming God or Moses, but I bet he had been saying something that could be construed in these terms by an unsympathetic audience. In other words, I don't think Stephen was speaking against Moses, but he probably was saying something that could lead someone to think that Stephen wanted to change the customs of Moses.

And what Stephen is accused of saying about the temple—that Jesus would destroy it—sounds a whole lot like what Jesus is accused of saying at his own trial before the Sanhedrin, where the false witnesses accused Jesus of saying, "I will destroy this temple made with human hands, and in three days I will build another not made by hands" (Mark 14:58; cf. Matt 26:61). But these again are false witnesses; we don't have a record of Jesus actually saying that he would destroy the temple. But the Gospel of John records Jesus as saying, "Destroy this temple, and I will raise it up three days later" (John 2:19)—not a threat to destroy the temple, but a promise to rebuild it. But, of course, "he was speaking about the temple of his body" (v. 21). And then there was the prediction Jesus made that the actual temple would be destroyed so that "not one stone will be left on another that will not be thrown down" (Matt 24:2). So, I bet Stephen had been saying something about a temple being destroyed, and as he points out in his speech, even the Old Testament prophets talked about how God doesn't really need a temple (Acts 7:49–50; cf. Isa 66:1–2). Jeremiah (7:12–15) and

Ezekiel (ch. 10) had both proclaimed that God had abandoned his (first) temple. And even Solomon, at the dedication of the temple, acknowledged that the temple isn't really God's dwelling place (1 Kings 8:27).

But back to Moses, or what Stephen is supposed to have said about Moses. What might Stephen have been saying that would lead people to think that he wanted to change the Torah? Later on, the idea of Gentiles being circumcised will become a major point of contention (Acts 11:2–3; 15:1), but Stephen probably hasn't been talking about circumcision because there weren't any Gentile Christians yet. The same is probably true about the Levitical food laws and the Sabbath observance—these things would become controversial only when Gentiles started entering the church, so not yet in the days of Stephen. He could have talked about how sacrifice was no longer necessary after the sacrifice of Jesus, or how Christ fulfills the Passover, but it seems like these issues were only worked out later. In the book of Acts, Christians can still engage in offerings at the temple (21:26), though probably not sin offerings. But what Stephen was probably telling people is to worship Jesus, to acclaim him the Lord of heaven and earth. Given the commitment to monotheism among most Jews—a commitment grounded in the daily repetition of the Shema (Deut 6:4–9)—such teaching on the part of Stephen would surely have sounded to many Jews like he wanted to change the customs of Moses.

The speech that Luke records in Acts 7 is the longest speech in either Luke or Acts. By no means does Stephen directly address the accusations leveled against him. Instead, he tells the history of Israel in such a way that he is not contradicting Moses but affirming everything he said, while at the same time Stephen's own accusers are standing in a long tradition of the Israelite people rejecting the prophets sent to them, including Moses.

On the other hand, the charge about the destruction of the temple seems to be more-or-less on target. It seems to me that Stephen essentially pleads guilty as charged on that count (vv. 44–50). He anchors his teaching about the temple in the Israelite prophetic tradition by quoting Isaiah 66, which, as we have seen, is merely the tip of the iceberg, as Jeremiah and Ezekiel and even Solomon the temple-builder insist on the contingent nature of the temple. It is not something that God needs or even particularly desires. Stephen was not the only Jew at this time that was talking about the temple in this way. The Qumran community (= the authors of the Dead Sea Scrolls) considered the temple to be basically defiled and operated by a corrupt priesthood; the impurity of the temple was probably part of the reason the Qumran community withdrew into the desert around the Dead Sea.

Unlike in Hebrews 11, Stephen does make Moses the main character of his speech, no doubt because it was Moses whom he had been accused of blaspheming. Like Hebrews, Stephen mentions that Moses was beautiful (v. 20; cf. Exod 2:2), but he stresses that Moses was beautiful in God's sight. Stephen adds what should have been obvious to us anyway, that Moses received a first-rate Egyptian education.¹² Stephen is the one who tells us that Moses was 40 years old in Exodus 2:11 when he visited the Israelites (Acts 7:23), but unlike the writer of Hebrews, Stephen does not speculate on why Moses made this visit.

Stephen then narrates in some detail (vv. 23–29) the incident of Moses killing the Egyptian that we find in Exod 2:11–15.¹³ Stephen agrees with Hebrews that Moses' flight from Egypt was not out of fear of the king's wrath, although neither does Stephen mention the "reproach of Christ." But Stephen does draw a fairly obvious connection between Moses and Christ: Moses was supposed to be the deliverer of the Israelites (Acts 7:25), but the Israelites rejected him (vv. 27–28, quoting Exod 2:14). That's the main point Stephen wants to make about Moses—that the Israelites rejected him at first, just as the Israelites always rejected God's prophets, just as the Jewish leaders rejected Jesus, just as the Jewish leaders are at this moment rejecting Stephen. It is not the Jewish leaders who adhere to the customs of Moses, but

---

12. Philo elaborates: "Teachers at once arrived from different parts, some unbidden from the neighbouring countries and the provinces of Egypt, others summoned from Greece under promise of high reward. But in a short time he advanced beyond their capacities; his gifted nature forestalled their instruction, so that his seemed a case rather of recollection than of learning, and indeed he himself devised and propounded problems which they could not easily solve" (*Life of Moses* 1.21). Philo continues describing Moses' education through § 24.

13. According to Philo (*Life of Moses* 1.44), the Egyptian killed by Moses was "the cruellest of all." "Moses considered that his action in killing him was a righteous action. And righteous it was that one who only lived to destroy men should himself be destroyed."

rather it is Stephen who is fulfilling the role of Moses, the rejected prophet.

Stephen quickly summarizes the narrative of Moses meeting Zipporah and her father Reuel (or Jethro), the priest of Midian (Exod 2:15–22), and having sons. Only one son is mentioned in Exod 2, but both of Moses' sons are named at Exod 18:2–4. But Stephen doesn't want to talk about Moses' family or speculate on what kind of priest Reuel/Jethro was.

Stephen wants to talk about the burning bush (Exod 3–4), the moment when God appointed Moses as a deliver for Israel "through the angel who appeared to him in the bush" (v. 35; see v. 30). The text of Exodus says that it was the "angel of YHWH"[14] in the bush (Exod 3:2), though this angel is not mentioned in the rest of the burning bush narrative. There is a long Christian tradition of identifying this angel with the pre-incarnate Christ. We have explicit testimony to this interpretation only after the time of Stephen, starting in the second century,[15] but Stephen may already be hinting at this interpretation by even mentioning the angel and acknowledging that the angel was somehow involved in Moses' commission.

At any rate, Stephen briefly narrates the commission without mentioning all of Moses' hesitations and questions that take up so much of the narrative of Exod 3–4. The main point Stephen wants to make here is that Moses was

---

14. The next chapter explains why I'm using YHWH instead of "the Lord."

15. See Justin Martyr, *Dialogue with Trypho* 58–60; Irenaeus, *Proof of the Apostolic Preaching* 46.

commissioned to deliver those people who had previously rejected his leadership (v. 35). And "this is the Moses who said to the Israelites, God will raise up for you a prophet like me..." (v. 37, quoting Deut 18:15).[16] Again, there's a parallel between the "prophet to come" (Jesus) and the prophet who came (Moses). The prophet to come will be "like me," said Moses, and it turns out he was so much like Moses that the people rejected him just as they rejected Moses. After all, Moses received "living oracles" (v. 38) but "our ancestors were unwilling to obey him" (v. 39), and so far did they stray from the teaching of Moses that they even made a golden calf to worship (vv. 40–41, quoting Exod 32:1). The Israelites have always been idolaters, have always had improper conceptions of God (as if he really lived in a temple), have always rebelled against God's appointed leaders. So even now:

> You stiff-necked people with uncircumcised hearts and ears.[17] You are always resisting the Holy Spirit. As your ancestors did, you do also. Which of the prophets did your ancestors not persecute? They even killed those who foretold the coming of the Righteous One, whose betrayers and murderers you have now become. You

---

16 Peter quotes the same passage in Acts 3:22–23.

17. Stephen draws these images from his Bible; see Exod 32:9; 33:3, 5; 34:9 (stiff-necked); Deut 10:16 (heart circumcision); Jer 6:10 (uncircumcised ears).

received the law under the direction of angels and yet have not kept it.[18]

Who is truly keeping the customs of Moses? Who is fulfilling the living oracles delivered by Moses? Not these Jewish leaders who "have not kept it," but rather those who believe in Jesus, who fulfills those living oracles. It is the Jewish leadership, the Sanhedrin, and that Synagogue of the Freedmen, who have betrayed Moses, not Stephen and the other believers. But Stephen knows that he is playing a role scripted out for him centuries earlier, a role similar to that of Moses himself, and especially similar to the later prophets who announced the coming of the Righteous One. Stephen himself has announced the coming of the Righteous One, so he knows full-well what his role requires him to do: proclaim God's oracles to a stiff-necked people who will refuse to listen and put him to death. They are also playing a role that has been re-enacted many times throughout Israel's history. It is Stephen's job in this speech to assure them that they are not playing the role of Moses, but he himself is.

---

18. Stephen mentions the "angel who spoke to him [Moses] on Mount Sinai" (v. 38), and again, "the law under the direction of angels" (v. 53). The idea that an angel was involved in delivering the Sinai legislation is also mentioned in Gal 3:19 and Heb 2:2, and was a feature of some retellings of the Sinai narrative in contemporary Jewish literature (e.g., the book of Jubilees). This angel of Mt. Sinai is not mentioned in the book of Exodus.

CHRISTIANS AND MOSES

Moses is never criticized in the New Testament, he is always esteemed as one who spoke God's words to his people, who obeyed God's commands, and sometimes as a model of faith or even a type of Christ. But in light of the coming of Jesus, the authority of Moses—which had for so long seemed absolute—was seen to be only contingent, derivative. Like a lamp that appears so bright in a dark room but can only seem less brilliant when the shades are drawn and the sunlight pours in, so also the glory of Moses, which had seemed so radiant, now pales in comparison to the glory of Christ.[19] Moses appears along with Elijah on the mount of Transfiguration, but the heavenly voice speaks only of the other figure, the beloved son: "Hear ye him" (Mark 9:7). And yet this beloved son came to fulfill the living oracles delivered by Moses and proclaimed by the prophets. In the debate on who is truly representing the views of the Founding Father of Israel, the New Testament insists that Jesus and his followers are standing on Moses' side.

---

19. This is something like what Hebrews is getting at in 3:1–6; and Paul in 2 Corinthians 3:7–18.

2

God's Name[1]

> After making purification for sins, he sat down at the right hand of the Majesty on high, having become as much superior to angels as the name he has inherited is more excellent than theirs. (Hebrews 1:3–4)

What is God's name? Christians in America—at least in my experience—have usually used the word "God" as if it were a name, even asserting that the flippant phrase "O my God" abuses God's name in violation of the Third Commandment (Exod 20:7). Of course, we use the same word for pagan gods—Zeus is a Greek god, Baal is a Canaanite god—in which case we don't capitalize the word. I guess we could say that "God" (capital letter = proper noun) is the English name of the Christian God, whereas the term "god" (lower-case letter = common noun) can be used for pagan

---

1. The Bible Project has produced an excellent 4-minute video on this topic. Go to YouTube and search "Bible Project YHWH" and you'll find it.

(i.e., fake) gods.[2]

But, whereas most Christians I know probably use "God" as if it were God's name (and I guess I do too), if you actually asked these people the question, "What is God's name?," they probably wouldn't answer, "God." My guess is that the answer they would give might be Jehovah, or Yahweh, or "I AM." In any case, the answer would have something to do with Exodus 3:14, the passage about the burning bush where Moses (basically) asks God the question, "What is your name?"

Context: Exodus 3

Long after Moses escaped from Egypt, when he was about 80 years old (Exod 7:7),[3] Moses had gotten married and had two sons (cf. Exod 18:3; only one son mentioned at Exod 2:22; 4:24–26). He was living in Midian, south of Edom, but he led his flock of sheep to "Horeb, the mountain of God" (3:1).[4]

---

2. N. T. Wright thinks such usage is dangerous for Christian theology; see his *The New Testament and the People of God* (Minneapolis: Fortress, 1992), xiv–xv.

3. If you were reading Exodus for the first time, you wouldn't know how old Moses was at this point, because a notice of his age doesn't come for a few more chapters. My guess is you would probably think he was a young father (cf. 2:21–22), maybe around 30 years old. You wouldn't expect that a man described as "shepherding the flock of his father-in-law" (3:1) would be 80 years old.

4. We don't really know where Mt. Sinai is, though the traditional location puts it pretty far from Midian, in the southern part of what is now called "the Sinai Peninsula." On the other hand, some Bible maps locate Sinai within the land of Midian; see Richard Elliott Friedman, *The Exodus: How It Happened and Why It Matters* (New York: HarperOne, 2017), 126. (You should be able to find online maps that place Mt. Sinai in each of these locations.) For an argument that Sinai is not in Midian, see James K. Hoffmeier, *Ancient Israel in Sinai: The Evidence for the Authenticity of the Wilderness Tradition* (Oxford: Oxford University Press, 2005), 121–22, 130–40. If the traditional site of Mt. Sinai is correct, then the Gulf of Aqaba lies between Midian and Sinai. According to Google Maps, the path from a random Saudi Arabian city (Al Bad, located in what would have been ancient Midian), around the Gulf of Aqaba, to Saint Catherine's Monastery, at the foot of the mountain (Gabal Musa) traditionally identified as Sinai—that path would be about 220 miles. For a consideration of the location of biblical Mt Sinai and an argument that it is located somewhere in the southern Sinai Peninsula, see Hoffmeier, *Ancient Israel in Sinai*, 111–48.

Horeb might be another name for Sinai, or Horeb (meaning "dry") might be a region in which Sinai is located. In that case, Exod 3:1 would mean something like, "to the region of Horeb, specifically, to the mountain of God."[5] The name "Horeb" (17x in the Hebrew Bible) is used mostly in Deuteronomy,[6] Sinai (21x in the Hebrew Bible) is used in Exodus, Leviticus, and Numbers,[7] though there is some overlap. Horeb appears three times in Exodus, including in our passage (also 17:6; 33:6). I'm not sure why we have two different names for this mountain (or two different names for Moses' father-in-law, for that matter).[8] At any rate, this is the "mountain of God," the location to which Moses will return with the liberated Israelites in order to worship God "on this mountain" (3:12).

It is here that Moses witnesses a "remarkable sight" (3:3), a bush apparently on fire but not burning up.[9] The text tells

---

5. For this proposal, see Hoffmeier, *Ancient Israel in Sinai*, 114–15, and see the translation of 3:1 he offers at p. 121.

6. Deut 1:2, 6, 19; 4:10, 15; 5:2; 9:8; 18:16; 29:1. Horeb is used also at Exod 3:1; 17:6; 33:6; 1 Kings 8:9; 19:8; 2 Chron 5:10; Psa 106:19; Mal 4:4.

7. Exod 19:11, 18, 20, 23; 24:16; 31:18; 34:2, 4, 29, 32; Lev 7:38; 25:1; 26:46; 27:34; Num 3:1; 28:6; Deut 33:2; Judg 5:5; Neh 9:13; Psa 68:8, 17; Acts 7:30, 38; Gal 4:24–25. Mt. Sinai is in the wilderness of Sinai, which is mentioned at Exod 16:1; 19:1–2; Lev 7:38; Num 1:1, 19; 3:4, 14; 9:1, 5; 10:12; 26:64; 33:15, 16. On the appearances of the word Sinai in the Bible, see Hoffmeier, *Ancient Israel in Sinai*, 38.

8. Jethro: 3:1; 4:18; 18:1–12. Reuel: Exod 2:18. And there's a third name, Hobab: Judg 4:11. There's a footnote in my Bible that says, "Jethro's clan or last name was Reuel," which might be right. This interpretation might be suggested by Num 10:29.

9. Hollywood has given us several depictions of this scene, which can easily be found online. There's the classic Charlton Heston version from 1956 (search "charlton heston burning bush") or the reimagined Christian Bale version from 2014 (search "exodus gods and kings burning bush"), but probably my favorite movie depiction of this scene is in the cartoon *Prince of Egypt* from 1998 (search "prince of egypt burning bush"). It would be a good exercise in a Bible class to watch all three versions and discuss their strengths and weaknesses in depicting this scene from Exod 3.

us that "the angel of the LORD" was in the bush (3:2), which is maybe what it means that there was a flame in the bush—maybe the angel was the flame of fire (cf. Heb 1:7, quoting Psa 104:4).[10] But then, of course, God speaks to Moses and commissions him to free his people from Egypt. (Perhaps we should then see God as the fire.)[11]

This is the first time in the Bible that God calls someone to serve him on behalf of others (he didn't really call Abraham for that purpose), and when God does that, people often resist. Gideon had several tests that he wanted performed (Judg 6); Isaiah was concerned about his own impurity (Isa 6:5); and Jeremiah thought he was too young (Jer 1:6). Moses was the first called, so he was the first to protest. He had some questions, and one of the first answers he sought was the identity of the God he was talking to. So God told him.[12]

---

10. Justin, *Dialogue with Trypho* 127, interprets the angel as the fire.

11. See Chapters 12 and 13 below; and Benjamin D. Sommer, *The Bodies of God and the World of Ancient Israel* (Cambridge: Cambridge University Press, 2009), 41–42: "The famous fire in this passage, which burned *in* the bush without burning the bush, is nothing other than a small-scale manifestation of God." He suggests translating the verse: "Yhwh's small-scale manifestation appeared to him as [or: in the form of] a flame of fire from the midst of the bush."

12. According to R. W. L. Moberly, *The Old Testament of the Old Testament: Patriarchal Narratives and Mosaic Yahwism* (Minneapolis: Fortress, 1992), 15, God speaks about his name in the entire Hebrew Bible only here and in Exod 33:19; 34:5–7, 14.

God Reveals His Name

Apparently God expected Moses to know him by the title "The God of your father, the God of Abraham, the God of Isaac, and the God of Jacob," since that is how he initially identifies himself to Moses (v. 6). Moses seems to think that the Israelites know this title for God as well, because he imagines telling them "The God of your fathers has sent me to you" (v. 13). But Moses wants to know the personal name for God.

The main answer to the question is in vv. 14–15. (The rest of the chapter gives instructions on what Moses should do once he gets to Egypt.) Actually, verse 15 answers the question, and the answer is ... obscured by our English translations. Most English translations I've seen use the term LORD in all capital letters to represent the name of God. This is not universal practice: the French translations of Scripture that I have seen use L'Eternel (= the Eternal One) for the name of God, and I know of one English translation that does this.[13] But the name in Hebrew is represented by four letters, all consonants (just like all written Hebrew words).

$$יהוה = YHWH$$

We'll talk more about this name in a little bit, but for now let's see what God says about the name. "This is my name

---

13. *The Voice Bible* (Nashville: Thomas Nelson, 2012).

forever; this is how I am to be remembered in every generation."

But before answering Moses' question directly, God gave a description of himself. "I AM WHO I AM.[14] This is what you are to say to the Israelites: I AM has sent me to you" (v. 14). Some English translations use the future tense instead: I will be who/what I will be. The Hebrew phrase (with the vowels) is *ehyeh asher ehyeh*.[15] This phrase that sounds a little funny in English has a relatively straightforward significance, I think. God is telling us that we should connect his name to the verb "to be," that the significance of the name has something to do with existence. Though "I AM" doesn't actually substitute for the name YHWH in the Bible, God suggests in v. 14 that "I AM" (*Ehyeh*) is equivalent to his name.

This verse should tell us something pretty important about God. He is the Existent one—the one who exists. I figure that's probably why those French translations I mentioned use the term L'Eternal for God's name, "the Eternal One." Our God is Existence itself, the only one who can be described as the great I AM. His existence is not contingent, not dependent on anything else. His existence has no beginning or end. But our existence is completely contingent, we depend completely on God, on his creating us,

---

14. I am relying here on Moberly, *Old Testament of the Old Testament*, 21. Other scholars think that this is one of God's names, or that this answer from God demonstrates his refusal to answer the question (but then he goes on in the next verse to offer a direct answer).

15. For help with pronouncing this phrase, watch the Bible Project video mentioned in the first note of this chapter.

sustaining us, providing for us. As Epimenides said, "In him we live and move and have our being" (as quoted by Paul in Acts 17:28). Hardly any other major deity is described in these terms. Certainly the chief god of the Babylonians, Marduk, was not thought of as ever-existent—he was born from previous gods. Same for Baal; same for Zeus. But the Israelites never told stories about the beginning of the God of Abraham. His name accurately describes his being, "I AM." This meaning seems to be the one codified in the Septuagint, which translates *ehyeh asher ehyeh* as "I am the one who exists."[16]

And God is the Present one—the one who is present with his people. God has just promised Moses that when he returns to Egypt on this mission, "I will certainly be with you" (Exod 3:12). And now God uses the very same word, *Ehyeh*, "I will be," as his own name. This word does not imply merely existence but also presence. Again, we can think of Paul's quotation of Epimenides (Acts 17:28): because we live and move within God, he is always present with us. His very name tells us that.

---

16. There have been suggestions that the Hebrew should be translated this way; for discussion and rejection of this idea, see Bertil Albrektson, "On the Syntax of אהיה אשר אהיה in Exodus 3:14," in *Words and Meanings: Essays Presented to David Winton Thomas*, ed. Peter R. Ackroyd and Barnabas Lindars (Cambridge: Cambridge University Press, 1968), 15–28.

God's Name Newly Revealed

After God tells Moses his name, YHWH, he tells him to speak to the Israelites in this name (v. 16) and then speak to Pharaoh in this name (v. 18). That's exactly what Moses does. The people of Israel respond favorably (4:19–31), but Pharaoh does not. The problem is, he has never heard of a god named YHWH (5:1–2). So Moses resorts to the descriptive phrase "the God of the Hebrews" to explain who YHWH is (5:3; cf. 3:18). This goes all wrong—at least, in Moses' mind—so Moses complains to God that speaking to Pharaoh "in your name" has led only to problems (5:22–23). But YHWH's response makes it sound like this is all a part of the plan (6:1).

At that point, God speaks more about his name.

> Then God spoke to Moses, telling him, "I am YHWH. I appeared to Abraham, Isaac, and Jacob as *El Shaddai*, but I was not known to them by my name YHWH." (Exod 6:2–3)

This statement seems to mean that Moses is the first person to know God's name YHWH. Now, it is true that some stories in Genesis are told as if Abraham knows God as *El Shaddai* (cf. Gen 17:1; 28:3; 35:11). But there are also plenty of stories in Genesis that make it seem like Abraham knows God as YHWH, like at Gen 15:7, where God says to

Abraham, "I am YHWH." Two possible explanations[17]: (a) maybe Exod 6:3 actually just means that while the patriarchs knew the name YHWH, they didn't know the full meaning of the name, and that full meaning is only revealed now to Moses[18]; or (b) maybe the patriarchs really didn't know the name YHWH, but the stories about the patriarchs are told by a narrator who does know that name and knows that Abraham's God was YHWH, whether Abraham knew that name or not.[19]

If the second interpretation is correct, then God is telling Moses that this name YHWH has never been revealed before. Previous generations knew God under potentially a variety of names, but especially as *El Shaddai*, "God Almighty," but now that he is forming a nation from Abraham's descendents and rescuing them from slavery, he also reveals to them his everlasting name, YHWH.

The Tetragrammaton

This newly revealed name, YHWH, is the one that appears most commonly in the Hebrew Bible (over 6000

---

17. I do not take account here of the usual scholarly explanation, that different sources stand behind the biblical narratives, an explanation insisted upon by Friedman, *The Exodus*, 47–49. Aside from the inherent difficulties of the source critical explanation, I ignore it because I wish here to deal with the canonical text.

18. For an example of this common interpretation, see W. Ross Blackburn, *The God Who Makes Himself Known: The Missionary Heart of the Book of Exodus* (Downers Grove, IL: IVP, 2012), ch. 2, esp. pp. 26–28, 56–61.

19. For discussion, see Moberly, *Old Testament of the Old Testament*, chs. 1–2, who argues for the second idea.

appearances). It is the Tetragrammaton, the "four-letter word." This name appears in every book of the Hebrew Bible except for Song of Songs (but see 8:6), Ecclesiastes (which uses *elohim*, "God"), and Esther.[20] The Tetragrammaton gave rise to the English word "Jehovah," but the most common scholarly proposal for pronouncing it now is Yahweh. Let's talk about why we don't know for sure how to pronounce the word.

Hebrew was originally written without vowels. Of course, the Hebrew language was spoken with vowel sounds, because you can't pronounce anything without vowels, but you can write words with just the consonants. For example, we could write the English sentence:

Gd lvs ppl

It might take us a second to figure it out, but most people are going to read this sentence as "God loves people." It's easier to read it if you have the vowels written down, but it's not impossible even without the vowels. English writing was formulated to combine vowels and consonants, but Hebrew writing was designed to use only the consonants. The Hebrew alphabet consists of 22 letters, all consonants, no vowels. It's not just Hebrew; the Israelites adopted the Phoenician alphabet, which also used only consonants. The

---

20. Reinhard Feldmeier and Hermann Spieckermann, *God of the Living: A Biblical Theology* (Waco, TX: Baylor University Press, 2011), 23–24. On the possibility of an acronym of the Tetragrammaton in Esther 5:4 and other verses, see John M. Manguno Jr., "Accident or Accronymy: The Tetragrammaton in the Masoretic Text of Esther," *Bibliotheca Sacra* 171 (2014): 440–51.

Phoenicians spread the alphabet to the Greeks, and it is the Greeks who get the credit for converting some of the letters into vowels.[21]

The Dead Sea Scrolls give a picture of what Hebrew Scripture looked like around the time of Jesus. Here's a picture of the Great Isaiah Scroll.[22]

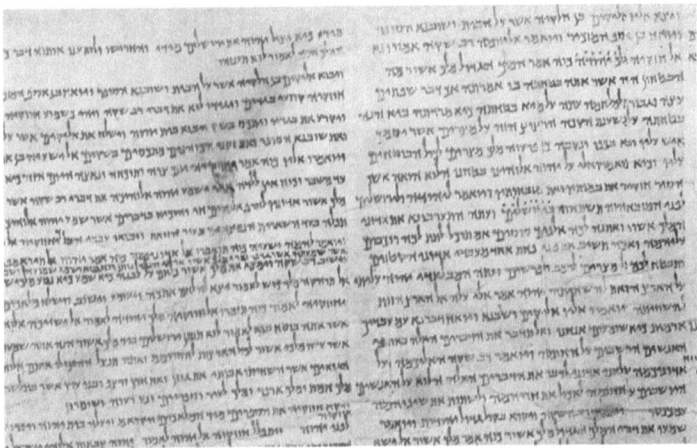

Figure 1. *Great Isaiah Scroll.* Photograph by Ardon Bar-Hama. The Israel Museum.

There are only consonants there. To read the text, you'd have to mentally insert the vowels, just like earlier we had to mentally insert the vowels into that vowelless sentence, "Gd lvs ppl."

---

21. On the Greek alphabet, see Willemijn Waal, "The Greek Alphabet: Older than You May Think?" *The Ancient Near East Today* 7.3 (March 2018), online at http://www.asor.org/anetoday/2019/03/Greek-Alphabet-Older-Than-You-Think.

22. Images available online at http://dss.collections.imj.org.il/isaiah.

Eventually, Jewish scribes invented vowel signs and inserted these signs into manuscripts of the Bible. Today, if you buy a copy of the Hebrew Bible, it will most likely have vowel signs or vowel points.[23] Here's what a modern edition looks like.

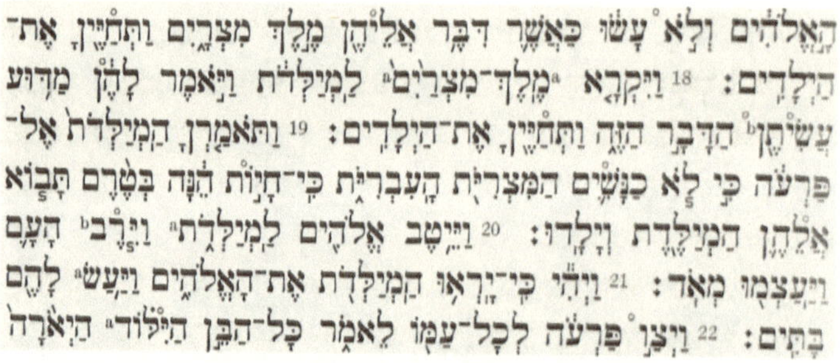

הָאֱלֹהִים וְלֹא עָשׂוּ כַּאֲשֶׁר דִּבֶּר אֲלֵיהֶן מֶלֶךְ מִצְרָיִם וַתְּחַיֶּיןָ אֶת־הַיְלָדִים: 18 וַיִּקְרָא מֶלֶךְ־מִצְרַיִם לַמְיַלְּדֹת וַיֹּאמֶר לָהֶן מַדּוּעַ עֲשִׂיתֶן הַדָּבָר הַזֶּה וַתְּחַיֶּיןָ אֶת־הַיְלָדִים: 19 וַתֹּאמַרְןָ הַמְיַלְּדֹת אֶל־פַּרְעֹה כִּי לֹא כַנָּשִׁים הַמִּצְרִיֹּת הָעִבְרִיֹּת כִּי־חָיוֹת הֵנָּה בְּטֶרֶם תָּבוֹא אֲלֵהֶן הַמְיַלֶּדֶת וְיָלָדוּ: 20 וַיֵּיטֶב אֱלֹהִים לַמְיַלְּדֹת וַיִּרֶב הָעָם וַיַּעַצְמוּ מְאֹד: 21 וַיְהִי כִּי־יָרְאוּ הַמְיַלְּדֹת אֶת־הָאֱלֹהִים וַיַּעַשׂ לָהֶם בָּתִּים: 22 וַיְצַו פַּרְעֹה לְכָל־עַמּוֹ לֵאמֹר כָּל־הַבֵּן הַיִּלּוֹד הַיְאֹרָה

Figure 2. *Portion of Exodus 1*.
From *Biblia Hebraica Stuttgartensia* (German Bible Society).

All the letters of the alphabet are still consonants, but the dots and lines around the letters—usually below the letters, but sometimes above them—are the newly invented vowel signs. The most popular set of vowel signs were invented by Jewish scribes called the Masoretes from the Israeli town of Tiberias, and these Masoretic scribes worked in the second half of the first millennium AD (i.e., around 500–1000 AD). Here's a picture of a section of text from one of the most famous manuscripts they produced, the Aleppo Codex, from 925 AD.[24] You can clearly see the vowels around the letters.

---

23. For an explanation, see Wikipedia's entry on Niqqud.
24. Images of the codex are available online at http://www.aleppo-codex.org/.

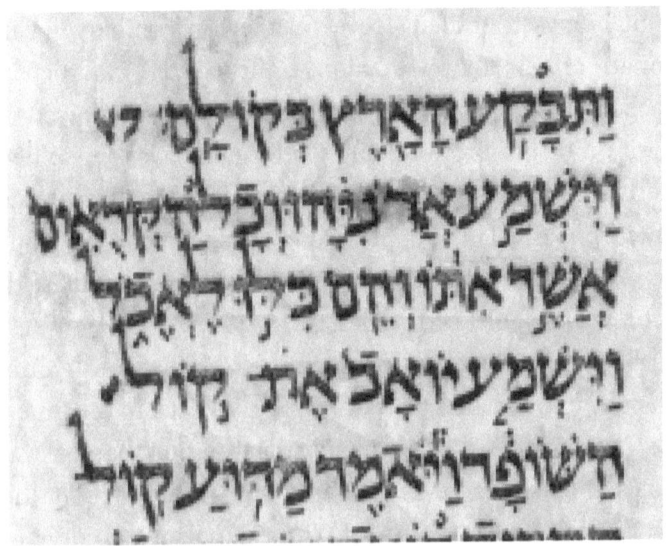

Figure 3. *Aleppo Codex.* Photograph by Ardon Bar-Hama. Ben Zvi Institute (The Israel Museum).

But the Masoretes did not put the correct vowels on the word YHWH (יהוה)—or, at least, this is what most scholars think happened. Apparently the Masoretes did not want people to pronounce the name of God (we'll talk about that later), so they did not put the vowels on YHWH that reflected how the word was actually pronounced. This is why we don't know exactly how to pronounce God's name.[25]

There is a long tradition in Judaism—going back to before the time of Jesus—of not saying God's name. (This tradition is not universal, as we will see; that is, even in the Second Temple Period, Jews sometimes pronounced God's

---

25. See the cautions in this regard expressed by Feldmeier and Spieckermann, *God of the* Living, 30.

name.) I myself studied Hebrew at a Jewish seminary in Cincinnati called Hebrew Union College, so I had Jewish teachers and Jewish fellow-students. We always followed the tradition of not pronouncing God's name YHWH. Whenever we came across it in the Hebrew Bible—which we did quite a bit; as I said, it appears more than 6000x—we would always use the word "Lord." Well, actually, we would use the Hebrew word for Lord, which is *Adonai*.

This tradition of pronouncing the Hebrew word *Adonai* whenever you see the word YHWH goes back to the time of the Chronicler.[26] This is probably the tradition that the Masoretes themselves practiced, and the tradition that they inscribed in their manuscripts. Take a look at a random example from the Aleppo Codex of how the Masoretes treated the name of God, the Tetragrammaton:

Figure 4. Detail of the Tetragrammaton. *Aleppo Codex*. Photo by Ardon Bar-Hama. Ben Zvi Institute.

---

26. This is especially evident when comparing David's prayer in 2 Sam 7 to its parallel in 1 Chron 17. See Koog P. Hong, "The Euphemism for the Ineffable Name of God and Its Early Evidence in Chronicles," *Journal for the Study of the Old Testament* 37 (2013): 473–84, esp. pp. 481–84.

The four letters here are יהוה, YHWH. Under the first letter—remember to read right to left—there are two dots, arranged vertically, like this ְ, which together form a *shewa*, a vowel sign. Under the third letter (from the right), there is a T-looking mark called a *qamets*, another vowel mark. So the Masoretes did put vowel signs on the Tetragrammaton, but these are not the right vowel signs. They are the vowel signs for *Adonai*.[27] They are supposed to remind the reader not to pronounce the name of God but to say *Adonai* instead. When European scholars looked at this Hebrew word—God's name with the vowels of *Adonai*—they transferred it into Latin as Jehovah (or something close to it).[28] Most scholars accept that the original pronunciation of the name was, however, Yahweh.[29] The first syllable, Yah, is

---

27. Some scholars interpret the vowel signs as deriving not from *Adonai* but from another substitution, *Shma*, "the name." I find Martin Rösel's arguments against this position persuasive; see his "The Reading and Translation of the Divine Name in the Masoretic Tradition and the Greek Pentateuch," *Journal for the Study of the Old Testament* 31 (2007): 411–28.

28. See the Wikipedia entry on Jehovah under the section "Similar Latin and English Transcriptions."

29. See, for instance, the standard Hebrew grammar by Gesenius-Kautzsch-Cowley, *Gesenius' Hebrew Grammar* (Oxford: Oxford University Press, 1910), §17c; or, for much more detail, see D. N. Freedman and M. O'Connor (with H. Ringgren), "יהוה *YHWH*," *Theological Dictionary of the Old Testament*, 15 vols. (Grand Rapids: Eerdmans, 1977–2012), 5.500–521. However, there are many people who argue that Jehovah or Yehowah is an approximate pronunciation of the Tetragrammaton. These people think that the Masoretes did include the correct vowel signs on the Tetragrammaton. Admittedly, they have some evidence (such as the pronunciation of certain Israelite names with theophoric elements, such as Jehoshaphat), and the Masoretes never actually own up to their substituting the wrong vowels on the Tetragrammaton. So, we cannot say this view is impossible, but most scholars do not accept it.

established through comparison of other Hebrew words, such as Hallelujah, which appears frequently in the Psalms. The final syllable of Hallelujah is a short form of God's name.

So Jehovah is probably not the name of God. It is an English form of the Latin form of the Hebrew form that combined the consonants of God's name (YHWH) with the vowels of Adonai. But this form has become established in English, through hymns ("Hallelujah, Praise Jehovah") and a few influential translations of Scripture, particularly the KJV, which has the form "Jehovah" four times (Exod 6:3; Psa 83:18; Isa 12:2; 26:4). The ASV from 1901 prints "Jehovah" for every appearance of the Tetragrammaton in Hebrew, that is, more than 6000 times.

But, as I said, the name was probably pronounced Yahweh. This is established not only through Hebrew evidence but also through the evidence of other languages, such as Greek and Latin, when writers would transliterate the name of God. For instance, a fifth-century AD Christian writer named Theodoret reported that the Samaritans known to him pronounce the name "Yave" (Ιαβέ in Theodoret's Greek).[30]

There is also a shorter form that often appears in Greek, Latin, and Aramaic, pronounced Yaho or Yaō. Jerome comments on Psa 8:1, which has the Tetragrammaton followed by the Hebrew word *Adonai*, which, when it doesn't refer to God, can simply refer to people ("master"):

---

30. *Questions on Exodus* 15.

> The first name, Lord, among the Hebrews consists of the four letters *yod, he, vav, he,* which properly is a word for God and can be pronounced *Yaho,* and the Hebrews think it unpronounceable. But the second, Adonai, is very common, frequently used for people.[31]

Jerome mentions a pronunciation *Yaho*. This is an alternative pronunciation for which we have other evidence. It was, in fact, fairly common to spell God's name in Greek as Ιαω = Yaō.[32] A few of the Dead Sea Scrolls were in Greek, and we have one Greek Leviticus scroll that has the name of God as Ιαω (or, actually, ΙΑΩ, all capital letters).[33] Diodorus Siculus, a pagan writer from just before Jesus' birth, also knows that Moses taught the Jews that the name of God was Ιαω.[34] This pronunciation is also the one attested in Aramaic among the fifth-century BC Jewish community in Egypt in the village called Elephantine.[35]

So, obviously not all Jews had ceased pronouncing the Divine Name by the time of Jesus. But the refusal to

---

31. *Commentarioli in Psalmos* 8:2.
32. Frank Shaw, *The Earliest Non-Mystical Jewish Use of Iaw* (Leuven: Peeters, 2014).
33. See the good images available at the Wikipedia entry on 4Q120. Or better images here: color, https://www.deadseascrolls.org.il/explore-the-archive/image/B-503715; infrared, https://www.deadseascrolls.org.il/explore-the-archive/image/B-503717.
34. Diodorus Siculus, *Hist.* 1.94.2 (cf. Loeb Classical Library, vol. 1 of Diodorus Siculus, p. 321).
35. See Bezalel Porten, *The Elephantine Papyri in English: Three Millennia of Cross-Cultural Continuity and Change* (Leiden: Brill, 1996). See, for instance, the document numbered B19, dating to 25 Nov 407 BC, at p. 140 line 9; p. 142 line 4; p. 143 line 10; p. 144 lines 2–3. See also the Wadi Daliyeh Samaria Papyri #8 (DJD 28, p. 88 line 7).

pronounce the name seems to have been the dominant tendency in Judaism at the time. Let's consider why.

SUBSTITUTION

This is going to get a little bit complicated, but stick with me, because this whole discussion is going to have important implications for Christian theology.

In the time of the Israelite and Judean monarchy, there is no evidence that anyone harbored reservations about pronouncing the name YHWH. Like I've said, the Tetragrammaton appears all over the Hebrew Bible, 450x in the book of Isaiah, for instance. Surely when Isaiah condemned the people for forsaking YHWH (Isa 1:4), he actually pronounced God's name. But not long after the exile, a good many Jews did feel uncomfortable saying God's name. We saw earlier that there is evidence already in Chronicles that some Jews were substituting *Adonai* for YHWH. Most scholars would connect this reticence to pronounce God's name to the Third Commandment: "Thou shalt not take the name of YHWH your God in vain" (Exod 20:7).

The Third Commandment is not a prohibition of pronouncing the name of God, but such a prohibition was written into the Greek translation of Leviticus. The Hebrew text of Lev 24:16 says: "Whoever blasphemes the name of YHWH shall surely be put to death." But in the Septuagint, this verse reads, "Whoever names the name of the Lord shall surely be put to death." The apocryphal book of Sirach warns its readers from "habitually uttering the name of the

Holy One" (Sir 23:19). The Mishnah—an early rabbinic document from around 200 AD, but recording much earlier tradition—reports the opinion that "one who utters the Divine Name as it is spelled" has no share in the World to Come.[36] The important Dead Sea Scroll known as the *Community Rule* codifies this prohibition:

> If any man has uttered the [Most] Venerable Name, even though frivolously, or as a result of shock or for any other reason whatever, while reading the Book or praying, he shall be dismissed and shall return to the Council of the Community no more.[37]

The most common substitute throughout history has been the word for "Lord" in the language of the speaker or reader. In Hebrew, that's *Adonai*; in Greek, it's *kurios* (κύριος); in Latin, it's *Dominus*; and in English, it's "LORD."

When the Septuagint (LXX) began to be translated in the third century BC, it seems that the translators used the word *kurios* (κύριος) as the substitute for YHWH, probably reflecting the tradition of using *Adonai* as the substitute in Hebrew.[38]

---

36. Mishnah, *Sanhedrin* 10.1; text available online at https://www.sefaria.org/Mishnah_Sanhedrin.10?lang=bi.

37. The *Community Rule* is known by the abbreviation 1QS, and the quoted passage comes from column 6, line 27, through column 7, line 2 (i.e., 1QS 6.27–7.2). The translation of the entire document by Geza Vermes is available online here: http://ccat.sas.upenn.edu/gopher/other/courses/rels/225/Texts/1QS.

38. But the LXX is not completely consistent in rendering the Tetragrammaton with κύριος, and it does use κύριος for a variety of other Hebrew words; see David B. Capes, *Old Testament Yahweh Texts in Paul's Christology* (1992; Repr.: Waco, TX: Baylor University Press, 2017), 34–43.

This is a debated point.[39] Almost all of our manuscripts of the LXX have *kurios* for the Tetragrammaton, but almost all of our LXX manuscripts were copied by Christians, and so they might not reflect the earliest form of the LXX. On the other hand, we have several fragmentary copies of the

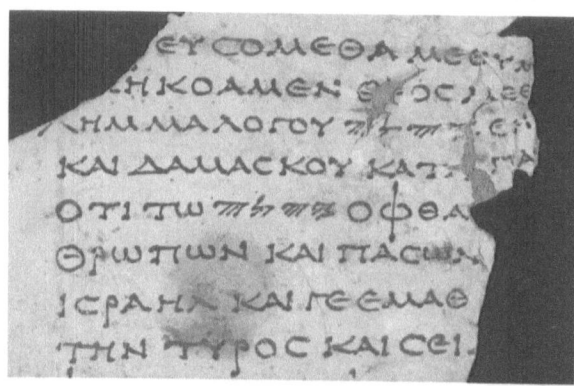

Figure 5. Courtesy of the Leon Levy Dead Sea Scrolls Digital Library. Israel Antiquities Authority. Photograph by Shai Halevi.

LXX from before the time of Christ, and not a single one of them features *kurios* for the Tetragrammaton. They do not follow any uniform practice. As mentioned above, one of the manuscripts—a copy of Leviticus from the Dead Sea Scrolls—has the form Ιαω. Other copies of the LXX feature the actual Hebrew Tetragrammaton within the Greek text, such as in the Greek Minor Prophets Scroll from Naḥal Ḥever.[40] Above is an image, which features the (paleo-)Hebrew Tetragrammaton in the third line and the fifth line.[41]

---

39. Wikipedia has a good overview of the debate; in the article on the Tetragrammaton, go to the section labeled "Septuagint and other Old Greek Translations."

40. There's a Wikipedia entry on this scroll.

41. Image available at https://www.deadseascrolls.org.il/explore-the-archive/image/B-370936.

This is one example of several from ancient manuscripts (especially the Dead Sea Scrolls) in which the name of God is treated in a visually distinctive way. Sometimes in a Hebrew manuscript, the Tetragrammaton is written in distinctive Hebrew letters (paleo-Hebrew), sometimes it is not written at all but four dots appear instead of four letters. For example, see this non-biblical manuscript from the Dead Sea Scrolls.[42] The four dots in the middle of this image is the substitution for the name of God.

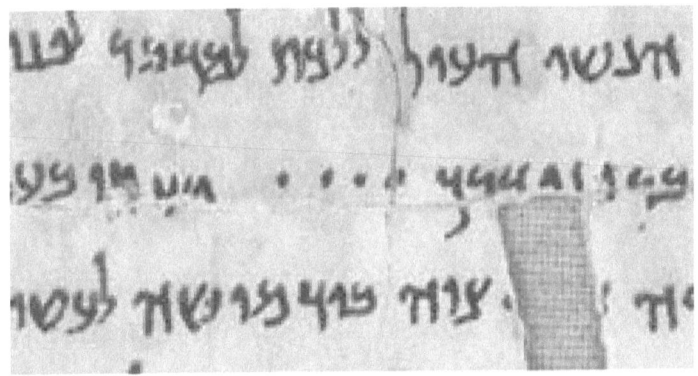

Figure 6. Courtesy of the Leon Levy Dead Sea Scrolls Digital Library. Israel Antiquities Authority. Photograph by Shai Halevi.

Some scholars have argued that the LXX originally featured the Hebrew Tetragrammaton, and this was later changed to *kurios*, or some have even argued that Iaω was the original LXX version of God's name.[43] It's hard to prove

---

42. This image is from 4Q176, https://www.deadseascrolls.org.il/explore-the-archive/image/B-360381.

43. See Patrick W. Skehan, "The Divine Name at Qumran, in the Masada Scroll, and in the Septuagint," *Bulletin of the International Organization for Septuagint and Cognate Studies* 13 (1980): 14–44.

one technique over another was original to the LXX, and it is not necessarily the case that every LXX translator adopted the same practice: maybe some translators used *kurios*, while some used Ιαω, and others retained the Hebrew Tetragrammaton. I myself think that Ιαω could not be the original LXX name for God, particularly not in Leviticus, which explicitly forbids pronouncing God's name (24:16), as we have seen.[44]

The most prominent practice for writing God's name in Greek biblical manuscripts at the time of Jesus was either (a) to retain the Hebrew Tetragrammaton or (b) to substitute the Greek word *kurios*. But evidence from Philo and other sources indicates that even if a reader of Greek Scripture came across the Hebrew Tetragrammaton in his Greek biblical manuscript, this reader would not actually pronounce the Hebrew name but would say *kurios* instead,[45] just as when I am reading the Hebrew Bible and I encounter the Tetragrammaton I automatically say *Adonai*. I imagine if a reader of Hebrew saw four dots in place of God's name, he or she would not say "four dots" but *Adonai* or some other substitute.

So, in Greek, almost certainly, the most common practice was to pronounce the name of God as *kurios*, whether the word *kurios* was written in the text or not.

---

44. This argument is from Rösel, "Reading and Translation of the Divine Name."

45. For the evidence, see James R. Royse, "Philo, ΚΥΡΙΟΣ, and the Tetragrammaton," *Studia Philonica Annual* 3 (1991): 167–83, esp. 178–83, who bases his case mostly on Philo's *Life of Moses* 2.114, 132.

Jesus and the Name of God

Here's where this whole discussion about substitutions for the Tetragrammaton becomes relevant for Christian theology. In the New Testament, Jesus is *kurios*.

> For although there may be so-called gods in heaven or on earth—as indeed there are many "gods" and many "lords"— yet for us there is one God, the Father, from whom are all things and for whom we exist, and one Lord [*kurios*], Jesus Christ, through whom are all things and through whom we exist. (1 Cor 8:5–6)

As most scholars recognize, Paul seems to be re-working the Shema here, the basic Jewish confession of their God derived from Deut 6:4: "Hear O Israel, YHWH your God is one YHWH," which in Greek would have been read as "*Kurios* your God is one *kurios*." Paul wants somehow to fit Jesus into this confession of faith, and so for Christians ("for us") there is one God, the Father, and one Lord, Jesus Christ.

The Greek way of referring to YHWH—using the word *kurios*—is the way that Paul refers to Jesus. This is also reflected in Paul's quotations of the Old Testament.[46] Fourteen times Paul quotes a verse from the Old Testament that has the Tetragrammaton in Hebrew but *kurios* in Paul's Greek quotation. Seven times Paul applies the title *kurios* to

---

46. For detailed discussion of the evidence, see Capes, *Old Testament Yahweh Texts*.

God the Father,[47] and seven times he applies the title to Jesus.[48]

Or think about what Paul is saying in Philippians 2:9: "For this reason God highly exalted him and gave him the name that is above every name." We might think that Paul means that the name "Jesus" is the name above every name, since he goes on in the next verse to say, "so that at the name of Jesus every knee will bow...." But actually Jesus is not in any way a unique name; even today a bunch of people are named Jesus, particularly native Spanish speakers, and certainly many ancient Jews had this name (*Yeshua*, the equivalent of the name Joshua). But the name YHWH—now that is a unique name. Nearly every scholar I have looked at argues that "the name above every name" could describe only YHWH, and this is the name that Jesus bears.[49] That is why every knee will bow at the name of Jesus, because the name Jesus wears is YHWH. After all, Paul is actually echoing Isa 45:23 here,

---

47. Rom 4:7–8 (quoting Psa 32:1–2); Rom 9:27–29 (quoting Isa 10:22–23 and Isa 1:9); Rom 11:34 (quoting Isa 40:13); Rom 15:11 (quoting Psa 117:1); 1 Cor 3:20 (quoting Psa 94:11); 2 Cor 6:18 (quoting 2 Sam 7:14).

48. Rom 10:13 (quoting Joel 2:32); Rom 14:11 (quoting Isa 45:23); 1 Cor 1:31 (quoting Jer 9:24); 1 Cor 2:16 (quoting Isa 40:13); 1 Cor 10:26 (quoting Psa 24:1); 2 Cor 10:17 (quoting Jer 9:24); 2 Tim 2:19 (quoting Num 16:5). Capes, *Old Testament Yahweh Texts*, also discusses allusions in Paul to Hebrew biblical texts that use the Tetragrammaton (pp. 149–60).

49. To cite one example: Larry W. Hurtado, *God in New Testament Theology* (Nashville: Abingdon, 2010), 43–44. On the other hand, Blackburn, *The God Who Makes Himself Known*, 60, seems to think the name is "Jesus."

> By myself I have sworn; truth has gone from my mouth,
> a word that will not be revoked: Every knee will bow to
> me, every tongue will swear allegiance.

Immediately before this statement in Isaiah, YHWH says, "For I am God, and there is no other" (Isa 45:22). It is this statement, proclaiming the uniqueness and sovereignty of YHWH, that Paul applies to Jesus, who will fulfill this promise that "every knee will bow... and every tongue will confess that Jesus Christ is *Kurios*" (Phil 2:10–11).

It is not only Paul who sees Jesus as an incarnation of YHWH. Mark's Gospel begins by quoting Isa 40:3 to the effect that a voice in the wilderness is preparing the way for YHWH/*Kurios*. The rest of the chapter reveals that the *Kurios* whose way has been prepared is Jesus.[50] Luke's Gospel explicitly applies the title *kurios* to Jesus a number of times.[51] The Gospel of John does the same thing (6:23; 11:2; 20:20), but it has even more overt connections to YHWH by applying the meaning of the name to Jesus. When Jesus told the crowds, "Before Abraham was born, I am," they wanted to kill him (John 8:58–59), no doubt because they correctly recognized that Jesus was claiming for himself the Divine Name, "I AM," with its implication of eternal existence. I assume that some power inherent in the Divine Name, at least on the lips of Jesus, is why the soldiers fell back when Jesus said, "I AM" (John 18:6).

---

50. For more, see Daniel Johansson, "*Kyrios* in the Gospel of Mark," *JSNT* 33 (2010): 101–24 (available online to the savvy googler).

51. Luke 7:13, 19; 10:1, 39, 41; 11:39; 12:42; 13:15; 17:5–6; 18:6; 19:8; 22:61; 24:3. See C. Kavin Rowe, *Early Narrative Christology: The Lord in the Gospel of Luke* (Berlin: de Gruyter, 2006).

The main point of this is to say that Jesus shares in the divine identity,[52] he bears the name above every name, he is the incarnation of YHWH, he is Lord, he is *kurios*.

Just one more point: Christian writers shortly after the time of the New Testament—such as Justin Martyr, from the mid-second century—identified the "angel of YHWH" who appeared to Moses in the bush (Exod 3:2) as the pre-incarnate Christ.[53] If we follow that reading, then even in its Old Testament context, Jesus is revealed as YHWH. In fact, God says about the angel who will lead the Israelites into the promised land that the Israelites should obey him because "my name is in him" (Exod 23:20–23). Justin Martyr makes the connection (*Dialogue* 75).

Conclusion

God reveals his name YHWH to Moses, a name that had great significance for Israel as signifying the eternal existence and the eternal presence of their God. The Divine Name also has great significance for Christians, since our Lord Jesus is the LORD who bears the name above every name. Reflecting on the name of God helps us understand who Jesus is.

---

52. This way of putting the matter is especially associated with Richard Bauckham; see his *Jesus and the God of Israel: God Crucified and Other Studies on the New Testament Christology of Divine Identity* (Grand Rapids: Eerdmans, 2008).

53. See Justin's *Dialogue with Trypho* 58–60. On the early Christian reading of this text as an appearance of the pre-incarnate Christ, see Bogdan Gabriel Bucur, *Scripture Re-envisioned: Christophanic Exegesis and the Making of a Christian Bible* (Leiden: Brill, 2019), ch. 3.

3

Pharaoh's Hard Heart

> The king's heart is a stream of water in the hand of
> YHWH; he turns it wherever he will. (Prov 21:1)

I'm pretty proud of my kids. They're good people, and I'm not entirely sure why. I think part of it is that they're my kids—my wife and I have intentionally provided a good environment to form them morally. So, in a sense, they're good not by their own choice but because we have made them good. But that doesn't explain everything, not by a long shot. First of all, my kids are all different, and they make choices differently. One finds it generally easier to be obedient, another finds it relatively more difficult. I don't know why they're different in that way. We've probably treated them differently in ways we don't understand. I think the birth order thing explains some of it: usually (but not always) the first child is more obedient; the second child is more rebellious. All of this suggests that it's not entirely up to the children themselves. It's like they were fated to be the way they are. Our family has also adopted a couple of kids who had lived for several years in other places before they got to our house. Their differences from our biological children can be explained partially by nurture—they've had vastly different experiences than they would have had in our household—but also by nature—they don't have our DNA. Either way, it has nothing to do with their choice.

Have you wondered what your life would be like if some of your experiences were different from what they were? If you had a different set of parents? If you had grown up in the family next door? In another country? In another religion? How many people do you know who change religion from the one in which they were raised? I don't mean a Baptist becoming a Presbyterian; I mean a Muslim becoming a Christian, or a Buddhist becoming a Jew? Sure, it happens, but not much, not in America, anyway. What if you had grown up in a Muslim household? How would that have determined the rest of your life?[1]

If you grow up poor in the inner-city, we expect that you'll live your whole life there. We aren't surprised if the son of a drug dealer becomes a drug dealer. When we hear about a murderer, we automatically wonder what happened in his childhood to make him turn out that way. When we hear that he was abused (physically or sexually) as a child, we say, "Oh, that explains it."

Of course, that's not always the way. LeBron James is impressive in part because of where he came from, the fact that he spent part of his childhood living in a car, the fact that he grew up without a father, and yet not only did he become a great basketball player but also a responsible family man and an articulate spokesman for various causes. Alexander

---

1. Origen discusses these things in *On First Principles* 2.

Hamilton has been recently lionized by Lin-Manuel Miranda for the same reason. We like to hear such stories of success, partly because they are so unexpected. Why does the accident of birth make success so difficult for some people, so easy for others? I know that people who have pulled themselves up from poverty will say that their experiences made them the people that they are. But more often such experiences crush people.

Paul said, "By the grace of God I am what I am" (1 Cor 15:10). But God almost forced his grace upon Paul in such a way that even "a blasphemer, persecutor, and insolent opponent" (1 Tim 1:13) could not deny the glory of Jesus. If God could do that for someone like Paul, why does he not do it for others? Why does God not similarly intervene in everyone's life to prevent anyone from being lost? It doesn't seem like Paul earned this special dispensation of grace in the form of a special revelation of Jesus Christ—if anything, Paul earned the opposite, since he was the chief of sinners (1 Tim 1:15)—so is it possible that God chooses certain people without any conditions? And could he then reject people eternally equally unconditionally, based on nothing within themselves or what they have done but simply his own arbitrary choice?[2]

The idea I have just outlined has a rich and venerable tradition within Christianity. It is most closely associated with John Calvin, the Genevan Reformer from the sixteenth century, whose views are still widely influential within

---

2. Calvinists probably would object to the term "arbitrary" here, but as Roger E. Olson shows (*Against Calvinism* [Grand Rapids: Zondervan, 2011], 110–21), the concept fits their doctrine.

conservative (evangelical) Christianity across the globe. (In the Calvinistic system, the idea we're discussing would be the "U" of TULIP, "unconditional election.")[3] But versions of predestination have also been championed by many Christian leaders throughout history, such as Martin Luther,[4] Augustine,[5] and, of course, the apostle Paul. In all these articulations of a doctrine of predestination—I don't want to say *the* doctrine of predestination—the hardening of Pharaoh's heart has had a role to play.

Context

As soon as Moses gets to Egypt, he does exactly what God had told him to do (3:16–22): he approaches the Israelites to inform them that YHWH, the God of their fathers, is about to redeem them (4:29–31); and then he approaches Pharaoh (5:1), asking him to grant Israel permission to leave (on a 3-day journey—we'll get to that). But God has already told Moses that Pharaoh will refuse to grant the request.

> I know that the king of Egypt will not allow you to go, even under force from a strong hand. But when I

---

3. For an explanation of this doctrine by a Calvinist, google "John Piper Five Points of Calvinism." For a brief history and explanation of the term TULIP, see Exploration 3.3 p. 75.

4. See Luther's *The Bondage of the Will*, which presents a rather Calvinistic view (to be anachronistic), in *Erasmus-Luther: Discourse on Free Will*, trans. Ernst F. Winter (New York: Ungar, 1961), 95–138.

5. See, for example, Augustine, *On the Predestination of the Saints*, trans. John A. Mourant and William J. Collinge, in *Saint Augustine: Four Anti-Pelagian Writings*, Fathers of the Church 86 (Washington, D.C.: Catholic University of America Press, 1992), 218–70.

stretch out my hand and strike Egypt with all my miracles that I will perform in it, after that, he will let you go. (Exod 3:19–20)

These are God's initial instructions to Moses, still at the burning bush. God is warning Moses that Pharaoh's refusal will not surprise God and should not disappoint Moses. It's all a part of the plan.

What do we know about Pharaoh at this point? Hardly anything at all. Remember, this is a different Pharaoh from the one who was in office at the beginning of the book. That previous Pharaoh, who "knew not Joseph" (Exod 1:8), is the one who ordered the death of the Israelite baby boys (1:22), the one whose daughter raised Moses as her son (2:5–10), the one who wanted to kill Moses for having killed an Egyptian (2:15). But that Pharaoh had died (2:23). Moses had been gone for a long time, so this new Pharaoh is either the son or the grandson (or even great grandson?) of that previous Pharaoh. This new Pharaoh certainly does not give the impression that he knows Moses very well; they do not interact as if they are long-lost brothers. I don't think we ever learn how old Pharaoh's first-born son is, the one who dies in the last plague, but we usually think about him being a pretty young boy, which might suggest that this Pharaoh himself is not an old man, nowhere near as old as Moses (which would again suggest that they were not raised together in the same household, Moses and this Pharaoh).

We do know that this Pharaoh belongs to a family that oppresses the Israelites, a family that makes itself rich and powerful off of the back of slave labor. Under this new Pharaoh, the Israelites are still groaning and crying out because of their difficult labor (2:23). And the initial response of Pharaoh to Moses is not simply to refuse the request for liberation, but to increase the difficulty of Israel's slave labor, apparently just to be mean (5:6–9). We do know—not from the Bible but from Egyptian sources, and this idea is probably assumed in the Bible—that Pharaoh was considered at least partially divine and would become a god at his death.[6] And we can assume that Pharaoh is a polytheist who encourages worship of the traditional Egyptian deities.

Hardening Pharaoh's Heart

Our initial impression of Pharaoh would probably be that he would be a poor candidate to respond obediently to a message from the Israelite God. Then again, Moses seems to have been a poor candidate, but God overcame his objections. Not so with Pharaoh. Quite the opposite, in fact. We have already seen that God warns Moses that Pharaoh will reject the request to liberate the Israelites. Later, after Moses has left the burning bush, collected his family, and has started returning to Egypt God explains to Moses just why Pharaoh will be so hard-hearted.

---

6. Explained at Wikipedia (https://en.wikipedia.org/wiki/Pharaoh or at Encyclopedia Britannica (https://www.britannica.com/topic/pharaoh). At times Pharaoh was thought of as the incarnation of Horus (https://en.wikipedia.org/wiki/Horus#Horus_and_the_pharaoh) and at other times as an embodiment or "son" of Ra (https:// en.wikipedia.org/wiki/Ra#Worship).

YHWH instructed Moses, "When you go back to Egypt, make sure you do before Pharaoh all the wonders that I have put within your power. But I will harden his heart so that he won't let the people go." (Exod 4:21)

God takes responsibility for Pharaoh's refusal. This is the first in a string of verses over the next ten or so chapters in which we read about Pharaoh's hard heart. Sometimes God hardens Pharaoh's heart, sometimes Pharaoh hardens his own heart, and sometimes Exodus reports merely that Pharaoh's heart was hard.

> **EXPLORATION 3.1**
> **REFERENCES TO PHARAOH'S HARD HEART**
>
> 1. God will stiffen (piel of חזק; σκληρύνω) Pharaoh's heart (4:21)
> 2. God will harden (hiphil of קשה; σκληρύνω) Pharaoh's heart (7:3)
> 3. Pharaoh's heart is stiff (qal of חזק; κατισκύω), this in response to the first sign, when Aaron's rod became a snake and swallowed the other rods (7:13).
> 4. Pharaoh's heart is heavy (כָּבֵד; βαρέω), this in God's instructions to Moses and Aaron immediately after Aaron's magic rod failed to impress Pharaoh (7:14).
> 5. Pharaoh's heart is stiff (qal of חזק; σκληρύνω), this in response to the first plague, water to blood (7:22).
> 6. Pharaoh makes his heart heavy (hiphil of כבד; βαρύνω), this in response to the frogs leaving as a result of Moses' intercession (8:15; Heb. 8:11).

7. Pharaoh's heart is stiff (qal of חזק; σκληρύνω), this in response to the gnats, and his own magicians' inability to imitate the plague (8:19; Heb. 8:15).

8. Pharaoh makes his heart heavy (hiphil of כבד; βαρύνω), this in response to the swarm of insects leaving as a result of Moses' intercession (8:32; Heb. 8:28).

9. Pharaoh makes his heart heavy (qal of כבד; βαρύνω), this in response to the plague on the cattle that did not affect Israelite cattle (9:7).

10. God stiffened (piel of חזק; σκληρύνω) Pharaoh's heart, this in response to the boils (9:12).

11. Pharaoh makes his heart heavy (hiphil of כבד; βαρύνω), this in response to the cessation of hail (9:34).

12. Pharaoh's heart is stiff (qal of חזק; σκληρύνω), as a summary statement (9:35).

13. God makes Pharaoh's heart heavy (hiphil of כבד; σκληρύνω; 10:1).

14. God stiffened Pharaoh's heart (piel of חזק; σκληρύνω; 10:20).

15. God stiffened Pharaoh's heart (piel of חזק; σκληρύνω; 10:27).

16. God stiffened Pharaoh's heart (piel of חזק; σκληρύνω; 11:10).

17. God will stiffen Pharaoh's heart (piel of חזק; σκληρύνω; 14:4)

18. God stiffened Pharaoh's heart (piel of חזק; σκληρύνω; 14:8).

> 19. God is stiffening the Egyptians' hearts (piel participle of חזק; σκληρύνω; 14:17)
> - חזק Piel 8x (4:21; 9:12; 10:20, 27; 11:10; 14:4, 8, 17). God stiffens Pharaoh's heart.
> - חזק Qal 4x (7:13, 22; 8:19; 9:35). Pharaoh's heart is stiff.
> - כבד Hiphil 3x (8:15, 32; 9:34). Pharaoh makes his heart heavy.
> - כבד adjective 1x (7:14). Pharaoh's heart is heavy.
> - כבד Qal 1x (9:7). Pharaoh's heart is heavy.
> - כבד Hiphil 1x (10:1). God makes Pharaoh's heart heavy.
> - קשה Hiphil 1x (7:3). God hardens Pharaoh's heart.

What are we to make of this? In the past I have approached the issue this way: aside from the two predictions that God will harden Pharaoh's heart (4:21; 7:3), when we actually get to the action of the plagues, the text speaks only of Pharaoh hardening his own heart,[7] or Pharaoh's heart being hard,[8] until the sixth plague, when the text starts attributing the hardening to God (9:12), at which point God becomes the active agent of hardening,[9] except for one further reference to Pharaoh hardening his own heart (9:34) and to Pharaoh's heart being hard (9:35). So maybe we could interpret this hardening in terms of Romans 1, "God gave them up...." Once Pharaoh had chosen his path, God gave

---

7. Exodus 8:15, 32; 9:7.
8. Exodus 7:13, 14, 22; 8:19.
9. Exodus 10:1, 20, 27; 11:10; 14:4, 8, 17.

him over to that path.[10] I would still like for this interpretation to be valid, but I don't think it really works in terms of the plot of Exodus.

Another possible explanation would be that God hardens Pharaoh in the sense that he presents him with an opportunity for obedience or disobedience, and because of the type of person Pharaoh chooses to be, this opportunity itself results in hardening. That is, God doesn't really actively harden Pharaoh or desire his hardening, but God's actions (sending Moses) result in the hardening nonetheless.[11] Again, I wouldn't mind this interpretation if we could get it to work out. But I don't think that it will work in terms of the plot of Exodus.

It seems to me—no matter how much I have tried to think of ways around this interpretation—that God is actively involved in hardening Pharaoh, ensuring that he is disobedient. Let me say now that I do not think that God's dealings with Pharaoh provide a model for how God deals with people generally (i.e, Pharaoh is a special case), and I

---

10. The fifth-century commentator Theodoret of Cyrus emphasized that Pharaoh had free will and chose to harden his heart before God acted; see *The Questions on the Octateuch*, vol. 1: *On Genesis and Exodus*, trans. Robert C. Hill, Library of Early Christianity (Washington, D.C.: Catholic University of America Press, 2007), 237–43 (= question 12 on Exodus).

11. This is how Origen understands Pharaoh's hardening (*On First Principles* 3.1.8–14). See also Theodoret, *Questions on the Octateuch*, 1.243 (question 12 on Exodus), who gives the following analogy: "The sun with its heat melts wax but dries mud: softening one and hardening the other. As the same heat produces opposite effects, so from God's lovingkindness some reap benefit, others harm; some are softened, others hardened."

certainly do not believe that God foreordained from all eternity that Pharaoh would be lost in hell. I do not interpret Pharaoh's hard heart as a point leading inextricably to the Unconditional Election of Calvinism. But in terms of what God wanted to accomplish through the exodus, God wanted Pharaoh to be resistant.

What if Pharaoh had acquiesced to Moses' initial request? What if at Exodus 5:2—instead of saying, "I don't know YHWH, and I'm not going to let the people go!"—what if he had said, "Sure, go ahead"? Without any conflict, God could not have displayed his power.

It's the same reason we're not quite sure how good of a basketball player George Mikan was: who did he play against? What was the level of competition? Or we're not sure where to rank Pete Sampras as a tennis player because he didn't play the greats that came before him (McEnroe, Connors) or the greats that came later (Federer, Nadal, Djokovic). To establish greatness, there needs to be some level of competition. For a lot of basketball fans, the recent run of the Golden State Warriors means less for the greatness of the individual players than what other dynasties have done because the collection of talent on the Warriors was so absurdly superior to any collection of talent in history; because the team was so good, it's hard to judge how good the individual players were. There's not enough competition.

When we're talking about God versus a human, there's always going to be an infinite gap in ability; it'll always be a one-sided competition. But humans are pretty bad at accepting that truth, and so sometimes God wants to demonstrate his power. "Give me the greatest king in the world, king of the greatest empire in the world, rich and powerful beyond human comprehension, even thought to be son of a god. And let's go toe-to-toe and see how it turns out." It's not much of a competition, but God wants to show us how lopsided the competition is, precisely because we are so accustomed to ooo-ing and ahh-ing at the power of the pharaohs. This narrative shows that Pharaoh—and his heart—is putty in YHWH's hands. God wanted to broadcast his power to the entire world, and particularly to his own people (Deut 7:18). According to the Bible, the strategy worked: Rahab reports how concerned her countrymen are because they have heard reports about what Israel's God did to Egypt (Josh 2:9–11; cf. 1 Sam 4:8).

God could have gone all Sodom-and-Gomorrah on Egypt. At the first sign of Egyptian resistance to the word of God, he could have rained fire and brimstone on them and set Israel free. But, in this case, he apparently didn't want the competition to end too quickly. He wanted to create a lasting effect. Remember that nobody knows who YHWH is, and the process of the plagues is not really about freeing Israel but about revealing YHWH. Pharaoh's first response to Moses is, "Who is YHWH?" (Exod 5:2). Look what God tells Moses before his next encounter with the king.

> See, I have made you like a god to Pharaoh, and Aaron your brother will be your prophet. You must say whatever I command you; then Aaron your brother must declare it to Pharaoh so that he will let the Israelites go from his land. But I will harden Pharaoh's heart and multiply my signs and wonders in the land of Egypt. Pharaoh will not listen to you, but I will put my hand

into Egypt and bring the military divisions of my people the Israelites out of the land of Egypt by great acts of judgment. The Egyptians will know that I am YHWH when I stretch out my hand against Egypt and bring out the Israelites from among them. (Exod 7:1–5)

What is the point of this whole battle between God and Pharaoh? "The Egyptians will know that I am YHWH." Why does God harden Pharaoh's heart? So that he can "multiply my signs and wonders in the land of Egypt."

EXPLORATION 3.2

THE TEN PLAGUES (EXOD 7-12)

Aaron turns his staff into a snake; the magicians do also, but Aaron's staff swallows theirs (7:8–13)

1. Water to Blood (7:14–25)—the magicians can do this (7:22)
2. Frogs (7:26–8:11)—the magicians can do this (8:3); Pharaoh offers to let the people go to sacrifice (8:4)
3. Gnats (8:12–15)—the magicians say this is the finger of God (8:15)
4. Insects (8:16–28)—Goshen is not affected (8:18–19); Pharaoh offers to release the people for a short distance (8:21–24)
5. Animals die (9:1–7)—Israelite cattle not affected (9:4)
6. Boils (9:8–12)—magicians could not stand before Moses because of the boils (9:11)

7. Hail (9:13–35)—Goshen is not affected (9.26); Pharaoh offers to release Israel (9:27–28)

8. Locusts (10:1–20)—Prior to the plague, Pharaoh offers to release the Israelite men to serve YHWH (10:7–11), and during the plague Pharaoh says he has sinned (10:16; cf. 9:27), but does not explicitly offer release.

9. Darkness (10:21–29)—Goshen is not affected (10:23); Pharaoh offers to release all Israelites, but not their animals (10:24).

10. Firstborn die (11:4–10; 12:12–13, 29–42)

Psalm 78:43–51 presents a reduced list of plagues, in this order: water to blood, insects, frogs, locust, hail, cattle, death of firstborn. Using the narrative in Exodus as the standard, Psalm 78 presents the order 1, 4, 2, 8, 7, 5, 10, and it omits any reference to plagues 3, 6, 9.

Psalm 105:27–36 presents a reduced list of plagues, in this order: darkness, water to blood, frogs, flies, hail, locusts, death of firstborn. So, the order that this psalm presents the plagues is 9, 1, 2, 4, 3, 7, 8, 10, omitting altogether numbers 5–6.

Apparently the first time the phrase "ten plagues" is used is in the first-century writer known as Pseudo-Philo, in his *Book of Biblical Antiquities* 10:1, where he names off the plagues as "blood and frogs and mixed creatures and hail and pestilence upon cattle and locusts and lice and palpable darkness and the death of the first-born," which is, of course, only nine plagues. The order is 1, 2, ?,

> 7, 5, 8, 3, 9, 10. I'm not sure what the "mixed creatures" would be (maybe the insects, #4?). This list does not include #6.[12]
>
> The apocryphal Wisdom of Solomon interprets the plagues not only as judgments against the gods of Egypt but also as acts of mercy designed to bring the Egyptians to an understanding of their own folly. "The ones who weren't brought back to their senses by this mocking judgment would experience the just judgment of God. They were plagued by the very things they once took to be gods, and came to hate them" (Wis 12:26–27).

Can we call this rope-a-dope? I don't know, something like that. Anyway, it seems to me that God is actively engaged here in ensuring Pharaoh's refusal to acquiesce to Moses' demands. Maybe God is using agents to accomplish this task; the classic movie *The Ten Commandments* (1956) with Charlton Heston has Pharaoh's wife harden her husband's heart by goading him into displaying his own superiority to Moses and his God. However, God accomplished it, the prolonged battle would demonstrate God's power and make his name known throughout the world as the God who made mincemeat out of Pharaoh.

> For this time I am about to send all my plagues against you, your officials, and your people. Then you will

---

12.. Trans. Howard Jacobson, "Pseudo-Philo, Book of Biblical Antiquities," in *Outside the Bible: Ancient Jewish Writings Related to Scripture*, 3 vols., ed. Louis H. Feldman, James L. Kugel, and Lawrence H. Schiffman (Philadelphia: JPS, 2013), 1.470–613, at 493.

> know there is no one like me on the whole earth. By now I could have stretched out my hand and struck you and your people with a plague, and you would have been obliterated from the earth. However, I have let you live for this purpose: to show you my power and to make my name known on the whole earth. (Exod 9:14–16)

> Go to Pharaoh, for I have hardened his heart and the hearts of his officials so that I may do these miraculous signs of mine among them and so that you may tell your son and grandson how severely I dealt with the Egyptians and performed miraculous signs among them, and you will know that I am YHWH. (Exod 10:1–2)

I do not mean to say that Pharaoh has no culpability here. The text does say at times that Pharaoh hardened his heart and thereby sinned (e.g., 9:34). And it's hard for me to believe that God would have treated Pharaoh in this manner if Pharaoh had shown more signs of openness toward God, less arrogance. Maybe it is this aspect—Pharaoh's arrogance, his hardening of his own heart—that explains why God seems to be upset with him sometimes for not releasing the Israelites (e.g., 9:17), though at other times the text indicates that God has brought this circumstance about.

I don't understand this whole section of Scripture as well as I would like, but it seems to me that taking the text at face value—that God is actively engaged in hardening Pharaoh—makes more sense of the Scriptural statements than any alternative that I know about. I understand that there are theological difficulties with this approach, but I think they are not insurmountable.

God's ultimate goal with Pharaoh and Egypt seems to be to bring judgment upon them, and God's hardening Pharaoh's heart aids him in bringing that judgment. The plagues themselves are judgments,[13] certainly the Tenth Plague is a judgment, and then the destruction of the Egyptian army in the Red Sea is a judgment. This judgment would not have come about in the same way—apparently the way that God wanted to accomplish it, apparently the way that would make God's name renowned throughout the world—had Pharaoh permitted the Israelite exodus early on, or really at any point in the narrative.

> "Pharaoh will not listen to you, so that my wonders may be multiplied in the land of Egypt." Moses and Aaron did all these wonders before Pharaoh, but YHWH hardened Pharaoh's heart, and he would not let the Israelites go out of his land. (11:9–10)

> As for me, I am going to harden the hearts of the Egyptians so that they will go in after them, and I will receive glory by means of Pharaoh, all his army, and his chariots and horsemen. The Egyptians will know that I am YHWH when I receive glory through Pharaoh, his chariots, and his horsemen. (14:17–18)

I trust God's justice. I believe 1 Tim 2:4, that God desires all men to come to a knowledge of the truth. I believe God knew who he was dealing with in this Pharaoh, and dealt with him

---

13. See the apocryphal Wisdom of Solomon (Wis 12:23–27).

appropriately. Perhaps God waited so long to liberate Israel from Egyptian bondage because he wanted to demonstrate his power over this particular Pharaoh. That bit of speculation is in part based on Gen 15:16, where God says that the conquest of Canaan will happen when "the sin of the Amorite" is complete. The conquest of Canaan was delayed a long time until judgment upon the Canaanites (Amorites) became most appropriate. Perhaps the exodus from Egypt was similarly delayed until judgment upon Pharaoh became most appropriate.

One more point here: Pharaoh is a special case, I think, but he is not a unique case. God did the same thing (on a smaller scale) with Sihon, king of Heshbon (Deut 2:30). And there are other Bible passages that attribute to God actions that probably make us uncomfortable (e.g., 2 Thess 2:11–12), all of which are hard to explain. But, again, at the end of the day I trust God's justice and his love.

The 3-Day Journey

This competition with Pharaoh might explain the strange, recurring request from Moses that Pharaoh allow the Israelites to go on a 3-day journey to sacrifice to their God.[14] Readers of Exodus are sometimes surprised and confused to find this theme; it's not something that we have talked a lot about in our churches (in my experience). But it is God who tells Moses to make this request. God tells Moses to...

---

14. Films such as *The Ten Commandments* omit this troublesome part of the story.

> ...go to the king of Egypt and say to him: YHWH, the God of the Hebrews, has met with us. Now please let us go on a three-day journey into the wilderness so that we may sacrifice to YHWH our God. (3:18)

The idea that Israel is just going to go celebrate a festival and sacrifice to God in the wilderness recurs often in the text.[15] There are several things to say about this theme.

*The first assignment for Israel really is to "worship God at this mountain," i.e., Sinai (3:12), and they did sacrifice to God at Sinai (24:5–6).

*The time period "3 days" seems in the Bible to be an expression for a short period of time (sort of like when we tell someone to wait for "just a minute," which might actually be 5–10 minutes).

*The 3-day journey apparently refers not to how long the Israelites would be away from Egypt but to how long the trip would take to get to the location to worship God.[16] The actual travel time was, however, about six weeks (Exod 19:1; cf. Num 33:3).

*Moses didn't tell Pharaoh that the Israelites would return to their enslaved status once the festival was done, and Pharaoh certainly seems to have been dubious about the whole

---

15. Cf. Exodus 4:23; 5:1, 3; 7:16; 8:1, 8, 20, 25–29; 9:1, 13; 10:3, 7–11, 24–28; 12:31.

16. William H. C. Propp, *Exodus 1–18*, Anchor Bible (New York: Doubleday, 1998), 206–7.

thing. At one point he wanted the Israelites to sacrifice within Egypt (8:25), or at least not far in the wilderness (v. 28). At another point he wanted just the males to go (10:8-11). At another point, Pharaoh offered to let all the Israelites go if they left their animals behind (10:24). These all seem to be offers designed to ensure that Israel continues to be slaves to Egypt. Pharaoh knew that the request to go on a 3-day journey—and stay who knows how long!—was really a request for permanent liberation.

But why would God tell Moses to express it in these terms? Why not just come out with it and say that God demands Pharaoh release permanently the Israelites? The only reason I can imagine is that this seemingly small request exhibits Pharaoh's hard heart all the more, since he refused to grant even a 3-day journey.

Paul's Use of Pharaoh's Hard Heart

> What shall we say then? Is there injustice on God's part? By no means! ¹⁵ For he says to Moses, "I will have mercy on whom I have mercy, and I will have compassion on whom I have compassion" [Exod 33:19]. ¹⁶ So then it depends not on human will or exertion, but on God, who has mercy. ¹⁷ For the Scripture says to Pharaoh, "For this very purpose I have raised you up, that I might show my power in you, and that my name might be proclaimed in all the earth" [Exod 9:16]. ¹⁸ So then he has mercy on whomever he wills, and he hardens whomever he wills. (Rom 9:14–18)

This is a passage that has caused a great deal of controversy over the centuries. "If Romans is the arena of the predestination debate, then Romans 9 is the cage that the gladiators get locked in for their combat."[17] We're not going to solve the issues here. Let me just present a way of thinking about what Paul is doing with Pharaoh's hard heart.

Romans 9–11 considers the election of Israel in the context of (1) God's promises to Israel and (2) Israel's rejection of God's Messiah. Paul interprets this rejection as indicating some sort of hardening of Israel (Romans 11:7)—but not in the same sense as Pharaoh was hardened, because God made no promises to Pharaoh, but he has made promises to Israel. So Paul says this hardening is only partial, and he is still convinced that the promises will all be fulfilled so that "all Israel will be saved" (Rom 11:26), at which point he quotes Isaiah 59:20–21 as a prooftext: "The Deliverer will come from Zion; he will turn godlessness away from Jacob. And this will be my covenant with them when I take away their sins." Now, I have no desire to jump out of the frying pan (predestination) and into the fire (Paul's hopes for Israel), so let's get back into the frying pan, right after we notice that this whole convoluted (to me, anyway) discussion ends in wonder at how unsearchable are God's judgments and inscrutable are his ways (11:33). Paul thinks this stuff is so complex as to be inscrutable. I agree.

God moves in mysterious ways. Sometimes God even hardens people. God accomplished his purpose by hardening Pharaoh, and maybe he is involved in some similar way

---

17. Michael F. Bird, *Evangelical Theology: A Biblical and Systematic Introduction* (Grand Rapids: Zondervan, 2013), 519.

now in regard to Israel. Similar, but different. Israel has stumbled, but not so as to fall (11:11). The difference, again, is that God has made certain promises to Israel, and we cannot imagine that the word of God has failed (9:6). I'm not really sure that Paul has a firm idea about how God is going to show himself faithful to Israel, but he is certain that God will show himself faithful.

None of this, I think, supports a Calvinistic view of predestination, about which, more in just a moment. Now I certainly see how someone could get a Calvinistic view form this text (by not paying much attention to the rest of the Bible), since Paul says that God hardens whomever he wants. I think every professing Christian would agree with Paul: God certainly does harden whomever he wants to harden. Many of us would just want to insist that God does not really want to harden people as a general rule. And, as we've already seen, Paul seems to regard the case of Pharaoh as somewhat exceptional—as an example of what God can do, to be sure, but not as an example of what God is in the habit of doing. It is an example that has some interesting parallels with what is going on with Israel, but it is not exactly the same thing as what is going on with Israel.

Pharaoh's Hard Heart and Predestination[18]

We should probably end it with Paul, but let's take the matter a step further.

---

18. For an extensive treatment of the history of the doctrine, see Matthew Levering, *Predestination: Biblical and Theological Paths* (Oxford: Oxford University Press, 2012).

Predestination is a biblical doctrine, as long as it is defined biblically. The classic biblical texts are in Paul's letters.

> And we know that for those who love God all things work together for good, for those who are called according to his purpose. ²⁹ For those whom he foreknew he also predestined to be conformed to the image of his Son, in order that he might be the firstborn among many brothers. ³⁰ And those whom he predestined he also called, and those whom he called he also justified, and those whom he justified he also glorified. (Rom 8:28–30)

> Blessed be the God and Father of our Lord Jesus Christ, who has blessed us in Christ with every spiritual blessing in the heavenly places, ⁴ even as he chose us in him before the foundation of the world, that we should be holy and blameless before him. In love ⁵ he pre-destined us for adoption to himself as sons through Jesus Christ, according to the purpose of his will… (Eph 1:3–5)

> In him we have obtained an inheritance, having been predestined according to the purpose of him who works all things according to the counsel of his will, ¹² so that we who were the first to hope in Christ might be to the praise of his glory. (Eph 1:11–12)

Calvinists[19] interpret these passages along with Romans 9 as indicating that before the creation of the world, God selected specific individual people to be saved—God

---

19. See Exploration 3.3 for a brief overview of the Five Points of Calvinism.

predestined people individually. Since Calvinists and most other Christians also affirm that human beings are sinful (Calvinists would say "totally depraved") and without hope of salvation unless God saves them, God's act of choosing specific individuals and not others for salvation necessarily means that he chooses specific individuals to be damned.[20] Furthermore, this "election"[21] is unconditional —God's choice of individuals has nothing to do with the individual, whether the person would be good or have faith or whatever.

> ### EXPLORATION 3.3
> ### A BRIEF HISTORY OF THE FIVE POINTS OF CALVINISM
>
> The so-called Five Points of Calvinism or the "doctrines of grace" were not formulated as such by John Calvin (1509–1564). To what extent he affirmed them all is actually a matter of dispute. At any rate, his writings can be interpreted as affirming, or at least inspiring, the later formulation of the five points. But he did not particularly emphasize these precise teachings any more than others; his *Institutes of the Christian Religion* covers a lot more ground than just what we think of as TULIP.
>
> It was the opponents of Calvinism that formulated five points of anti-Calvinism, a.k.a, Arminianism (= The Remonstrance).[22] Jacob Arminius (1560–1609) was a

---

20. For Calvin's exposition of this teaching, see *Institutes of the Christian Religion* 3.21–24.

21. "Election" is of course a biblical word: Titus 1:1; 1 Pet 1:1.

22. For an English translation of the brief section of the Remonstrance that lays out the positive views of the Remonstrance, see *Creeds and Confessions of Faith in the Christian Tradition*, vol. 2: *Reformation Era*, ed.

Reformed theologian who lived a little bit after Calvin and came to disagree with some of the teachings of other Reformed theologians.[23] The year after his death, some of the followers of Arminius presented five points on which they disagreed with general Reformed theology.[24] This move led several years later (1618–19) to the Synod of Dort,[25] which rejected all five points of Arminianism and articulated in response what has come to be known as the Five Points of Calvinism.[26]

In English-speaking territories, these five points are commonly denoted by the acronym TULIP, thus:[27] (1) Total Depravity: due to Adam's sin, human nature is

Jaroslav Pelikan and Valerie Hotchkiss (New Haven: Yale University Press, 2003), 547–50.

23. For a basically sympathetic account of the theology of Arminius, see Keith D. Stanglin and Thomas H. McCall, *Jacob Arminius: Theologian of Grace* (Oxford: Oxford University Press, 2012).

24. See on Wikipedia "Five Articles of Remonstrance."

25. Dort = Dordrecht, a city in the Netherlands, with a population today of about 120,000, located about 50 miles south of Amsterdam. On the Synod, see Wikipedia, "Canons of Dort."

26. For an English translation of the canons of the Synod of Dort, see Creeds and Confessions, ed. Pelikan and Hotchkiss, 569–600.

27. What I present here is an unsympathetic oversimplification of these doctrines. For a Calvinist explanation of each of these points, see the exposition of John Piper mentioned in note 3 above.

totally evil and unable to come to God or do anything good. (2) Unconditional Election: God elects the saved, and condemns the reprobate, unconditionally, based on nothing within the person, or what the person has done, not even in regard to whether the person has faith. No one has faith unless God's irresistible grace calls them. Otherwise, everyone is totally depraved. The elect have faith because of God's grace and not *vice versa*. (3) Limited Atonement: Christ died only for the elect, not for everybody. (4) Irresistible Grace: the elect cannot resist God's grace—they cannot not be saved. (5) Perseverance of the Saints = once saved, always saved.

Wikipedia shares a little bit about the history of the acronym TULIP.[28] Apparently the acronym was coined by Cleland Boyd McAfee, the author of the hymn "Near to the Heart of God" (written in the wake of the death of McAfee's two nieces). In 1913, William H. Vail reported that eight years earlier he had heard a lecture by "Dr. McAfee" on the five points of Calvinism in which McAfee had made use of the word "tulip" as a

---

28. https://en.wikipedia.org/wiki/Calvinism#Five_points_of_Calvinism.

> mnemonic device.²⁹ So, apparently McAfee came up with this mnemonic (unless he adopted it from someone else) at least by 1905. The TULIP acronym was later adopted by Loraine Boettner in his popular book *The Reformed Doctrine of Predestination* (1932).³⁰ Thereafter, the TULIP formulation of Calvinism has become almost the unquestioned "canonical" version of Calvinism, for Calvinists and non-Calvinists, alike. It is interesting to read in Vail's article from 1913 the several different versions of the Five Points that he discovered in his searches, before TULIP became standard. (The first version Vail lists even has "free will" as one of the five points!)

This is the way Calvin put it:

> We call predestination God's eternal decree, by which he determined with himself what he willed to become of each man. For all are not created in equal condition; rather, eternal life is foreordained for some, eternal damnation for others. Therefore, as any man has been created to one or the other of these ends, we speak of him as predestined to life or to death.³¹

---

29. See William H. Vail, "The Five Points of Calvinism Historically Considered," *The Outlook* 104 (1913): 394–95, available at https://babel.hathitrust.org/cgi/pt?id=iau.31858033603428;view=1up;seq=400.

30. Available at https://babel.hathitrust.org/cgi/pt?id=inu..32000007725304;view=1up;seq=8.

31. Calvin, *Institutes of the Christian Religion* 3.21.5.

There are some verses that could lend support to this way of interpreting predestination.

> No one can come to me unless the Father who sent me draws them, and I will raise them up at the last day. (John 6:44)
>
> You did not choose me, but I chose you and appointed you so that you might go and bear fruit. (John 15:16)[32]
>
> All who were appointed for eternal life believed. (Acts 13:48)

The Calvinistic idea of unconditional election—with the concomitant idea of unconditional reprobation and damnation—assumes that there is no genuine free will. In the introduction to this chapter, we noticed that some very important aspects of our lives are completely outside of our control, such as where we are born and what sort of family raises us. Moreover, different scientific fields question whether humans truly have free will, as judged from a purely physical standpoint irrespective of religion.[33]

All that to say that Calvinists have highlighted certain biblical verses that need to be considered in thinking about

---

32. See Augustine's comment on this verse quoted by Bird, *Evangelical Theology*, 521.

33. Listen to the physicist Brian Greene discuss free will here: https://soundcloud.com/onbeing/brian-greene-on-free-will-1; and here is a NYT Blog post on free will from the perspective of neuroscience: https://opinionator.blogs.nytimes.com/2011/11/13/is-neuroscience-the-death-of-free-will/.

God's relationship with humans, and some Calvinistic ideas have a strange resonance with some scientific ideas.

And Calvinists emphasize the sovereignty of God, for which we should be thankful. I believe that emphasis lines up well with the point of God's hardening Pharaoh's heart—God is in control, much more powerful than the most powerful human monarch.

"In him we live and move and have our being" (Acts 17:28). We could reflect on what implications this statement has for our free will. All of our decisions are made "within God," since we depend on him for life—more than that, for holding the particles of our bodies together, for enabling our brains to work, for not snapping his fingers so that the universe ceases to exist.

But ... the Bible consistently represents humans as having the ability to choose the path they go down, to choose whether to follow God or not.

> Choose life, that you and your offspring may live. (Deut 30:19)

> Choose this day whom you will serve. (Josh 24:15)

> Say to them, As I live, declares the Lord YHWH, I have no pleasure in the death of the wicked, but that the wicked turn from his way and live; turn back, turn back from your evil ways, for why will you die, O house of Israel? (Ezek 33:11)

> And Peter said to them, "Repent and be baptized every one of you in the name of Jesus Christ for the

forgiveness of your sins, and you will receive the gift of the Holy Spirit." (Acts 2:38)

Yes, admittedly, it does not seem (to me, anyway) to be the case with Pharaoh in the Plague Narrative of Exodus that he had much of a choice. When the text says that God hardened Pharaoh, I interpret that to mean that Pharaoh didn't really have a choice in the matter, that if he were going to choose to release the Israelites, that God would have overruled that choice until all God's purposes were fulfilled. But I also assume that early in his life Pharaoh did have a genuine choice as to what kind of person he would be. The divine hardening during the Plague Narrative is a special case in human history and even within the life of this particular Pharaoh.

Moreover, the Bible represents God as love (1 John 4:8), and as loving the whole world (John 3:16), and as wanting everyone to be saved (1 Tim 2:4). It is difficult to see how unconditional election and unconditional damnation fits with these Scriptural depictions of God.

Calvin himself says that 1 Tim 2:4—God "desires all people to be saved and to come to the knowledge of the truth"—does not really mean that God wants every individual human to be saved.

> By this he assuredly means nothing more than that the way of salvation was not shut against any order of men; that, on the contrary, he had manifested his mercy in such a way, that he would have none debarred from it.[34]

---

34. Calvin, *Institutes of the Christian Religion* 3.24.16.

According to Calvin, the passage speaks about "any order of men," not about individual people. God doesn't want any type of person—Asians, Africans, Americans, Europeans, etc.—barred from salvation, but Paul didn't mean to say that God wants all human beings to be saved.[35]

That is not a compelling interpretation of the passage.

Though the Bible consistently represents God as loving and merciful, the Calvinist scheme represents him as arbitrarily condemning the non-elect to hell. This scheme calls into question the nature of God's love, not to mention the purpose of evangelism.

Calvinist biblical scholar Michael Bird responds

> The Calvinistic scheme does not mean that God has no love for the nonelect. God desires all persons to be saved, and none who come to him will ever be rejected. That is God's general love for all of people. Yet God also has a special love, and he demonstrates that love by choosing a people for salvation even though neither they nor anybody deserved it. God loves generally in his

---

35. Augustine, *On Rebuke and Grace*, 14.44, offers the same interpretation as that of Calvin. See also Augustine's *Handbook on Faith, Hope, and Love (Enchiridion)*, 27.103, written somewhat earlier, where he advises his readers to pray to God "to will our salvation, because if he will it, it must necessarily be accomplished." He concludes the paragraph by asserting, "He certainly did not will to do anything that he has not done." In terms of the types of people in view in 1 Tim 2:4, Augustine names "kings, subjects; noble, plebeian, high, low, learned, and unlearned; the sound in body, the feeble, the clever, the dull, the foolish, the rich, the poor, and those of middling circumstances; males, females, infants, boys, youths; young, middle-aged, and old men; of every tongue, of every fashion, of all arts, of all professions, with all the innumerable differences of will and conscience, and whatever else there is that makes a distinction among men."

> willingness to receive all, and he loves particularly in ensuring that a remnant of humanity will be saved. ... If God has determined who will be saved, is there any point in engaging in evangelism? Should we only preach to people who, the hyper-Calvinists say, show signs of election? God's instrument to bring the elect into salvation is the proclamation of the gospel by the church. God has determined not only the end of salvation, but also its means. Far from stifling evangelism, God's predestination of believers motivates evangelism since we know that God's Word does not fail and those whom he elects will be saved through our message.[36]

Again, that line of thought is hard to follow. A "special love" that he grants unconditionally only to certain people, while his general love ensures only eternal damnation? That's some kind of love! And we need to preach the gospel to peo-ple whose eternal destiny is already secure, ordained from all eternity. Hmm. This type of interpretation is harshly crit-icized by John Wesley in his two sermons "Predestination Calmly Considered" and "Free Grace."[37]

Rather than unconditional election of individual humans, a better, more consistent way of understanding the Bible's teaching on election is to say that God elects the group—Israel, or the church—and individuals become a part of the elect according to their faith. This idea is specifi-cally denied by Bird: "The point is not that the church is elect and one joins the elect by faith. Faith is

---

36. Bird, *Evangelical Theology*, 529.
37. You can easily find these sermons online. The first one mentioned is pretty long; the second one is pretty short.

created by God's word (Rom 10:17). Faith is not the means to election, but the sign of it (see Rom 4)."[38] But taking the biblical teaching as a whole, this idea is easier to hold than the other.[39]

Conclusion

A few points at the end of this discussion:

*If you are lost, you have no one to blame but yourself. You sinned and God didn't make you sin. You cannot use Pharaoh's hard heart to blame God for your own sin.

*If you are saved, "what do you have that you did not receive?" (1 Cor 4:7). I don't mean that God unconditionally elected you, but you have certainly received blessing upon blessing that has aided you in coming to faith. Just because you responded to these blessings positively while others responded negatively is no cause for boasting. This is a traditional Calvinist emphasis, and it's a point well taken.

*God gives us a choice of how to respond. I don't see how to make any sense out of anything in the Bible if this point is not true. In my view, the Plague Narrative presents an exceptional circumstance in which God had a particular purpose in ensuring Pharaoh's disobedience. Clearly the text of Exodus does not use God's relationship with Pharaoh

---

38. Bird, *Evangelical Theology*, 520.
39. For a defence of this idea, see Olson, *Against Calvinism*, 128–35.

as a model for God's relationship with people generally, and neither does Paul.

*God upholds all things by his power. Even our free choice is enabled by God's providence.

*We trust God's justice and grace. Even if we can't interpret Scripture as well as we would like, even if we don't know exactly what God is up to all the time, we trust his justice and grace.

4

Passover

Passover today is a lot different from the way it was celebrated in the Bible,[1] whether we're talking about the New Testament or Old Testament. A big part of the difference is that there is no Temple (or Tabernacle) anymore, so no particular need to get to Jerusalem for the celebration, and no sacrifice. According to Deuteronomy 16:6, the sacrifice of the Passover lamb should happen "only at the place where YHWH your God chooses to have his name dwell" (= Jerusalem, at the Tabernacle/Temple). The Feast of Unleavened Bread immediately follows Passover, and it is one of the three pilgrimage festivals.

---

1. If you're not sure how Jews celebrate Passover today, you should go online and find some videos about it. You can even find a video of Mayim Bialik explaining Passover. In that video, Dr. Bialik describes Passover as an eight-day holiday, meaning she (like most modern Jews) combines the whole biblical Feast of Unleavened Bread within the title 'Passover' (cf. Luke 22:1). You can also find videos teaching popular Jewish songs, including the most popular Passover song, *Dayenu*. And, of course, you can turn to Wikipedia for more information on the Passover Seder.

> Celebrate a festival in my honor three times a year. ¹⁵ Observe the Festival of Unleavened Bread. As I commanded you, you are to eat unleavened bread for seven days at the appointed time in the month of Abib, because you came out of Egypt in that month. No one is to appear before me empty-handed. ¹⁶ Also observe the Festival of Harvest [= Pentecost] with the firstfruits of your produce from what you sow in the field, and observe the Festival of Ingathering [= Booths] at the end of the year, when you gather your produce from the field. ¹⁷ Three times a year all your males are to appear before the Lord YHWH. (Exod 23:14–17; cf. Deut 16:16)

So, back in Jesus' day, and for about the entire millennium prior, there would have been a large crowd in Jerusalem for these three feasts, including Passover, and there would have been a Passover sacrifice. But there is no lamb at the Passover meal these days; there is, instead, a lamb bone, to remind participants of what used to happen. Already the Mishnah, in the early third century, points out this change in the celebration of Passover. After detailing certain obligations in regard to Passover, the Mishnah says:

> And in the Holy City they used to bring before him the body of the Passover offering.²

The modern celebration of Passover also differs from what we read in the Bible because what we read in the Bible is a

---

2. Mishnah, tractate *Pesahim* 10.3; trans. Herbert Danby, *The Mishnah* (Oxford: Oxford University Press, 1933), 150.

pretty bare bones description of the celebration, and Jews have, over the centuries, filled out the holiday with many further traditions

But what hasn't changed is that Passover is a celebration, a joyous time, as you can tell in any of the online videos. The Bible certainly presents it in that same manner. While the songs may have changed, celebrants have been singing at Passover from the very beginning (Exod 15; cf. Mark 14:26). In the Old Testament, the Passover festival is a celebration of the defining moment in God's relationship with Israel, when he rescued them from Egyptian slavery. In the New Testament, Passover becomes the defining moment in world history, the time of the Crucifixion of our Lord, the rescue of humanity from the power of sin.

Context

The battle between God and Pharaoh began in earnest in Exod 7 with the first of the plagues, and since then—over a period of what must have been a few weeks, at least—Egypt was devastated by a steady succession of predicted disasters: their water had turned to blood for a week (7:14–24), frogs were everywhere (8:1–15), gnats afflicted people and animals (8:16–19), flies got so bad that "the land was ruined" (8:24; 8:20–32), the cattle suffered from a plague (9:1–7), the Egyptians and their animals endured "festering boils" (9:8–12), hail destroyed the Egyptian fields (9:13–35), locusts ate what was left (10:1–20), and the country had fallen into "thick darkness" for three days (10:21–29)—all except for one place, the land of Goshen (10:23). These plagues would be remembered as God's great victory over the oppressive forces of Egypt (Psa 105:24–38).

> YHWH displayed before our eyes great and awesome signs and wonders against Egypt, against Pharaoh and all his household. (Deut 6:22)

> You performed signs and wonders against Pharaoh and all his servants and all the people of his land, for you knew that they acted insolently against our ancestors. You made a name for yourself, which remains to this day. (Neh 9:10)

> You showed signs and wonders in the land of Egypt, and to this day in Israel and among all humankind, and have made yourself a name that continues to this very day. [21] You brought your people Israel out of the land of Egypt with signs and wonders, with a strong hand and outstretched arm, and with great terror. (Jer 32:20–21)

After nine plagues, now was the time for the Lord to strike his decisive blow, a blow that would not only repay Egypt for the death of Israelite boys earlier in the story (Exod 1:15–22) but also throw the Egyptian royal family into confusion and despair while also throwing the succession into doubt. As the Lord had said to Moses at the beginning of their relationship, he would kill the firstborn son of Pharaoh (Exod 4:23). Thus he would "execute judgments against all the gods of Egypt" (Exod 12:12; cf. Num 33:4).

The Tenth Plague

As it turns out, more than just Pharaoh's child is under threat in this final plague.

> So Moses said, This is what YHWH says: About midnight I will go throughout Egypt, ⁵ and every firstborn male in the land of Egypt will die, from the firstborn of Pharaoh who sits on his throne to the firstborn of the servant girl who is at the grindstones, as well as every firstborn of the livestock. (Exod 11:4–5)

But not in Goshen:

> But against all the Israelites, whether people or animals, not even a dog will snarl, so that you may know that YHWH makes a distinction between Egypt and Israel. (v. 7)

God had Pharaoh exactly where he wanted him. He knew very well that this final plague would bring about Israel's deliverance (Exod 11:1), and he had been saving it up for just this time. Egypt would be begging Israel to leave after this night (11:8). God has announced that Israel would not be affected by this final plague, just as he had saved them from some (at least) of the other plagues.[3] But the Israelites are going to have to obey some instructions in order to receive this protection.

---

3. The text of Exodus makes explicit that the Israelites were not affected by these plagues: #4, insects (8:18–19); #5, cattle die (9:4); #7, hail (9:26); #9, darkness (10:23).

Here are the instructions (12:1–11): on the 10th of Abib (cf. 13:4)—which now should be considered by the Israelites to be the first month—each family or group of families should select a male lamb or goat, unblemished and one year old. A few days later, on the 14th at twilight, the Israelites should slaughter their goat or lamb, and use some hyssop (12:22) to paint around the door of their house with the blood. Then they roast the meat and eat it with unleavened bread and bitter herbs, and burn any leftovers. For this meal, they must dress in traveling clothes, with staff in hand.

> The blood on the houses where you are staying will be a distinguishing mark for you; when I see the blood, I will pass over you. No plague will be among you to destroy you when I strike the land of Egypt. (12:13)

Notice that God will "pass over" the houses of the Israelites when he sees the blood. In Hebrew, the term "pass over" is one word (*pasaḥ*) which gives its name to the festival. Jews call it Pesach.

So far, it sounds like all of this will be a one-time event, a way to avoid the temporary threat that is coming from God onto the land of Egypt. But then God instructs the Israelites that "this day is to be a memorial for you, and you must celebrate it as a festival to YHWH" (v. 14). We'll talk about the festival in a little bit.

God had been communicating all this to Moses (and Aaron; 12:1–20). Moses then tells Israel's elders all these instructions, about what to do during the Tenth Plague, and about the annual celebration (12:21–28). Then the plague happens.

> At midnight YHWH struck down all the firstborn in the land of Egypt, from the firstborn of Pharaoh who sat on his throne to the firstborn of the prisoner who was in the dungeon, and all the firstborn of the livestock. ³⁰ Pharaoh arose in the night, he and all his officials and all the Egyptians; and there was a loud cry in Egypt, for there was not a house without someone dead. ³¹ Then he summoned Moses and Aaron in the night, and said, "Rise up, go away from my people, both you and the Israelites! Go, worship YHWH, as you said. ³² Take your flocks and your herds, as you said, and be gone.[4] And bring a blessing on me too!" ³³ The Egyptians urged the people to hasten their departure from the land, for they said, "We shall all be dead."

THE EXODUS AND THE SEA

And so the Israelites leave Egypt. According to Exodus 12:40, they had been in Egypt 430 years, in accordance with what God had previously announced to Abraham (Gen 15:13–14). This is the defining moment of God's relationship with Israel. When God introduces himself at Sinai, he identifies himself as "YHWH your God, who brought you out of the land of Egypt, out of the place of slavery" (Exod

---

4. Does Pharaoh still want the Israelites to come back after they're done worshiping, as we discussed in the third lesson, on "Pharaoh's Heart"? That seems to be the implication of Exodus 14:5, where it sounds like Pharaoh is surprised that the people had fled.

20:2). Centuries later, Israelites will look back on this moment as the pivotal action of grace and power from their all-gracious and all-powerful God.

> When Israel went out from Egypt, the house of Jacob from a people of strange language,
> [2] Judah became God's sanctuary, Israel his dominion.
> [3] The sea looked and fled; Jordan turned back.
> [4] The mountains skipped like rams, the hills like lambs.
> [5] Why is it, O sea, that you flee? O Jordan, that you turn back?
> [6] O mountains, that you skip like rams? O hills, like lambs?
> [7] Tremble, O earth, at the presence of YHWH, at the presence of the God of Jacob,
> [8] who turns the rock into a pool of water, the flint into a spring of water.
> (Psalm 114)
>
> When Israel was a child, I loved him, and out of Egypt I called my son. (Hos 11:1)[5]

Other nations had heard about these mighty actions and grew frightened (Josh 2:10; 4:23).

In some ways, the Lord became the God of Israel through this event. He redeemed a people, bought and paid for.

---

5. Other references to the exodus in the Old Testament: Isa 11:16; Ezek 20:5–10; Hos 2:17; 12:9, 13; Amos 2:10; 3:1; 9:7; Mic 6:4; 7:15; Hag 2:5; Psa 78:12, 43; 81:11; 105:23–38; 106:7.

> Yet I have been YHWH your God ever since the land of Egypt; you know no God but me, and besides me there is no savior. (Hos 13:4)

Jeremiah repeatedly refers to the exodus as the origin of Israel, though he also predicts future judgment on Israel, and a coming salvation that will even eclipse the exodus from Egypt.

> Therefore, the days are surely coming, says YHWH, when it shall no longer be said, "As YHWH lives who brought the people of Israel up out of the land of Egypt," [15] but "As YHWH lives who brought the people of Israel up out of the land of the north and out of all the lands where he had driven them." For I will bring them back to their own land that I gave to their ancestors. (Jer 16:14–15; cf. 23:7)[6]

There are several uncertainties about the account of the exodus. How many Israelites left Egypt? Six hundred thousand soldiers (12:37) would imply a total population of perhaps three million, an enormous number that some scholars consider absurdly large. Perhaps there has been a mistranslation, or a problem in the transmission of the

---

6. Other references to the exodus from Egypt in Jeremiah: 2:6; 7:22, 25; 11:4, 7; 31:32; 32:20–21; 34:13.

numbers.[7] What route did the Israelites take upon leaving Egypt? The problem is that we don't know the location of some of the place names mentioned in Scripture, such as Succoth (12:37), Etham (13:20), and Pi-hahiroth (14:2).[8] As mentioned in a previous chapter, we are not even really sure where Mt. Sinai is.

The same difficulties surround the location of the most famous event of the whole narrative, the crossing of the Red Sea—if that's what we should call it. For even the name of this body of water is a mystery. The Hebrew term is *Yam Suf* (Exod 10:19; 13:18; 15:4). *Yam* means "sea," and *suf* means "reeds" or "weeds," such as in Jonah's prayer, "weeds were wrapped around my head" (Jonah 2:5), or earlier in Exodus when Jochebed placed baby Moses "among the reeds" (2:3). So some scholars refer to this sea as the "Reed Sea" instead of the Red Sea. *Yam Suf* was translated "Red Sea" in the Septuagint (ἡ ἐρυθρὰ θάλασσα), and this identification became traditional. Remember that the Red Sea is like an arm stretching up along the east of Egypt, with two fingers split

---

7. For an argument that the word "thousand" has been mistranslated here, with the conclusion that the Israelite population was actually much smaller than traditionally thought, see Hoffmeier, *Ancient Israel in Sinai: The Evidence for the Authenticity of the Wilderness Tradition*, 157–59. But this interpretation is rejected by Friedman, *The Exodus: How It Happened and Why It Matters*, 21. For theological reflections on the problem, see R. W. L. Moberly, *Old Testament Theology: Reading the Hebrew Bible as Christian Scripture* (Grand Rapids: Baker, 2013), 88–91.

8. See P. Enns, "Exodus Route and Wilderness Itinerary," in *Dictionary of the Old Testament: Pentateuch*, ed. T. Desmond Alexander and David W. Baker (Downers Grove, IL: IVP, 2003), 272–80.

apart on either side of the Sinai Peninsula.⁹ The left finger is the Gulf of Suez—connected to the Mediterranean Ocean since the mid-1800s by means of the Suez Canal—and the right finger is the Gulf of Aqaba. When the *Yam Suf* is identified as the Red Sea, usually one of these gulfs is meant. But maybe we shouldn't think of it as the Red Sea at all; rather, maybe "Reed Sea" refers to a smaller body of water somewhere, perhaps north of the Gulf of Suez. According to one theory, "the marshy region in the vicinity of the Nile Delta is a likely candidate for Israel's departure from Egypt."¹⁰ But the Bible apparently uses the term *Yam Suf* to refer to different bodies of water,¹¹ and the name and location of the sea of the exodus crossing is so uncertain that scholars often now just leave it untranslated, *Yam Suf*.¹² The bottom line is that we don't know where the *Yam Suf* is that the Israelites crossed, though there are several guesses.

Who all exited Egypt at this time? We know that some of the Egyptians paid a little more attention to Moses than did Pharaoh. Some of them sheltered their cattle from the threatened hail, for instance (9:20), and some of them recognized that Moses was the instrument of God (8:19). Is it

---

9. To remind yourself of what this looks like, just go to Google Maps and search "Red Sea."

10. Enns, "Exodus Route," 276, relying on Hoffmeier.

11. See again Enns, "Exodus Route," 275. Another good discussion: D. Matthew Stith, "Red Sea, Reed Sea," in *The New Interpreter's Dictionary of the Bible*, 5 vols, ed. Katharine Doob Sakenfeld (Nashville: Abingdon, 2007), 4.750–51.

12. A recent example: Philip Y. Yoo, "Once Again: The *Yam Sûp* of the Exodus," *Journal of Biblical Literature* 137 (2018): 581–97, at n. 1.

possible that some of these people left with the Israelites? Exodus 12:38 contains the interesting statement, "a mixed multitude also went up with them." Ross Blackburn even suggest that some of the Egyptians listened to Moses and were saved from the Tenth Plague, and then left with the Israelites.[13]

Wherever the *Yam Suf* is, the Lord "turned the sea into dry land" so that Israel could cross it (14:21), and he held back the advancing Egyptians by means of his pillar of fire and cloud (14:24). Then the Lord allowed the Egyptians into the midst of the sea, where he destroyed Pharaoh's army (14:26–28). The miraculous intervention on behalf of the oppressed and the simultaneous devastation of the oppressor is immediately celebrated in song (15:1–21), and this moment of the reversal of fortunes comes to define God.

> He has toppled the mighty from their thrones and exalted the lowly. He has satisfied the hungry and sent the rich away empty. (Luke 1:52–53)

---

13. Blackburn, *The God Who Makes Himself Known: The Missionary Heart of the Book of Exodus*, 50. But Hoffmeier, *Ancient Israel in Sinai*, 154, thinks the mixed multitude was all non-Egyptian. Philo comments: "They were accompanied by a promiscuous, nondescript and menial crowd, a bastard host, so to speak, associated with the true-born. These were the children of Egyptian women by Hebrew fathers into whose families they had been adopted, also those who, reverencing the divine favour shewn to the people, had come over to them, and such as were converted and brought to a wiser mind by the magnitude and the number of the successive punishments" (*Life of Moses* 1.147).

The Celebration of Passover

It's interesting that when Exodus 12 talks about the annual festival—rather than the night of the Tenth Plague—that it doesn't talk about an animal but it talks about bread, calling the festival the Feast of Unleavened Bread (12:17). Obviously, there is an animal involved, because Moses imagines that later on, in the Promised Land, children will be asking their parents about the rituals, and the parents should respond, "It is the Passover sacrifice to YHWH" (v. 27). But whereas in the story of the Tenth Plague and the exodus, the failure of the bread to rise is barely more than a footnote (12:34, 39), it becomes the basis for a weeklong celebration.

Passover starts at sundown on the 14th of the month Abib (= Nisan), meaning that the Passover Seder (meal) really happens on the 15th of the month (i.e., after sundown, according to the Jewish way of reckoning time, in which the day begins at sundown). This is also the start of the Feast of Unleavened Bread, which lasts a full week, until the 21st of the month, at sundown (Lev 23:4–8; Exod 12:18; Num 28:16–25; Deut 16:1–8). Only circumcised Israelites may eat at the Passover meal (Exod 12:43–49). The meal serves as a time for Israel to remember their deliverance by God and to teach the next generation (12:26–27; 13:8, 14–15).

One aspect of the holiday that children enjoy is tracking down all the leaven in the house in order to banish it for a week. It's sort of a Jewish equivalent of hunting for Easter eggs. The biblical commandment is for the house to be free of leaven for a week (Exod 12:15, 19; 13:7). Of course, this becomes another teaching opportunity, explaining how the

Israelites leaving Egypt ate of necessity unleavened bread (12:34, 39). As Blackburn says, "the ceremonies draw future generations and the events of the exodus together, so that Israel's descendants might, through ritual, *participate* in the Egyptian deliverance."[14]

The Crucifixion as Passover Sacrifice

Jesus was crucified at Passover. The Triumphal Entry into Jerusalem (Mark 11:1–11) took place during the week leading up to Passover (cf. John 11:55; 12:1, 12–16). There is some confusion about whether the Friday when the Crucifixion took place would have been the 15th of Nisan/Abib (= the first full day of the holiday) or the 14th of the month (= the time when the lambs would be slaughtered).[15] In any

---

14. Blackburn, *The God Who Makes Himself Known*, 51.

15. The chronology in the Gospel of John suggests the latter, that the Crucifixion happened before the actual holiday but at the time when the lambs were being slaughtered (cf. John 13:1; 18:28; 19:31). The Synoptic Gospels seem to support the other chronology, that the Crucifixion happened on the first day of the Festival, so that the Last Supper would have been the Passover meal (cf. Mark 12:12). For discussion of this issue, see J. Dennis, "Death of Jesus," in *Dictionary of Jesus and the Gospels*, 2d ed., ed. Joel B. Green (Downers Grove, IL: IVP, 2013), 172–93, esp. 177; and H. W. Hoehner and J. K. Brown, "Chronology," in Green, *Dictionary of Jesus and the Gospels*, 134–38, esp. 136–37. N. T. Wright argues (along with some others) that the Last Supper was actually not on the day of Passover, but that Jesus observed the Passover meal a day early, as it were. Wright thus accepts the Johannine chronology and harmonizes the Synoptic Gospels toward John. See his *Jesus and the Victory of God* (Minneapolis: Fortress, 1996), 555–57. As Wright points out, the Talmud has a passage that agrees with the chronology of John (*Sanhedrin* 43a).

case, the Crucifixion is closely associated with the Passover, which helps to interpret the significance of Jesus' death.

During Passover week, Jerusalem would have been hopping, with hundreds of thousands of extra people. Like revelers in Times Square on New Year's Eve, they were there to celebrate, and they would have been thinking about the mighty act of deliverance that God had accomplished against the pagan oppressor. In light of the new pagan empire currently oppressing the people, Rome, the Passover could get a little rowdy. I'm thinking of college football; a few years ago, one Alabama fan became so emotionally involved in the sport that he vandalized a revered landmark on Auburn's campus. And this was a middle-aged man, not some college kid. Well, multiply that level of emotion by some degree, due to actual oppression from a foreign power, and the belief that God will one day liberate his people as he did in the past. And now we're observing the very festival that celebrates that ancient liberation. And here comes Jesus the wonder-worker riding on a donkey, in fulfillment of prophecy about a coming king. The season of Passover helps to explain why things got so emotional that last week of Jesus' life. And why Jesus chose to enter Jerusalem on that particular occasion.

But Passover is also one of the ways of understanding what Jesus' death means. The phrase "the ultimate sacrifice" refers to someone dying in some worthy cause, perhaps in the military. We frequently use the term sacrifice in metaphorical terms, not in reference to the slaughter of an animal but to a financial contribution or a major time investment in some project: we talk about people sacrificing their time or means for some goal. The metaphor of sacrifice is such a part of our language that we hardly even realize it's a metaphor.

When Paul used the metaphor of sacrifice for Christ's death, he did not do so in the offhand way that we sometimes use that metaphor, but rather he tried to offer a deeper interpretation of Christ's sacrifice. At Eph 5:2, he mentions that "Christ loved us and gave himself up for us, a fragrant offering and sacrifice to God," thus borrowing the description of Israelite sacrifice (cf. Lev 1:9). The writer of Hebrews also explicitly interpreted Jesus' death in terms of the Levitical sacrifices (cf. Heb 7:27; 9:26; 10:12).

Since the Crucifixion happened at Passover, it's not too much of a stretch to think about Jesus as a Passover sacrifice specifically. And so Paul does.

> Cleanse out the old leaven that you may be a new lump, as you really are unleavened. For Christ, our Passover lamb, has been sacrificed. (1 Cor 5:7)

Paul does not elaborate, but the typological interpretation almost writes itself. A century after Paul, Melito of Sardis preached an Easter sermon in which he drew out several of the resonances between Passover and Crucifixion.

> For, himself led as a lamb and slain as a sheep, he ransomed us from the world's service as from the land of Egypt, and freed us from the devil's slavery as from the hand of Pharaoh; and he marked our souls with his own Spirit and the members of our body with his own blood. It is he that clothed death with shame and stood the

devil in grief as Moses did Pharaoh. It is he that struck down crime and made injustice childless as Moses did Egypt. It is he that delivered us from slavery to liberty, from darkness to light, from death to life, from tyranny to eternal royalty, and made us a new priesthood and an eternal people personal to him.[16]

Paul incorporates into his interpretation the other major element from the Festival, the removal of leaven from the home. But—in harmony with his usual motives for citing Old Testament Law (see chapter 8)—Paul does not stress the command to remove the leaven in a literal way, but figuratively, pointing to the need to avoid the dangerous leaven of sin. (Jesus had used the term "leaven" similarly; cf. Mark 8:15.) This is the entire point of bringing up the Passover sacrifice of Jesus in this context: there is an ethical dimension to Jesus' sacrifice. If the death of Jesus signals the time of our Passover, then it is time to remove the leaven of sin from our midst.

Let's just note in this connection that the Passover interpretation is not the only interpretation of Jesus' death in the New Testament.[17] The Epistle to the Hebrews presents Jesus' death in terms of the Day of Atonement (cf. Lev 16), the only time of the year that the high priest enters the Holy of Holies to make atonement for himself and for the people (cf. Heb 5:3; 9:6–12). This analogy also makes sense, and it shows us that there is not a single right way to understand the death

---

16. Melito, *On Pascha*, 67–68; trans. Stuart G. Hall, *Melito of Sardis: On Pascha and Fragments* (Oxford: Oxford University Press, 1979), 35–37.

17. See further Dennis, "Death of Jesus," 172–93.

of Jesus, or even a single, right sacrifice to which to connect it. The entire sacrificial system in the Old Testament has resonance with the death of Jesus, and sometimes New Testament writers intend a broad reference to the entire system, such as when Paul says that "God presented Jesus as an atoning sacrifice in his blood" (Rom 3:25).

But the Passover connection is prominent, and the Gospel writers make sure to mention the festival in each of their accounts of the Passion of Christ. They usually leave the significance unstated, allowing the reader to trace out the similarities. But John does explicitly quote the Passover ordinance.

> Then the soldiers came and broke the legs of the first and of the other who had been crucified with him. ³³ But when they came to Jesus and saw that he was already dead, they did not break his legs. ³⁴ Instead, one of the soldiers pierced his side with a spear, and at once blood and water came out. ³⁵ He who saw this has testified so that you also may believe. His testimony is true, and he knows that he tells the truth. ³⁶ These things occurred so that the scripture might be fulfilled, "None of his bones shall be broken." (John 19:32–36)

Here John quotes Exod 12:46, a verse referring to the Passover lamb, but the Evangelist finds the fulfillment of this verse in the Crucifixion. Jesus is the Passover lamb.

The Last Supper[18]

The other major New Testament connection to Passover is the Last Supper, which seems to be a Passover meal, at least according to the Synoptic Gospels. (The Last Supper does not exactly appear in the Gospel of John, though see John 13:2.)

> On the first day of Unleavened Bread, when the Passover lamb is sacrificed, his disciples said to him, "Where do you want us to go and make the preparations for you to eat the Passover?" [13] So he sent two of his disciples, saying to them, "Go into the city, and a man carrying a jar of water will meet you; follow him, [14] and wherever he enters, say to the owner of the house, 'The Teacher asks, Where is my guest room where I may eat the Passover with my disciples?' [15] He will show you a large room upstairs, furnished and ready. Make preparations for us there." (Mark 14:12-15)

During this meal, the gathered celebrants would have recalled the salvation their God had accomplished for his people so long before. Jesus uses this opportunity to explain what is about to happen, a new salvation, more all-encompassing than even the Passover and exodus. The Book of Exodus describes the establishment of God's kingdom in Israel; Jesus was about to usher in the kingdom of God through his own death, symbolized in the elements of the

---

18. N. Perrin, "Last Supper," in Green, *Dictionary of Jesus and the Gospels*, 492–501; N. T. Wright, *Jesus and the Victory of God* (Minneapolis: Fortress, 1996), 554–63.

Passover meal, that unleavened bread, those cups of wine (Mark 14:22–25).

The Passover context helps Christians to understand the significance of the Lord's Supper. The unleavened bread had reminded Israelites for centuries that God had once defeated the forces of evil and he would do so again; and it reminds Christians that God, through the body of Christ, has decisively defeated the forces of evil. The wine reminds Christians of the blood of the Passover lamb that marks us out as God's people and protects us from spiritual destruction.

Conclusion

Each week, Christians gather together to celebrate the salvation our God has accomplished. At Passover time, we can look back at the amazing events of the exodus, recognizing that those Israelites who emerged from Egypt were our ancestors in the faith (see again 1 Cor 10:1–11). We rejoice in God's liberation of our ancestors, and especially in his liberation of us from evil through our Passover sacrifice, Jesus Christ.

5

BREAD FROM HEAVEN

The people asked, and he brought quails, and satisfied them with the bread of heaven. (Psalm 105:40)

And he rained down on them manna to eat and gave them the grain of heaven. Man ate of the bread of the angels; he sent them food in abundance. (Psalm 78:24–25)

Exodus 16 is a story about grace, and the lack of it. The grace belongs all to God, the lack of it belongs all to the Israelites.

It is all too easy to be ungrateful, ungracious. It is not easy for God; he reveals his character as defined by grace (Exod 34:6). But for people, being ungracious just comes naturally, as demonstrated by spending a little time around children. Children have to be taught manners; they have to be taught to be grateful. They will not say "thank you" when they receive something unless they are taught to do so.

Recently I was in Gatlinburg with my family, and I gave my kids a choice. We were at a recreation area, that featured miniature golf and laser tag and bumper cars and other things like that. I told my kids that I would pay for them to do some of these fun activities, or we could go get ice cream: one or the other, but not both. Most of my kids chose the activities—partly, I'm sure, because we were there at the time, and the ice cream was not right in front of them—and one of the kids chose ice cream. So we played games while the one child waited. I played miniature golf with a couple of my kids. Then we went to the ice cream shop, and one of the children who had already played games whined and cried because of not getting ice cream. I took the opportunity to lecture this child on being grateful: "You got to do the fun activities that you chose. Do you think I'm going to pay for those activities in the future if this is the way you act?!"

I am under no illusion that that lecture solved the problem. Children have to be taught repeatedly about how to be grateful, just like any other lesson. I recall with shame some of my own childhood moments of selfishness, and I regret that I haven't completely grown out of it. There are plenty of times still that I get grumpy when I don't get my way, or when I make a suggestion that others fail to recognize as brilliant, or when I go over the budget and find too little money to buy some of the toys I crave.

I think C. S. Lewis was right: the "great sin" is pride.[1] I'm not sure exactly how pride and selfishness are related—they seem to overlap quite a bit, but they also seem a little different. If selfishness is not the great sin, it is close to it. It

---

1. C. S. Lewis, *Mere Christianity*, book 3, ch. 8.

was selfishness that the Apostle warned against at the beginning of Philippians 2:

> Do nothing out of selfish ambition or conceit, but in humility consider others as more important than yourselves. Everyone should look out not only for his own interests, but also for the interests of others. Have this mind in you which was also in Christ Jesus.... (Phil 2:3–5)

Selfishness is ultimately what causes someone to be ungrateful. Selfishness is what makes us forget to say "thank you." Selfishness is what led the Israelites to complain about God's providence immediately after celebrating his deliverance of them at the Red Sea.

Context

After the crossing of the Red Sea in Exod 14, and the victory song in Exod 15:1–21, the Israelites wind up in the Wilderness of Shur and cannot find water for three days (15:22). Then they came to a place called "Bitter" (Marah), where there was bitter water, which Moses was able to make sweet by throwing into the water a tree branch at the instruction of YHWH (15:23–25). This is the first episode after the exodus in which the Israelites "grumble." It is, incidentally, the first episode after the exodus.

There are two more "grumbling" episodes before the people reach Sinai in Exod 19. The first, in Exod 16, is the focus of our lesson. The second, in Exod 17:1–7, is about Moses getting water from the rock, and we'll look at it in chapter 6.

The manna story of Exod 16 takes place in the Wilderness of Sin (v. 1). Of course, "Sin" is a Hebrew place name (סִין) and does not mean what "sin" means in English, which corresponds to a different Hebrew word (*ḥattat*). The word "Sin" here should really be pronounced "seen." Having said that, it is easy for English readers to see a strange appropriateness of this Hebrew place name.

Between the Wilderness of Shur and the Wilderness of Sin, Israel camped in one other location, Elim, which is allotted only a single verse (15:27), though it must have been much the most pleasant stop on the journey to Sinai, what with its twelve springs and seventy date palms. Israel must have felt well provided for at Elim. Then they left, headed through the Wilderness of Sin.

Liberated and Ungrateful

It seems—at first—amazing how focused on their bellies these Israelites are. You would think they would recognize that they had just been through an amazing, unprecedented experience, that their God had not only liberated them from slavery, had not only brought a brutal tyrant to his knees, but had even split the waters of the Red Sea so that the Israelites could cross on dry ground while also bringing punishment on those who had oppressed them. The Song of the Sea (Exod 15:1–18) hits the right note.

> YHWH is my strength and my song; he has become my salvation. This is my God, and I will praise him, my father's God, and I will exalt him. (15:2; cf. Isa 12:2)

But what have you done for me lately? Liberation from slavery? That was a month ago (16:1; cf. Num 33:3). Now we're hungry.

I say that *at first* it seems amazing that the Israelites focus on their bellies, but on second thought this is hardly surprising at all. Most people I know—including me—complain if conditions aren't close to perfect, with "perfect" defined as "the way I want them" or "the way I'm used to." I will get on a jet airplane and travel halfway around the world in less than a day and complain about how long it takes. I won't bore you with more examples, though they're not hard to think of. This is selfishness. I'm sure if I were one of these liberated Israelites I'd be complaining about my growling belly, too. Immediately after typing the above, I went to our school's cafeteria for lunch, but they were out of the main course. I was not happy.

This whole aspect of the story of Israel is reminiscent of Esau, who sold his birthright to fill his belly (Gen 25:29–34). Hunger can make you do some dumb things. A big part of what God wants to teach us is how to control our bodies, our appetites.

Another aspect of this story that is amazing at first is the nostalgic reminiscences of Egypt.

> [in the land of Egypt] we sat by pots of meat and ate all the bread we wanted! (16:3)

Later they will voice similar memories.

> We remember the free fish we ate in Egypt, along with the cucumbers, melons, leeks, onions, and garlic. (Num 11:5)

At one point they—actually, some of the Israelites who were actively rebelling against Moses' leadership—speak of Egypt as "a land flowing with milk and honey" (Num 16:13). "Oh, wasn't life great back then! Everything used to be wonderful! Our lives are so much worse than they used to be!"

Surely, we shouldn't take these memories of Egypt seriously. Yes, it is true that there was plenty of food in Egypt ... for Egyptians; not for the slaves. There were probably some times that the Israelites got an unusually large ration of bread and maybe meat. But we cannot believe that these people whose daily jobs are described in Exod 5 actually sat around all day eating meat and bread, or that they routinely had full bellies.

Nostalgia distorts. We also—in the 21st century—live in a nostalgic world. The 1950s were the epitome of American culture; we were such a godly nation with a godly president and godly laws. Uh huh. Godly laws like Jim Crow? Give me a break. Now, I'm not saying that every time period is equal to every other time period; perhaps some times are better than other times. But I am saying that nostalgia distorts, and it does little good to imitate Miniver Cheevy and long for the days of old.

God's Gracious Response to Ungratefulness

The people complain about their bellies, so God says, "I am going to rain bread from heaven for you" (v. 4). God gives them what they want. More than that, he's going to make it simple—it'll rain bread. You just have to pick it up off the ground. Such overabundant kindness is almost absurd. We might think also of Elijah, for whom the ravens brought food (1 King 17:4–6).

This is early in God's relationship with his people. They're still getting to know this God, and God is wanting to train them to think of him as their provider. You probably remember that God did not always have this response to Israelite grumbling. In these early episodes after the exodus, the grumbling is met mostly with grace, hardly any rebuke at all. Later, after they've spent a year at Sinai (cf. Num 10:11–12), and the people are still complaining about food, even complaining about the bread that falls from heaven (Num 11:6), God gets a little irritated, and so does Moses. "YHWH was very angry; Moses was also provoked" (Num 11:10). That's when God promises so much meat (quail) that it will "come out of your nostrils and become nauseating to you" (11:20). God also struck them with a plague (v. 33). Another time that they complain about food—and this episode takes place 40 years after the exodus—God sends poisonous snakes (Num 21:5–6). In the book of Numbers, after Israel should have known and trusted her provider, God appears fed up with their ungratefulness.

But immediately after the exodus, he's willing to be patient with his people as they come to understand their relationship with God. Perhaps some of them don't understand that "it was YHWH"—and not Moses?—"who brought you out of the land of Egypt" (Exod 16:6). So also, the Israelite complaints impugn the character of YHWH more than of Moses (v. 8). So his glory appears to Israel (vv. 7, 10) and he sends them food.

A Blessing and a Test: Manna and Sabbath

I don't mean that manna is the blessing and Sabbath is the test; rather both manna and Sabbath are both a blessing and a test.

God promises both meat and bread (Exod 16:12), and he provides both quails and manna (v. 13). But this story is more concerned with manna; the quails are mentioned only in the single verse, and then not again until Num 11:31–32. On the other hand, the manna fell from heaven for 40 years (Exod 16:35; cf. Josh 5:12). So, the quails in Exod 16 seem to be a one-off, an initial gift of meat, that was not repeated often.[2] (Maybe you should raise quails; if you want some reasons to consider it, go to YouTube and search "six reasons to keep quail.")

The manna was, of course, an enormous blessing,[3] but it came with some conditions. "The people are to go out

---

2. On quails in the Sinai peninsula, see Hoffmeier, *Ancient Israel in Sinai: The Evidence for the Authenticity of the Wilderness Tradition*, 173–75.

3. For a description of manna, in addition to Exod 16:14, 31, see Num 11:7–9. For natural explanations of the manna, see Hoffmeier, *Ancient Israel in Sinai*, 171–73.

each day and gather enough for that day. This way I will test them to see whether or not they will follow my instructions" (Exod 16:4). According to one scholar, "God is apparently leery of confiding his revealed laws to a people that, despite having witnessed a tremendous series of miracles in Egypt and at the Sea, is so quick to complain and to doubt divine providence."[4] In this sense, the test has to do with seeing whether Israel can obey so simple an instruction as going out each morning to gather the bread, and then to gather twice as much on Friday (vv. 4–5). Of course, not everyone did follow these instructions (vv. 20, 27).

But maybe we should think of the test in a different light, not really as an investigation into the character of Israel but rather as a formative test, as a trial that edifies, that teaches Israel how to be God's people. As Walter Moberly says, "there is good reason to see the test as formative, as contributing to the shaping of Israel into the people that God wants them to be, a people who will live by divine instruction (torah)."[5] The idea is you start off with simple instructions—"go find your shoes and put them on and then go get in the car"—and correct the mistakes—"switch your shoes to the other feet"—and once they get used to being faithful in little things, they'll be ready to be faithful in much. According to Moses:

---

4. Stephen A. Geller, "Manna and Sabbath: A Literary-Theological Reading of Exodus 16," *Interpretation* 59 (2005): 5–16, at 6.

5. Moberly, *Old Testament Theology: Reading the Hebrew Bible as Christian Scripture*, 79.

> [God] humbled you by letting you hunger, then by feeding you with manna, with which neither you nor your ancestors were acquainted, in order to make you understand that one does not live by bread alone, but by every word that comes from the mouth of YHWH. (Deut 8:3)

But God provides the manna not just to get Israel accustomed to obeying God's laws in preparation for Sinai, but also to get them accustomed to the idea that God provides for their needs, so that when they enter Canaan and suddenly have an abundance, they'll know that the grain and land and rain all come from God, just as surely as the manna from heaven had come from God.

> When you eat [in Canaan] and are full, you will bless YHWH your God for the good land he has given you. (Deut 8:10)

Again, the purpose of the manna was "in order to humble and test you, so that in the end he might cause you to prosper" (Deut 8:16).

Manna was recalled centuries later as one of the great blessings from God (Neh 9:20; Psa 78:24). The Jews in the first century mention manna to Jesus (John 6:31). It may be that the Bread of the Presence that was housed in the tabernacle and temple (Exod 25:30) was supposed to call to mind the miraculous gift of manna each morning.[6]

---

6. Geller, "Manna and Sabbath," 6.

The word Sabbath appears for the first time in the Bible at Exodus 16:23. It is considered a gift—"YHWH has given you the Sabbath"—not a burden, as we might imagine from reading the New Testament (cf. Mark 2:23–3:6). Rules about the Sabbath will later form the Fourth Commandment given on Mt. Sinai (Exod 20:8–11; Deut 5:12–15), where again it is supposed to be a blessing to people, all people, and not just the wealthy.

Incidentally, this notice in Exodus 16 about a day of rest every seven days is the first indication in the Bible, and maybe the first indication in world history, of a people organizing their lives in periods of seven days. The solar year is a fairly obvious unit of time, as is the month, both based on observable cosmological phenomena. The week is wholly different,[7] and it seems to be a gift to mankind from the Jews (although some evidence also indicates that Babylonians divided time into seven-day periods). In Egypt, there was a 10-day "week," of which eight days were devoted to work.[8] Of course the concept of a week, and the observance of a rest day during that week, connects to the biblical account of creation, in which God had a six-day work week and stopped on the seventh day.

---

7. See Wikipedia, "Week."
8. Hoffmeier, *Ancient Israel in Sinai*, 173, who cites Ann Macy Roth, "Work Force," in *The Oxford Encyclopedia of Ancient Egypt*, 3 vols., ed. Donald B. Redford (New York: Oxford University Press, 2001), 3.519–24, at 523. On the "week" in the Roman world, see Jörg Rüpke, "Week," in *Brill's New Pauly*, ed. Hubert Cancik and Helmuth Schneider, vol. 15 (Leiden: Brill, 2010), cols. 612–14: "The Greek calendar was dominated by 'decades' (ten-day weeks), while the calendar of the city of Rome comprised a structure of three successive eight-day weeks […]" (col. 612).

The word "Sabbath" means "stop." Geller wants to translate Exod 16:25–26 as, "Because today is God's stop, you will not find any manna in the fields. Six days you shall gather it, but the seventh day is a stop, you will not find it in the fields."

The Rules for Manna and Sabbath

The rules for manna can seem a little tricky to work out, thousands of years removed from the incident and the composition of the text.

> Gather as much of it as each of you needs, an *omer* to a person according to the number of persons, all providing for those in their own tents. (v. 16)

> The Israelites did so, some gathering more, some less. [18] But when they measured it with an *omer*, those who gathered much had nothing over, and those who gathered little had no shortage; they gathered as much as each of them needed. (vv. 17–18)

The best guess I have heard about what this all means is that Moses tells the Israelites to get as much as you need, and each person needs about an *omer* of manna, but you need to gather for your own household.[9] Whatever the precise

---

9. See Moberly, *Old Testament Theology*, 81.

scenario for gathering and distributing, the idea is that no one hoarded, no one got cheated, everyone got the right amount.

But the right amount included nothing for the next day. Just as you don't want to feed a mogwai after midnight, so you don't want to keep manna until the next day: it'll stink and get worms (v. 20). Each new day, you had to go out and get more, but not get too much. There was no security in gathering up a stockpile, no bank account where extra manna could be stored. The only security was in trusting that God was going to provide the manna the next day as well. But the rules changed on the Sabbath, in that God did not provide any manna that day, but he provided extra the day before.

The spiritual lessons are simple and profound at the same time, both elementary and difficult to learn. As Moberly says:

> YHWH's bread is not the sort that can be kept overnight. It can only be collected afresh each new day.
>
> The implicit sense is of a need to appropriate the divine gift always in the present, in the here and now.[10]

Philo says something similar. The gift of manna, this "new and strange form of benefaction," was designed to teach the Israelites to endure bravely when trials came, to "bear it patiently in expectation of good to come" (*Life of Moses*

---

10. Both quotations from Moberly, *Old Testament Theology*, 82.

1.199). It was impossible to store up manna "since it was God's purpose to bestow gifts ever new" (1.204).[11]

This idea that we have to trust in God for our needs is at the heart of any relationship with God, but it's not one that is easily learned. We're still learning it. We like to store up for ourselves treasures on earth. It makes us feel better, like we have some control over our lives. God was teaching the Israelites that they had no control.

> The Lord addresses this lack by providing Israel with food one day at a time, save the special circumstance of the seventh day, effectively re-presenting every evening the very circumstance about which the Israelites were complaining—the lack of food. The lack of a sustainable food source would be a constant reminder that the Lord was Israel's provider.[12]

> It is a manifestation of divine care that one must trust will be there tomorrow. Manna is therefore the ideal substance with which to test Israel's loyalty.[13]

Manna in the New Testament

There are several New Testament connections with this chapter of Exodus. At the end of the New Testament, Jesus

---

11. See also the interesting reflections on manna in Wisdom of Solomon 16:20–29. And for more on the way manna was viewed in early Judaism, see Brant Pitre, *Jesus and the Last Supper* (Grand Rapids: Eerdmans, 2015), 153–59.
12. Blackburn, *The God Who Makes Himself Known: The Missionary Heart of the Book of Exodus*, 69.
13. Geller, "Manna and Sabbath," 10.

promises "to those who conquer" some of the "hidden manna" (Rev 2:17). Jesus teaches his followers to pray for their "daily bread" (Matt 6:11 // Luke 11:3), a phrase designed to provoke memories of manna.[14] In his battle in the wilderness with Satan—when Jesus, though hungry, does not imitate Israel by grumbling about his belly—Jesus quotes from Deuteronomy's reflections on the gift of manna (Matt 4:4; Luke 4:4) "precisely to relativize the importance of material hunger in favor of obedient responsiveness to God."[15] And Paul quotes Exodus 16:18 as precedent for his admonition that the Corinthian Christians need to provide for the needs of their poor brothers and sisters (1 Cor 8:15).

> As it is written, the person who had much did not have too much, and the person who had little did not have too little.

The most sustained reflection on the manna story is in John 6,[16] immediately after the feeding of the 5000. The feeding stories in the Gospels, whether feeding 5000 (Matt 14:13-21; Mark 6:30-44; Luke 9:10-17; John 6:1-15) or 4000 (Matt 15:32-39; Mark 8:1-10), resonate with the giving of the manna, but only John's Gospel makes this resonance explicit. Even the crowd with full bellies recognizes the parallel between what Jesus has just done and what happens in Exod 16. But the people think only in physical

---

14. See Pitre, *Jesus and the Last Supper*, 159–93.
15. Moberly, *Old Testament Theology*, 97.
16. See Pitre, *Jesus and the Last Supper*, 193–250.

terms, and they want more bread. They quote to Jesus Psalm 78:24 (John 6:31), the psalmic reflection on manna quoted also at the beginning of this chapter. Their point is that if Jesus is the prophet like Moses (Deut 18:18; cf. John 6:14; 7:40) then he should—like Moses—provide continual bread from heaven. In saying this, they have demonstrated significant spiritual insight, but not quite enough, for they have failed to understand the basic lesson of Exodus 16, that just as the complaints of the Israelites were really directed at God and not Moses (Exod 16:8), and just as they needed to learn that it was God and not Moses who rescued them from Egypt (v. 6), so also it was God and not Moses who provided the bread from heaven.[17]

> But Jesus' instruction in how to read goes beyond this simple corrective. Not only does he insist that it is God the Father who is the true giver, but he also changes the tense of the verb from past to present and suggests that the manna must be interpreted as a *prefiguration* of another, truer bread still to come. "It is my Father who *gives* you the *true bread from heaven*." Here is the paradigm shift: the manna story is not just about a past event in salvation history; rather, it points forward *figurally* to a different kind of bread altogether. Even though the manna was divinely given, it was still "the food that perishes" (another exegetical allusion: cf. Exod 16:19–21), and those who ate it still died (John 6:49). John is once again teaching his readers how to

---

17. Josephus, *Jewish Antiquities* 3.31, says that God sent the manna "as a favor to Moses."

reread Israel's Scripture; [...] Jesus reinterprets the manna story as prefiguring *himself*.[18]

Jesus continues by being more explicit: "I am the bread of life" (v. 35). "The one who eats my flesh and drinks my blood has eternal life, and I will raise him up on the last day" (v. 54).

God sustained the Israelites in the wilderness with bread from heaven, teaching them obedience and dependence on God, and pointing toward the much better bread from heaven that provides eternal life. Exodus 16, especially as interpreted by Jesus, compels us to echo the immortal words of William Williams:

> Guide me, O Thou great Jehovah,
> Pilgrim through this barren land;
> I am weak, but Thou art mighty,
> Hold me with Thy pow'rful hand.
> Bread of heaven, Bread of heaven,
> Feed me till I want no more;
> Feed me till I want no more.

ONE LAST POINT

We are supposed to be imitators of God. The manna story shows a God who commits himself to demonstrating grace each new day. It teaches us to demonstrate grace daily, to those we see every day, particularly our families. I reflect on this as a parent of children, for whom I need to provide every day. Daily meals. Daily dishes. Daily laundry. Daily

---

18. Richard B. Hays, *Echoes of Scripture in the Gospels* (Waco, TX: Baylor University Press, 2016), 322.

transportation. Daily grace.[19] Of course, this type of thing applies to every relationship, and the point I'm trying to make is that it can get very repetitive; it can wear us out. God committed himself to such grace over the period of an entire generation. Such grace is not about the one-time action, but about the repeated action. As followers of Jesus, we take up our cross daily (Luke 9:23), and show grace to others daily.

---

19. A good, recent exploration of how such "menial" tasks reflect our calling by God is Tish Harrison Warren, *Liturgy of the Ordinary: Sacred Practices in Everyday Life* (Downers Grove, IL: IVP, 2016).

6

WATER FROM A ROCK

Ours is a family of water-bottle lovers. I exclude myself. I drink water when I'm eating or after exercise; I don't need to keep a flask with me at all times. But my wife does. She won't go to bed without a water bottle on the nightstand. And my oldest daughter will hardly get in the car without a water bottle, even if we're going just a little ways down the road. I guess they're healthier than I am. Google says you're supposed to drink about a half-gallon of water per day. When we go on a long trip, all seven of us have to have our own water bottle. I consider this a fine practice, so I don't have to stop and get drinks for all of us, but it was not something I grew up doing. Before my wife changed my ways, I figured if I got thirsty on a road trip, I'd just stop somewhere and get a drink.

Then again, most of my road trips happen in an air-conditioned car. If I were hiking through a wilderness, not only would I take some water with me, but I would plan out ahead of time where I could refill my supply.

I say all this as someone who has never experienced any true lack of water. But there is a scarcity of water in many parts of the world. According to Wikipedia:

> One-third of the global population (2 billion people) live under conditions of severe water scarcity at least 1 month of the year. Half a billion people in the world face severe water scarcity all year round. Half of the world's largest cities experience water scarcity.[1]

In March 2019, Manila "experienced its worst water crisis in a decade after taps ran dry for over two weeks for six million customers of privately-owned service provider Manila Water."[2] Yikes! What would you do if water was turned off at your house for two weeks?

Two members of the church of which I'm a part work to make fresh water available in difficult locations. I can personally attest that when a new water well is dug in various locations in Haiti, it is used all day long. There are many people in the world who are desperate for water.[3]

After they came out of Egypt, the Israelites were hiking through a wilderness. As Moses remembers:

---

1. "Water Scarcity" on Wikipedia. You could also see http://www.worldwatercouncil.org/en/water-crisis.
2. The quotation is from the article "Explainer: What Caused Manila's Water Crisis and Why Duterte Is Asking Singapore for Help," by Cynthia Choo at todayonline.com, published March 25, 2019.
3. Go to YouTube and watch "The Three Amigos Canteen/Lip Balm scene." We Americans are used to being Chevy Chase here, but can you imagine being Martin Short or Steve Martin?

> [God] led you through the great and terrible wilderness with its poisonous snakes and scorpions, a thirsty land where there was no water. (Deut 8:15)

We're not exactly certain where Israel was in Exodus 17. The route of the exodus has long been debated, but most likely Mt. Sinai is located somewhere in the southern part of what is now called the Sinai Peninsula, which today is part of Egypt.[4] The traditional mountain is Jebel Musa or Gebel Musa, with St. Catherine's monastery at the foot of the mountain. In Exodus 17, Israel arrives at a place called Rephidim (v. 1), which is apparently modern Wadi Feiran.[5] Whether or not this geographical analysis is precisely correct, wherever in the peninsula Israel happened to be, we can be sure that there would not have been a whole lot of rainfall—25-50 millimeters (= 1–2 inches) per year[6]—and the temperature could be quite variable, with some extreme highs.

> The weather is another dynamic factor for one traveling through or living in Sinai. In July the mean temperature in North Sinai is in the range of 26-28°C (78–82°F); it is 23–25°C (72–78°F) in Central Sinai, and in the higher elevations of South Sinai, 15–20°C (60–69°F). In January, the mean temperatures for these three regions are,

---

4. On all these questions, an authoritative discussion is Hoffmeier, *Ancient Israel in Sinai: The Evidence for the Authenticity of the Wilderness Tradition*.

5. There are Wikipedia entries on all these locations. For Jebel Musa, also see https://www.bibleplaces.com/jebelmusa/.

6. Hoffmeier, *Ancient Israel in Sinai*, 45. Hoffmeier reports this rainfall total specifically for Central Sinai.

respectively, 12–14°C (54–59°F), 7–10°C (42–50°F), and 0–2°C (32–36°F). However, these temperatures, registered in the shade, are often difficult to find. In May 1998, while surveying in the open sun of North Sinai, we recorded a temperature of 48°C (120°F). In 1995, when climbing Gebel Musa in mid-May at around 7:00 A.M., a rain shower moved in, the winds picked up, and the temperature plummeted to 7–8°C (44–46°F). I had never been so cold in my life. A few hours lateR, as we departed the St. Catherine's area and exited the Wadi Feiran, I noticed the temperature was 40°C (104°F)! Clearly the temperatures in Sinai vary considerably, depending on one's location. The sudden changes in temperature make life a challenge indeed.[7]

In that situation, Israel—like billions of people in the world today—was desperate for water. So God gave them water.

Salvation at Rephidim

Israel left the Wilderness of Sin and arrived at Rephidim at Exodus 17:1, and then left Rephidim and arrived at Mt. Sinai at Exodus 19:1–2. The Book of Exodus locates three events at Rephidim: the first water-from-a-rock story (17:1–7), the attack of Amalek (17:8–16),[8] and the appointment of judges to aid Moses (ch. 18). This chapter focuses on the first of these episodes.

---

7. Hoffmeier, *Ancient Israel in Sinai*, 46.
8. Where did they get the weapons to fight Amalek? According to tradition (e.g., Wisdom of Solomon 10:20), they picked up the Egyptian weapons that washed ashore at the Red Sea.

When the people arrive at Rephidim, they complain to Moses about the lack of water (17:2). I suppose we might think this is a natural response to their situation. But we could probably also say that a more godly response would to pray to God for water rather than to complain to Moses, who can do nothing about it. In ch. 16, Moses had told the people that their complaints against Moses really amounted to complaints against the Lord (v. 8). Here at Rephidim, the people ask, "Is YHWH among us or not?" (17:7). The people need to learn to depend on God. They haven't learned it yet, and it seems that the Lord is trying to train them to see him as their provider. As we noticed in the last lesson, these three grumbling episodes immediately following the exodus (at Marah in 15:22–27; in the Wilderness of Sin in ch. 16; and now at Rephidim) do not elicit an angry response from God, though later in Numbers God does get angry at the people's complaining (Num 11:10). At this point in Exodus, God does not yet expect the people to fully trust in him. He's training them toward that trust.

But the grumbling has gotten worse, not better. The Israelites' complaint about water at Marah (15:24) seems downright polite compared to the vitriol they unleash against Moses at Rephidim. Earlier they had merely wondered where they might find water; now they accuse Moses of kidnapping them from their pleasant lives in Egypt in order to murder them in the wilderness (17:3).[9] Moses fears

---

9. My description of the Israelite complaint is a bit of an exaggeration, but earlier in the Wilderness of Sin they had longed for their lives in Egypt (16:3), as they will later do, as well (Num 11:4–5).

for his life (v. 4). God still treats them with patience and mercy.

God uses Moses and his staff to provide water for Israel out of a rock.[10] Not only that, but God says: "I am going to stand there in front of you on the rock at Horeb" (v. 6). What could this mean? This is the same book of the Bible in which God says, "You cannot see my face, for no one can see me and live" (33:20). Then again, that statement from God comes in a story in which he does show himself, or some aspect of himself, to Moses: "when my glory passes by, I will put you in the crevice of the rock and cover you with my hand until I have passed by. Then I will take my hand away, and you will see my back, but my face will not be seen" (33:22–23). Also, at the covenant ceremony in ch. 24, Moses and his companions...

> ...saw the God of Israel. Beneath his feet was something like a pavement made of lapis lazuli, as clear as the sky itself.[11] God did not harm the Israelite nobles; they saw him, and they ate and drank. (Exod 24:10–11)

So, what does all this mean? I don't know. My guess is that though God cannot normally be seen, he can make himself visible. To expand on that thought: God cannot normally be seen by mortal man, both because God is not visible to human vision—God is spirit (John 4:24)—and

---

10. For natural occurrences of this type of thing, see Hoffmeier, *Ancient Israel in Sinai*, 169–71. But I agree with Durham that such explanations miss the point of the passage, which is God's miraculous provision for his people; John I. Durham, *Exodus*, Word Biblical Commentary (Waco, TX: Word, 1987), 231.

because the revelation of his full glory would overwhelm and kill a mortal. But God can become visible to people in whatever way he wants to, whether as fire in the midst of a cloud (19:18) or as a man (Gen 18). So, at Rephidim, God makes himself visible in some way and stands on a rock. The traditional Christian interpretation has been that any visible manifestation of God in the Old Testament involved a pre-incarnate appearance of the Son of God.

So, God stood on a rock, and Moses struck the rock with the staff he had used in Egypt to work wonders, and water flowed from the rock. God wanted to put on a show, to do something memorable, to amaze the Israelites so that they would learn to trust him. And they did remember this event centuries later. The poets of Israel continued to reflect on the story of God providing water from the rock, as one of those moments when God was unbelievably gracious to his people.[11]

If the question is, "Is YHWH really among us or not?" (17:7), God answers that question in dramatic fashion, by providing water from the rock on which his visible presence is standing.

One other side point on this verse (Exod 17:6): God will stand on a rock at Horeb. Apparently Horeb is not an alternative name for Sinai—the people haven't arrived at Sinai yet—but rather the name of a region, and Sinai is the name of the mountain (or a wilderness around the mountain) within the region. That explanation seems to work out and take account of all the biblical data.[12]

---

11. Deut 8:15; Neh 9:15; Psa 78:20; 105:41; 114:8; Isa 48:21.
12. As argued by Hoffmeier, *Ancient Israel in Sinai*, 114–15.

The conclusion of the story features Moses giving the place a new name—actually, two new names: Massah (Hebrew for "testing") and Meribah (Hebrew for "contention"). This aspect of the story, this grumbling/contention aspect, becomes the basis for the warning issued in Psalm 95 (picked up in Hebrews 4; cf. also Deut 6:16).

> [8] Do not harden your hearts, as at Meribah,
> As in the day of Massah in the wilderness,
> [9] "When your fathers tested Me,
> They tried Me, though they had seen My work.
> [10] "For forty years I loathed that generation,
> And said they are a people who err in their heart,
> And they do not know My ways.
> [11] "Therefore I swore in My anger,
> Truly they shall not enter into My rest." (Psalm 95:8–11)

Trouble in Kadesh

Nearly forty years later (cf. 33:36–38), the Israelites entered the Wilderness of Zin and settled in Kadesh (Num 20:1), a location close to Canaan (and close to Edom; Num 20:14, something like 200 miles north of Mt. Sinai (Gebel Musa).[13] "It is an eleven-day journey from Horeb to Kadesh-barnea

---

13. On the location of Kadesh Barnea, see Hoffmeier, *Ancient Israel in Sinai*, 122–24. This map is helpful: www.biblicalarchaeology.org/wp-content/uploads/kadesh-barnea.jpg. Kadesh is most often identified with Tell el-Qudeirat, but archaeologists suggest that this site was not occupied at the time of Moses. For more information, google "where is kadesh" and read the article at the Biblical Archaeology Society website.

by way of Mount Seir" (Deut 1:2). In other words, the Israelites were now nowhere close to Rephidim.

The people again complain about a lack of water, and their complaint is eerily similar to their complaint decades earlier.

> Why have you brought YHWH's assembly into this wilderness for us and our livestock to die here? [5] Why have you led us up from Egypt to bring us to this evil place? It's not a place of grain, figs, vines, and pomegranates, and there is no water to drink. (Num 20:4–5)

The people have grown tired of wilderness life, and all they can remember about Egypt is that it was better than the desert. They continue to dream about the good life in Egypt (Num 11:5; 14:2–3; 16:13; 21:5), and at one point some of them want to appoint a new leader to take them back (14:4).

But at this point, at Kadesh, God is patient. (In the next chapter, he's had enough; Num 21:6.) God will again provide water from a rock. This time, Moses and Aaron should "speak to the rock" (v. 8). But they disobeyed.

> Moses and Aaron summoned the assembly in front of the rock, and Moses said to them, "Listen, you rebels! Must we bring water out of this rock for you?" [11] Then Moses raised his hand and struck the rock twice with his staff, so that abundant water gushed out, and the community and their livestock drank. [12] But YHWH said to Moses and Aaron, "Because you did not trust me to demonstrate my holiness in the sight of the Israelites, you will not bring this assembly into the land I have

given them. ¹³ These are the waters of Meribah, where the Israelites quarreled with YHWH, and he demonstrated his holiness to them. (Num 20:10–13)

Aaron dies later in this very chapter (20:28), explicitly because of the rebellion at Meribah (v. 24). This will also be the reason Moses is barred from the Promised Land (27:12–14; Deut 32:50–51; cf. Psa 106:32).¹⁴

The Rock that Followed Them

A close reading of Exodus 17 and Numbers 20 side-by-side reveals some strange similarities. I've already pointed out the very similar complaint of the people, 40 years apart. But also the name of the place is Meribah in both instances. Now, for people who want to explain away every strange feature of the text—and I am usually one of those people—this element could be considered just a nickname that is applied to two different locations. Rephidim is given the nickname "Meribah" because of the contentious Israelites, and Kadesh is given the same nickname because of the same reason. But if you wanted to see something peculiar in the text, this might be a feature that would raise your curiosity—it's like there's something similar about these two places. And it's not hard to find that something similar: the rock. Did you notice that when God tells Moses what to do in Num 20:8, he tells him to speak to "the rock"? What rock? No rock had

---

14. At Psa 81:7, it is the Lord who tests the people at Meribah. Meribah is mentioned also at Deut 33:8 in connection with the Levitical tribe.

been mentioned previously in the chapter. But the story does remind us of the rock in Exod 17. It's almost like that rock from Rephidim had made the 200-mile trek to Kadesh along with Israel.

Yes, I admit, that's a weird way of understanding what's going on, but the weirdness did not stop ancient people from making this very proposal; in fact, the weirdness may have been one of the appealing features of this reading. And there's a passage just a little later in Numbers that also contributed to this interpretation.

> From there they continued to Beer [= "well" in Hebrew]; that is the well of which YHWH said to Moses, "Gather the people together, and I will give them water." [17] Then Israel sang this song:
> "Go up, O well!—Sing to it!—
> [18] the well that the leaders dug,
> that the nobles of the people opened,
> with the scepter, with the staff."
> (Num 21:16–18)

Here, Israel sang to a well of water, encouraging the well to "go up." Sure, this probably just means that they want the well to produce water, but it's almost like they want the well itself to move, to go up. And do you see that they're singing to the well "of which YHWH said to Moses, 'Gather the people together and I will give them water'"? What well is that, except the rock? So one way of understanding this (yes, a strange way, but still) is that the rock at Rephidim is the same as the rock at Kadesh, and the people in Numbers 21 are singing to this rock (= well), imploring it to move around with them.

Do you think that's too weird of an interpretation for ancient people? You'd be wrong. Here's a passage from the rabbinic writing called the *Tosefta* (from maybe the third century AD).

> And so the well which was with the Israelites in the wilderness was a rock, the size of a large round vessel, surging and gurgling upward, as from the mouth of this little flask, rising with them up onto the mountains, and going down with them into the valleys. Wherever the Israelites would encamp, it made camp with them, on a high place, opposite the entry of the Tent of Meeting. The princes of Israel come and surround it with their staffs, and they sing a song concerning it: *Spring up, O Well! Sing to it; [the well which the princes dug, which the nobles of the people delved with the scepter and with their staves]* (Num. 21:17–18). And they well upward like a pillar on high, and each one [of the princes] draws water with his staff, each one for his tribe and each one for his family, as it is said: *The well which the princes dug.*[15]

An Aramaic translation (Targum Onqelos) from around the same time presented this rendering for Num 21:16–20.

---

15. *Tosefta Sukka* 3.11, trans. Jacob Neusner, *The Tosefta: Translated from the Hebrew with a New Introduction*, 2 vols. (Peabody, MA: Hendrickson, 2002), 1.576. Mere references to the moveable well, or to Miriam's well: *b. Šabb.* 35a; *b. Pesaḥ.* 54a; *Gen. Rab.* 62:4; *Num. Rab.* 1:2; 9:14. There is a more substantial discussion at *Num. Rab.* 19.25–26.

At that time the well was given to them, that is the well about which the Lord told Moses, "Gather the people together, and I will give them water." So Israel offered this praise, "Rise O well, sing to it." The well which the princes dug, the leaders of the people dug, the scribes, with their staffs, and it was given to them, since wilderness times. Now since it was given to them, it went down with them to the valleys, and from the valleys it went up with them to the high country. From the high country to the descents of the Moabite fields, at the summit of the height, which looks out towards Beth Yeshimon.[16]

So the Rabbis develop the interpretation I've already laid out, that the rock—which was also a well of water—followed Israel around in the wilderness.

How far back can we trace this interpretation? At least to the first century AD, because it is attested in a work known as the *Book of Biblical Antiquities* by an unknown author.[17] At §10.7 of this work, the author mentions that God "brought forth a well of water to follow them." A little later, he says that the water "followed them in the wilderness forty

---

16. Trans. Bernard Grossfeld in *The Targum Onqelos to Leviticus and The Targum Onqelos to Numbers*, Aramaic Bible 8 (Wilmington, DE: Michael Glazier, 1988), 126.

17. This work was traditionally attributed to Philo, but scholars unanimously reject that attribution, and so the author is now known as Pseudo-Philo. A translation of his book, in Latin called *Liber Antiquitatum Biblicarum*, is available in James H. Charlesworth, ed., *The Old Testament Pseudepigrapha*, 2 vols. (Garden City, NY: Doubleday, 1983–1985), 2.297–377. The translation is by D. J. Harrington.

years and went up to the mountain with them and went down into the plains" (11.15).

There's one more thought I want to introduce before getting to Paul. (I assume you guessed that's where this is going.) Philo—the older contemporary of Paul from Egypt—does not ever mention that the rock or the well followed the Israelites in the wilderness, but he does say something else that is interesting: the rock was a manifestation of the wisdom of God.

> For the flinty rock is the wisdom of God (ἡ γὰρ ἀκρότομος πέτρα ἡ σοφία θεοῦ ἐστιν), which He marked off highest and chiefest from His powers, and from which He satisfies the thirsty souls that love God. And when they have been given water to drink, they are filled also with the manna, the most generic of substances (γενικώτατον), for the manna is called "somewhat" (τί), and that suggests the *summum genus* (πάντων γένος), but the primal existence (τὸ γενικώτατον) is God, and next to Him is the Word of God (καὶ δεύτερος ὁ θεοῦ λόγος), but all other things subsist in word only, but in their active effects they are in some cases as good as non-subsisting.[18]

Philo can be a little hard to understand, but the main point I'm wanting to bring out is that Philo equates the rock with the wisdom of God and brings up in this context also the word (*logos*) of God.

---

18. Philo, *Allegorical Interpretation* 2.86; trans. F. H. Colson and G. H. Whitaker, *Philo*, vol. 1, Loeb Classical Library 207 (Cambridge, MA: Harvard University Press, 1962), 279.

So, in Jewish tradition outside the New Testament, we've got a rock that provides water following the Israelites around in the desert, and this rock is also a manifestation of the wisdom or word of God. Now for Paul.

> For I do not want you to be unaware, brothers, that our fathers were all under the cloud, and all passed through the sea, ² and all were baptized into Moses in the cloud and in the sea, ³ and all ate the same spiritual food, ⁴ and all drank the same spiritual drink. For they drank from the spiritual Rock that followed them, and the Rock was Christ. (1 Cor 10:1–4)

Once we have examined the Jewish tradition about the traveling rock, it is a short leap to see Jesus in this rock, who is the wisdom and word of God. I think there can be no doubt that Paul has heard this Jewish tradition about the rock. I do not know whether Paul actually thinks that an actual rock followed the Israelites in the desert. But I think it is possible that his words can be understood without attributing that belief to him. Let me explain.

The Hebrew word *ṣur* (צוּר), "rock," is found 9x in Deuteronomy. This is the very word used at Exod 17:6, where Moses strikes the rock and water comes out. (A different Hebrew word, *ṣela*, "rock," is used in Num 20.) Now, in Deuteronomy the water from the rock is mentioned one time, at Deut 8:15.

> ...who led you through the great and terrifying wilderness, with its fiery serpents and scorpions and thirsty

ground where there was no water, who brought you water out of the flinty rock (ṣur).

The other eight appearances of ṣur in Deuteronomy are all in the Song of Moses: 32:4, 13, 15, 18, 30, 31 (two times), 37. Almost every one of these appearances of the word "rock" refers to God: the Lord is our Rock.

Is this connection (God = rock) what helped Paul see Jesus in the rock? It is almost certain that he had Deuteronomy 32 on the brain as he was writing 1 Corinthians 10, because he nearly quoted it.

> They sacrificed to demons, not God. (Deut 32:17)
> …they sacrifice to demons and not to God. (1 Cor 10:20)

> They have provoked my jealousy. (Deut 32:21)
> Or are we provoking the Lord to jealousy? (1 Cor 10:22)

It seems to me that Paul is adapting the Jewish tradition about the moveable well or the traveling rock and tweaking it so that it becomes a sign of the presence of Jesus with the ancient Israelites, the spiritual ancestors of the Corinthian believers (note: "our fathers," 1 Cor 10:1). The point he wants to make is that God's people have always had access to the life provided by Christ, life symbolized by the manna and the water, and the water itself was a sign that Christ was with them (cf. John 4:14). And since those ancient Israelites were in the same position we are, we should take heed to the mistakes they made, for they are "examples for us" (v. 6), or, even more literally, they are "types of us,"[19] and their struggles pre-figure our own. "These things happened to them as a type [*typikōs*], and they were written for our instruction, on whom the ends of the ages have come" (v. 11).

This whole line of thought might strike us as strange, but I don't think it's any stranger than seeing the scarlet rope hung out of Rahab's window (Josh 2:18) as symbolizing the blood of Jesus, or Moses' outstretched arms later in Exod 17 as symbolizing the crucifixion.[20]

Conclusion

The end of the matter: God graciously provides for the physical needs of the complaining Israelites in Exod 17 in such a way that his power, mercy, and faithfulness should be obvious to all. In a more perfect way, God has shown his power, mercy, and faithfulness through our Lord Jesus Christ. In this way, the rock that provided water for those Israelites truly displays for us our Rock, the Christ.

---

19. For this translation, see Richard B. Hays, *The Conversion of the Imagination: Paul as Interpreter of Israel's Scripture* (Grand Rapids: Eerdmans, 2005), 11.

20. Both of these examples are common in Christian history and attested already in the mid-second century in Justin Martyr, *Dialogue with Trypho* 111 (cf. 90).

7

KINGDOM OF PRIESTS

Why did God choose Israel? What was the point of it all? There are different ways to look at this idea, different biblical responses to these questions—not contradictory, just different angles by which to approach the theme.

The Book of Deuteronomy reflects on this question.

> "For you are a people holy to YHWH your God. YHWH your God has chosen you to be a people for his treasured possession, out of all the peoples who are on the face of the earth. ⁷ It was not because you were more in number than any other people that YHWH set his love on you and chose you, for you were the fewest of all peoples, ⁸ but it is because YHWH loves you and is keeping the oath that he swore to your fathers, that YHWH has brought you out with a mighty hand and redeemed you from the house of slavery, from the hand of Pharaoh king of Egypt. ⁹ Know therefore that YHWH your God is God, the faithful God who keeps covenant and steadfast love with those who love him and keep his commandments, to a thousand generations. (Deut 7:6–9; cf. 9:4–6; 10:14–16)

Why did God choose Israel? Because he loves Israel and because he's keeping his oath to Abraham, Isaac, and Jacob. That doesn't exactly answer the question, it just pushes it off a little bit, raising further questions, such as: why does God love Israel? Does he love Israel more than other nations? And why did he make an oath to Abraham? Deuteronomy does not answer those questions. And I guess it's always hard to answer the "love" question. As Walter Moberly says, "The reality of love surpasses the realm of reason."[1] As to the question of why God chose Abraham, people have been wondering about that for a long time. Ancient Jewish writings sometimes guessed that maybe Abraham did something to set himself apart from others, somehow meriting God's love, perhaps by taking a stand against idolatry.[2] But this is just speculation; the Bible knows nothing of it. Instead, it leaves the original call of Abraham (Gen 12) completely unexplained. And as for Israel, Moses almost goes out of his way to eliminate from their mind any thought that God's love for them reflects what they deserve. "Understand that YHWH your God is not giving you this good land to possess because of your righteousness, for you are a stiff-necked people" (9:6).

We have the same trouble explaining why God would choose us. Sure, we express our faith in Christ, and he saves us through the blood of Jesus, but why in the world were we so valuable to God that he would send his Son to die for us?

---

1. Moberly, *Old Testament Theology: Reading the Hebrew Bible as Christian Scripture*, 44.

2. See the discussion in James L. Kugel, *The Bible as It Was* (Cambridge, MA: Harvard University Press, 1997), 131–48.

The Bible doesn't explain it. It is one of the mysteries of the gospel that leaves us in "astonished wonder."[3]

I think that's about as far as we can go with that particular angle on this question. So, let's take a different path. Does God's choice of Israel entail a disdain for other nations, or a lack of concern for them? Does God's choice of the church entail a disdain for people outside the church? Certainly not. In fact, God expects Christians to behave in such a way that others will come to glorify God (Matt 5:16), and God expects Christians to testify to his goodness (Matt 28:19). What about Israel? Is it possible that God had something similar in mind in bringing a special people to himself long before the creation of the church? This is where Exodus 19 might come into play. After all, the terms with which Peter described Christians (1 Pet 2:5–9)—a people of God's own possession, a holy nation, a royal priesthood—are direct quotations from Exodus 19:5–6 in a description of Israel, implying that whatever the church is, Israel was in some way that same thing much earlier. If Christians somehow serve as God's ambassadors in this world (cf. 2 Cor 5:20), perhaps we can say something similar about Israel.

Context

Israel arrives at Sinai in Exodus 19, two months after their exodus from Egypt (v. 1). They won't leave for almost a year (Num 10:11). Moses ascends the mountain (v. 3) and receives this message from God.

---

3. The expression is from Moberly, *Old Testament Theology*, 45.

> Thus you shall say to the house of Jacob, and tell the people of Israel: ⁴ You yourselves have seen what I did to the Egyptians, and how I bore you on eagles' wings and brought you to myself. ⁵ Now therefore, if you will indeed obey my voice and keep my covenant, you shall be my treasured possession among all peoples, for all the earth is mine; ⁶ and you shall be to me a kingdom of priests and a holy nation. These are the words that you shall speak to the people of Israel. (Exod 19:3–6)

Moses delivers this message (v. 7). The people respond: "We will do all that YHWH has spoken" (v. 8). The people are then consecrated (v. 10) in preparation for God's descent onto Mt. Sinai, which happens on the third day (v. 16). "Mt. Sinai was completely enveloped in smoke because YHWH came down on it in fire" (v. 18). This is all preparation for the delivery of the laws that Israel has already committed herself to obeying.

This scene in Exodus 19 is the making of the covenant, God's covenant with Israel, the covenant that forms the backbone of all of Scripture. The introduction to this covenant—the explanation of what God has in mind by taking this people to himself—must then be one of the most important passages in the Hebrew Bible. The first time that Israel commits herself to obeying the Lord is in response to the Lord's opening words at Sinai, which again adds weight to his declaration that Israel would be his special possession, a kingdom of priests, and a holy nation. In the words of Walter Brueggemann, "This speech [19:3–6] is likely the most programmatic for Israelite faith that we have in the entire tradition of Moses."[4]

On the other hand, we should not imagine that with this speech we witness the birth of a nation. Israel does not become God's people at Sinai. They have already been the Lord's people. Remember God's words to Moses at the bush: "I have surely seen the affliction of my people..." (3:7). Moses approaches Pharaoh with the words of the Lord, "Let my people go" (5:1). Israel is, in fact, God's "firstborn son" (4:22). The arrival at Sinai does not turn Israel into God's people; it establishes the covenant that reveals the implications of what it means to be God's people.

We could spend some time talking about the individual phrases and terms in this speech, each of which is filled with significance.[5]

> I bore you on eagles' wings and brought you to myself.
>
> If you will indeed obey my voice and keep my covenant...
>
> You shall be my treasured possession among all peoples...
>
> For all the earth is mine.

---

4. Walter Brueggemann, "The Book of Exodus," *NIB* (Nashville: Abingdon, 1994), 834.

5. See, e.g., Terence E. Fretheim, "'Because the Whole Earth Is Mine': Theme and Narrative in Exodus," *Interpretation* 50 (1996): 229–39.

> You shall be to me a kingdom of priests…
> And a holy nation.

But in this lesson, it is the fifth element listed above that concerns us. What does the phrase "kingdom of priests" indicate here? What implications does it have for the nature of the covenant, for the role of Israel in the world, for the purpose behind God's choice of Israel?

There are indications in Scripture that God wanted Israel to testify to his righteousness and goodness, and that such testimony would be for the benefit of the nations. In other words, there are indications that God's choice of Israel did not entail a disregard for the world, but rather that God's choice of Israel was a vital constituent of God's plans for the world. For Israel would be a kingdom of priests.

THE FATE OF THE NATIONS

Before jumping into those passages that seem to indicate that Israel had a mission, let's take a look at what the Old Testament says about the other nations of the earth.

We start with a well-known prophecy that appears twice, in two different prophetic books.

> It shall come to pass in the latter days
> that the mountain of the house of YHWH
> shall be established as the highest of the mountains,
> and shall be lifted up above the hills;
> and all the nations shall flow to it,
> [3] and many peoples shall come, and say:
> "Come, let us go up to the mountain of YHWH

> to the house of the God of Jacob,
> that he may teach us his ways
> and that we may walk in his paths."
> For out of Zion shall go forth the law,
> and the word of YHWH from Jerusalem.
> ⁴ He shall judge between the nations,
> and shall decide disputes for many peoples;
> and they shall beat their swords into plowshares,
> and their spears into pruning hooks;
> nation shall not lift up sword against nation,
> neither shall they learn war anymore.
>
> (Isa 2:2–4 // Mic 4:1–3)

The vision of the future that these two prophets present is one of peace and justice, in which the nations give up warfare because they have learned the way of the Lord. Their desire for conquest is overcome by their desire to learn Torah. "For out of Zion shall go forth the law." This very positive view of the nations imagines a time when the whole world—and not Israel alone—will recognize the sovereignty of the Lord.

Later, Isaiah imagines a time when the root of Jesse will come (11:1, 10) and "the nations will look to him for guidance" (11:10). At Isa 45:22–23, God tells "all the ends of the earth" to "turn to me and be saved," and he announces a day in which "every knee shall bow to me, every tongue shall swear allegiance." There are several similar passages in Isaiah, such as where the prophet predicts an altar in Egypt where people will worship the Lord (19:19).[6]

---

6. See also 25:6–8; ch. 56; 60:11; 66:19–23.

Other prophets share similar visions of the ingathering of the nations.

> Sing and rejoice, O daughter of Zion, for behold, I come and I will dwell in your midst, declares YHWH. [11] And many nations shall join themselves to YHWH in that day, and shall be my people. And I will dwell in your midst, and you shall know that YHWH of hosts has sent me to you. [12] And YHWH will inherit Judah as his portion in the holy land, and will again choose Jerusalem. (Zech 2:10–12)

> The inhabitants of one city shall go to another, saying, Let us go at once to entreat the favor of YHWH and to seek YHWH of hosts; I myself am going. [22] Many peoples and strong nations shall come to seek YHWH of hosts in Jerusalem and to entreat the favor of YHWH. [23] Thus says YHWH of hosts: In those days ten men from the nations of every tongue shall take hold of the robe of a Jew, saying, Let us go with you, for we have heard that God is with you. (Zech 8:21–23)

At the dedication of the temple, Solomon includes the foreigner in his prayer to God.

> Likewise, when a foreigner, who is not of your people Israel, comes from a far country for your name's sake [42] (for they shall hear of your great name and your mighty hand, and of your outstretched arm), when he comes and prays toward this house, [43] hear in heaven your dwelling place and do according to all for which the foreigner calls to you, in order that all the peoples of the

earth may know your name and fear you, as do your people Israel, and that they may know that this house that I have built is called by your name. (1 Kings 8:41–43)

The psalmist hopes for a day when "your way may be known on earth, your saving power among all nations" (Psa 67:2). He implores, "Let the peoples praise you, O God; let all the peoples praise you!" (v. 3). God sent Jonah to Nineveh, which led to the conversion of the sailors (Jonah 1:16) and the Ninevites (3:5–10). Apparently God sometimes spoke to prophets outside of Israel (think about Balaam; Num 22). And the Lord was involved in the national histories of other nations (cf. Amos 9:7).

So in the Old Testament there is some concern for other nations. There is the wish that other nations would come to recognize that the Lord is God, and there is the hope that in the future these other nations will stream to Zion because they want to serve Israel's God.

These ideas continue to be expressed in Jewish literature outside our Bible.[7] For example:

> Many nations will come from afar to the name of the Lord God, bearing gifts in their hands, gifts for the King of heaven. Generations of generations will give you joyful praise. (Tobit 13:11)
>
> Then all the Gentiles will turn to fear the Lord God in truth, and will bury their idols. All the Gentiles will praise the Lord. (Tobit 14:6–7)

---

7. See also 1 Enoch 90; 2 Baruch 72.

> And all the sons of men shall be righteous, and all the nations shall serve and bless me, and all shall worship me. (1 Enoch 10:21)

Of course, there are also some pretty negative statements and predictions about the nations in the Old Testament (just as there are about Israel). Not everything comes up smelling like a rose when the prophets describe what the future of the nations looks like; sometimes that future is one of judgment. See, for example, Joel's depiction of the Lord's judgment on the nations (ch. 3), when the Lord tells them to "beat your plows into swords and your pruning knives into spears" (v. 10) to prepare for the coming war. The prophetic books frequently contain "Oracles against the Nations" that cast the nations in the role of God's enemies and predict coming judgment upon them.[8] But even these oracles are not wholly negative; after all, it's in the midst of the oracle against Egypt that Isaiah predicts a time when the nations will turn to the Lord (Isa 19:19). And even when these oracles exhibit a negative view of the nations, they simultaneously show that God is concerned about the behavior of all nations, not just one.

Did Israel Have a Mission?

> I will watch over you, and I will appoint you to be a covenant for the people and a light to the nations. (Isa 42:6; cf. 49:6)

---

8. See the Oracles against the Nations in Isa 13–23; Jer 46–51; Ezek 25–32.

If the nations were going to recognize the sovereignty of Israel's God and seek out his law, how would this come about? Was Israel supposed to play a role in helping the nations understand the truth about God? There is no Great Commission in the Old Testament; there is no explicit command to Israel to evangelize. But there are passages that indicate that God intended for ancient Israel to have a positive impact on the nations with the result that the nations would come to know God. As we've talked about previously, part of God's intentions through the plague narrative was to make sure that not only would Pharaoh come to know who YHWH is (cf. Exod 5:2) but also that the whole world would know his name (Exod 9:16). God had (and has) intentions for the entire world, and he wanted his people to contribute toward realizing those intentions.

Pre-Israelite History (Gen 1–11). It cannot be insignificant that the Hebrew Bible begins with God's creation of the world, not God's creation of Israel.[9] Every human being is made in the image of God (Gen 1:26–27; 5:1–2; 9:6). The first transgression affects all of humanity in that the way to the Tree of Life is blocked (3:22–24), "and so death spread to all people because all sinned" (Rom 5:12). Soon God finds that "the wickedness of man was great in the earth, and that every intention of the thoughts of his heart was only evil continually" (Gen 6:5), and so he brought the flood. But even after the flood, God acknowledges that "the intention of man's heart is evil from his youth" (8:21). As humanity

---

9. See Terence E. Fretheim, "The Reclamation of Creation: Redemption and Law in Exodus," *Interpretation* 45 (1991): 354–65, at 356–57.

starts over through Noah's descendants, the basic problem of an evil heart clearly has not been resolved. It affects Noah's own family, evident in his curse of his own descendants (9:20–27), and it appears in the prideful plan of humans to build a tower to reach the heavens, a tower that will give them a name (11:4). The problem, then, that the early chapters present is a universal problem, affecting the whole world, all humans. It would require a universal solution. It is at this point that God elects a particular family.

The Call of Abraham. God enters into a relationship with one man, promising to grant him great blessings, including many descendants and a land of their own. In the storyline of Genesis, God's call of Abraham comes out of the blue. (Of course, even the original readers of the story already knew Abraham's importance.) Since the problem of human rebellion has been exhibited so forcefully in the previous narrative, this new event in Gen 12 is apparently the solution. Since humanity as a whole had rejected relationship with God, God would enter into a covenant specifically with one man. God promises to protect Abraham, to build up his family, to bless his friends and curse his enemies (12:1–2), while Abraham should trust God. We read a little more about Abraham's role later on.

> For I have chosen him so that he will command his children and his house after him to keep the way of YHWH by doing what is right and just. This is how YHWH will fulfill to Abraham what he promised him. (Gen 18:19)

So Abraham did have some responsibilities. This covenant should affect his behavior, and the behavior of his children. But what should it do for humanity?

> ...and all the peoples on earth will be blessed through you. (12:3)

> ...and all the nations of the earth will be blessed through him. (18:18)

> ...and all the nations of the earth will be blessed in your seed. (22:18)

> ...and all the nations of the earth will be blessed in your seed. (26:4; to Isaac)

> ...and all the peoples on earth will be blessed in you and your seed. (28:14; to Jacob)

The call of Abraham has worldwide significance because of the blessing that his seed will bring to people. Now, the meaning of this phrase is disputed in biblical scholarship (surprise, surprise!), and the Hebrew expression is not the same in all cases, as it often is in English (as above).[10] Some scholars think the two different Hebrew expressions both mean the same thing, and what they mean is that other people will "bless themselves" by Abraham and his offspring: that is, they will pronounce blessings (like the blessings in Ruth 4:11–12) using Abraham's family as the model—"may

---

10. The verb "blessed" is in the niphal conjugation in 12:3; 18:18; 28:14; it is in the Hithpael conjugation in 22:18 and 26:4.

we be like Abraham and his family!"[11] Other scholars think this (or something like it) might be the meaning of the Hebrew expression used in 22:18 and 26:4, but the expression used in 12:3; 18:18; and 28:14 should be translated as a passive (as it usually is), "all peoples/nations will be blessed."[12] This latter idea—that nations "will be blessed" through Abraham and his seed—is traditional in Christianity, having been articulated in this sense by Paul (see Gal 3) and, even before him, in the Septuagint, which translates the verbs as passive.

In any case, Abraham's relationship with God would somehow bring blessing to other nations. The apostle Paul insists that the ultimate fulfillment of this blessing is in Christ, the seed of Abraham (Gal 3:16), and through Christ people can likewise become the seed of Abraham (Gal 3:29). But this ultimate fulfillment would have been obscure to Abraham, who probably would have assumed that God meant that his family would become a blessing to others. The book of Genesis does not show Abraham blessing other nations all that much—quite the opposite at times (cf. Gen 12:17)—but his seed does bring blessing to other nations (cf. Laban, 30:27). The most prominent example is Joseph, who

---

11. See, e.g., R. W. L. Moberly, *The Theology of the Book of Genesis* (Cambridge: Cambridge University Press, 2009), ch. 8. Moberly still gets a somewhat traditional meaning out of the statement, in that the use of Abraham as the model for life would surely entail coming to know the God of Abraham.

12. For a recent argument for this view, see Chee-Chiew Lee, "Once Again: The Niphal and the Hithpael in the Abrahamic Blessing for the Nations," *Journal for the Study of the Old Testament* 36 (2012): 279–96.

is able to bless the entire world (cf. Gen 41:57). Not coincidentally, Genesis emphasizes that the Lord was with Joseph (cf. Gen 39:2-3, 21, 23).

I don't think Gen 12:3 can be interpreted as explicitly evangelistic, as if Abraham and his family were supposed to talk to people about God. But the covenant with Abraham does begin the solution to the worldwide problem laid out in Gen 1-11, and the solution to humanity in rebellion is humanity blessed through Abraham and his seed. And "all the nations of the earth will be blessed through him" (18:18) because "I have chosen him so that he will command his children and his house after him to keep the way of YHWH by doing what is right and just. This is how YHWH will fulfill to Abraham what he promised him" (18:19). The point, as I see it, is that Abraham and his family would be the light of the world, a city on a hill, through whose trust in God and obedience to his will the nations would be blessed by coming to know God and glorify him (cf. Matt 5:14-16).

A Kingdom of Priests[13]

You can probably tell where this is going. If Abraham's seed was the solution to the worldwide problem of human rebellion, then that same type of outlook also defines Israel's vocation. At Mt. Sinai, they are not created as a people, because they have already been God's people; God long earlier elected Abraham and his descendants as his special people.

---

13. See John A. Davies, *A Royal Priesthood: Literary and Intertextual Perspectives on an Image of Israel in Exodus 19.6* (London: T&T Clark, 2004).

But at Sinai Israel learns what it means to be God's people. At Sinai, they receive a vocation.[14] They become a kingdom of priests (Exod 19:6). Note that later, at the covenant ceremony in Exod 24, blood is sprinkled on the people (Exod 24:8) as if consecrating them to a priestly function (cf. Exod 29:19–21).[15]

Unfortunately, God doesn't really expound on what he means with this description, and the description appears nowhere else in the Old Testament. We cannot take it literally, as if the whole nation were going to be priests. After all, a few chapters later, God specifies that Aaron and his sons will serve as priests (Exod 28:1). It will be these literal priests who perform sacrifices and lead worship. So we need to understand the statement that the entire nation would be a kingdom of priests in some metaphorical sort of way.[16]

One way to approach the meaning of this phrase is to think about the role of priests. In the Old Testament, priests offer sacrifice (Lev 1–7), and priests teach people about God's ways (Lev 10:11; Deut 33:10; Jer 18:18; Mal 2:6–7; Hos 4:1–9). If these tasks metaphorically apply to Israel as a whole, then at the least we can say that Israel's priestly status

---

14. Emphasized in Fretheim, "Reclamation of Creation," 361.
15. Ernest W. Nicholson, *God and His People: Covenant and Theology in the Old Testament* (Oxford: Oxford University Press, 1986), 173.
16. For discussion, see Christopher J. H. Wright, *The Mission of God: Unlocking the Bible's Grand Narrative* (Downers Grove, IL: IVP, 2006), 224–25, 255–57, 329–33, 369–75.

means that this nation represents God in the world. According to Blackburn: "Through Israel, God would make himself known to the world."[17]

The fifth-century Christian writer Theodoret of Cyrus agreed.

> In other words, as he honored the Levites—though they were Israelites like the rest—over the other tribes, and consecrated them to the divine worship without neglecting, but actually showing care for, the others through the Levites, so he chose the offspring of Abraham, Isaac, and Jacob.[18]

In other words, choosing Israel as a special people demonstrated God's care for the other nations, just as the special status of the Levitical priesthood arose from God's care for the entire nation of Israel.

How would this happen, this revealing of God to the nations? Again, probably not through overt evangelism. Philo, the first-century Jewish philosopher, describes Israel as a nation "consecrated above all others to offer prayers for ever on behalf of the human race that it may be delivered from evil and participate in what is good" (*Life of Moses* 1.149). That's the way he saw Israel's vocation: Israel would pray for the nations. There is also another possibility, suggested in

---

17. Blackburn, *The God Who Makes Himself Known: The Missionary Heart of the Book of Exodus*, 95.

18. Theodoret, *Questions on Exodus* 35, in Theodoret of Cyrus, *The Questions on the Octateuch*, vol. 1: *On Genesis and Exodus*, trans. Robert C. Hill, Library of Early Christianity (Washington, D.C.: Catholic University of America Press, 2007), 281.

Scripture. Israel would reveal God to the nations by keeping God's law, by which they would become a light to the nations. On the plains of Moab, Moses tells the next generation of Israelites:

> See, I have taught you statutes and rules, as YHWH my God commanded me, that you should do them in the land that you are entering to take possession of it. ⁶ Keep them and do them, for that will be your wisdom and your understanding in the sight of the peoples, who, when they hear all these statutes, will say, Surely this great nation is a wise and understanding people. (Deut 4:5–6)

As in the case of the covenant with Abraham, so also the covenant with Israel would reach its proper fulfillment only through the trust and obedience of God's people. If Israel will obey the laws, the nations will notice.

Ancient Interpretations of Israel's Priestly Status

Later Jewish writers recognized this aspect about their nation. The *Testament of Levi* interprets Israel's calling this way:

> For just as the sky is purer than the earth in the Lord's eyes, so are you, the lights of Israel, than all the nations. But if you are darkened through impiety, what will be left for the nations to do, living in blindness? You will bring down a curse upon our people, because the light of the Torah, which was given to illuminate every man,

this you wish to destroy by teaching commandments contrary to God's requirements. (*T. Levi* 14.3–4)[19]

Philo believes that Israel was chosen because God wanted "to consecrate it to the priesthood, that it might for ever offer up prayers for the whole universal race of mankind, for the sake of averting evil from them and procuring them a participation in blessings" (*Life of Moses* 1.149).

Later Philo imagines that if the Jews could be prosperous again:

> I believe that each nation would abandon its peculiar ways, and throwing overboard their ancestral customs, turn to honoring our laws alone. For, when the brightest of their shining is accompanied by national prosperity, it will darken the light of the others as the risen sun darkens the stars. (*Life of Moses* 2.44)

As we have seen, the hopes that Philo expresses here is the same as the hope expressed by the Old Testament prophets, that the nations would one day want to learn about Israel's God. It's the brightness of the Jewish Law, displayed through Jewish piety, that will win people over.

Finally, we may have an indication that Paul interprets Israel's calling in the same way. Look at what he says at the beginning of Romans 3.

---

19. See the translation by James L. Kugel in *Outside the Bible: Ancient Jewish Writings Related to Scripture*, 3 vols., ed. Louis H. Feldman, James L. Kugel, and Lawrence H. Schiffman (Philadelphia: JPS, 2013), 2.1742.

> Then what advantage has the Jew? Or what is the value of circumcision? ² Much in every way. To begin with, they were entrusted with the oracles of God.

Paul uses what might seem a surprising word: "entrust."[20] What does he mean that they were *entrusted* with the oracles of God? Why doesn't he say that they were *given* the oracles of God? Is there some nuance to the word "entrust" that separates it from the word "give"? When we say that we're entrusting someone with something, we usually mean that we're handing something over to someone not specifically for that person's benefit but for the benefit of somebody else. You entrust your money to your financial agent, but you don't mean for your financial agent to keep it all. But when you give someone a birthday present, you don't *entrust* them with the present, you just give it to them. Maybe Paul means that Israel was entrusted with God's oracles not as their exclusive preserve, but as a deposit: they should demonstrate what life with God looks like, and thereby share God's word with the nations. "For out of Zion shall go forth the law."

That's not to say that Jews actively engaged in proselytizing. They did a little bit, as Jesus himself attests (Matt 23:15). According to one recent study of the question:

---

20. For the interpretation that follows, see N. T. Wright, "Romans 2.17–3.9: A Hidden Clue to the Meaning of Romans?" in *Pauline Perspectives: Essays on Paul, 1978–2013* (Minneapolis: Fortress, 2013), ch. 30, 489–509, esp. 490–95; idem, *Paul and the Faithfulness of God* (Minneapolis: Fortress, 2013), 836–38.

Not only did Second Temple Jews look forward to Gentile worship of God at the climax of history; some sought to encourage this worship in the normal course of history. They prayed for it, drew Gentile neighbours to the synagogue, engaged in ethical apologetic, and, on a few clear occasions, even took part in explicit teaching.[21]

CHRISTIANS AS PRIESTS

Peter adopts this terminology from Exodus 19:6 to describe Christians. The church, too, should see itself as "a royal priesthood, a holy nation, a people for his possession, so that you may proclaim the praises of the one who called you out of darkness into his marvelous light" (1 Peter 2:9). But whereas in Exodus, God eventually did specify a particular group of Israelites to become literal priests (Aaron's sons), he doesn't make any such specification in the New Testament. The only priests are the believers, the "royal priesthood." All Christians perform the spiritual sacrifices enjoined in the New Testament, whether we're talking about the living sacrifice of our bodies (Rom 12:1) or the sacrifice of praise (Heb 13:15), or any other type of "spiritual sacrifices acceptable to God through Jesus Christ" (1 Pet 2:5).

---

21. John Dickson, "Mission-Commitment in Second Temple Judaism and the New Testament," in *Introduction to Messianic Judaism: Its Ecclesial Context and Biblical Foundations* (ed. David Rudolph and Joel Willitts; Grand Rapids: Zondervan, 2013), 255–63, at 262. The clearest references to explicit Jewish proselytizing include Cassius Dio 57.18.5a (cf. Jos. *Ant.* 18.81–84); Josephus, *Ant.* 20.34–41.

The role that Israel had to represent God in the world is still the role that God's people play.

8

THE LAW AT SINAI

For two thousand years, Christians have struggled with the authority of the Old Testament. Most Christians have accepted that the Old Testament is authoritative in some sense, but the question has been, "in what sense?" Actually, this isn't that hard of a question for the majority of the Old Testament: it's authoritative in the same way that it's always been. In whatever way the Proverbs were authoritative for ancient Israel—giving divine advice for living—they're authoritative in that same way for Christians in the twenty-first century. Same thing for the Psalms and the prophetic books and the historical narratives.[1] The issue of the Old Testament's authority for Christians really centers around what we're supposed to do with the Mosaic Law.

---

1. On the other hand, in terms of the authority of the Psalter, Christians have often not followed literally its various commands to praise God on instruments of music (cf. e.g., Psalm 150) as most Christians around the world and throughout history have participated in *a cappella* worship. But even most modern praise bands do not strictly "Praise him with the sound of the trumpet: praise him with the psaltery and harp" (Psa 150:3).

Christians have come up with a variety of schemas by which to understand the authority of the Mosaic Law, and we'll look in this chapter at some of the most prominent of these schemas. The reason for the differences of opinion has everything to do with the way that the New Testament, especially the apostle Paul, handles the law. On the one hand, Paul celebrates the freedom that a Christian enjoys, freedom from the "yoke of slavery" that is represented by the law (Gal 5:1-4). Paul emphasizes that Christians "are not under the law but under grace" (Rom 6:14). On the other hand, the problem is not the law, "for we know that the law is spiritual" (Rom 7:14); "the law is holy, and the commandment is holy and just and good" (v. 12). And Paul frequently quotes from the Torah of Moses and expects his (usually Gentile) readers to see these quotations as authoritative pronouncements from God to them (see esp. Rom 9-11; Eph 6:1-3). The tension (at least for readers, if not for Paul) in Paul's position on the status of the law for Christians is well illustrated in his own words: "Circumcision does not matter and uncircumcision does not matter. Keeping God's commands is what matters" (1 Cor 7:19).[2]

But this is all, perhaps, to put to the cart before the horse. We need to understand the role of the Law within the Old Testament itself. What does Exodus say about the revelation

---

2. Other scholars also highlight this verse as an especially straightforward and succinct presentation of the two—seemingly contradictory—poles of Paul's view of the law; see, e.g., James W. Thompson, *Moral Formation according to Paul: The Context and Coherence of Pauline Ethics* (Grand Rapids: Baker, 2011), 111; Brian S. Rosner, *Paul and the Law: Keeping the Commandments of God* (Downers Grove, IL: IVP, 2013), 33.

at Sinai? Is the Law a blessing or a curse? Is it the source of life or of death? The answers to these questions are relatively straightforward.

The Ten Commandments

Before Israel arrived at Sinai, the Lord had given them a smattering of commandments: how to do the Passover (Exod 12), how to collect the manna, which included instructions about a Sabbath rest (Exod 16). At Sinai, once the people have been sanctified (19:9–15), "YHWH came down on [Mt. Sinai] in fire" (v. 18), and Moses went down to the people (v. 25). Then the Lord spoke the Ten Commandments directly to the people, the only words the Lord spoke in this public way without using Moses as the intermediary. The people did not like it, but it did make an impression.

> Now when all the people saw the thunder and the flashes of lightning and the sound of the trumpet and the mountain smoking [cf. 19:16–19], the people were afraid and trembled, and they stood far off [19] and said to Moses, "You speak to us, and we will listen; but do not let God speak to us, lest we die." [20] Moses said to the people, "Do not fear, for God has come to test you, that the fear of him may be before you, that you may not sin." [21] The people stood far off, while Moses drew near to the thick darkness where God was. (Exod 20:18–21; cf. Deut 5:23–27)

Forty years later, Moses recalls this moment.

> Only take care, and keep your soul diligently, lest you forget the things that your eyes have seen, and lest they depart from your heart all the days of your life. Make them known to your children and your children's children—¹⁰how on the day that you stood before YHWH your God at Horeb, YHWH said to me, "Gather the people to me, that I may let them hear my words, so that they may learn to fear me all the days that they live on the earth, and that they may teach their children." ¹¹ And you came near and stood at the foot of the mountain, while the mountain burned with fire to the heart of heaven, wrapped in darkness, cloud, and gloom. ¹² Then YHWH spoke to you out of the midst of the fire. You heard the sound of words, but saw no form; there was only a voice. ¹³ And he declared to you his covenant, which he commanded you to perform, that is, the Ten Commandments, and he wrote them on two tablets of stone. (Deut 4:9–13)

The Lord spoke directly to the people to make a point, both about how terrifying the Lord could be, and also that the Lord had no form that could be cast as an idol. This is the point God makes to Moses immediately after the Israelites beg Moses to serve as the go-between. "You have seen that I have spoken to you from heaven. Do not make gods of silver to rival me; do not make gods of gold for yourselves" (Exod 20:22–23). Of course, people are fickle, and it wouldn't take Israel long to get over her fear and forget the lesson of God's formless voice (cf. Exod 32).

The Ten Commandments stand out,[3] then, because they were spoken directly by God to the people and they were the first commandments given at Sinai. Moreover, these commandments appear twice as a group. On the plains of Moab before Israel's entrance into Canaan, Moses gives the "second law" (= literal definition of "Deuteronomy") to Israel; he does not repeat every commandment from Exodus, Leviticus, and Numbers, but he does repeat the Ten Commandments at Deut 5. The two versions (Exod 20; Deut 5) are basically identical; the most obvious difference between the two versions is that the rationale for the Sabbath command is different: in Exodus God commands the Sabbath as a reflection of his own rest after the six days of creation (Exod 20:11), whereas in Deuteronomy the commandment for rest is connected to Israel's experience in Egypt as slaves (Deut 5:15).

The Ten Commandments were also the only commandments written on the stone tablets. Some passages might make us think otherwise (e.g., Exod 24:12; 31:18), but other verses clarify the matter. Immediately after reminding Israel about the Ten Commandments, Moses declares:

> YHWH spoke these commands in a loud voice to your entire assembly from the fire, cloud, and total darkness on the mountain; he added nothing more. He wrote them on two stone tablets and gave them to me. (Deut 5:22)

---

3. We won't deal here with the numbering of the Ten Commandments, which can be somewhat confusing; see Wikipedia.

This verse also alerts us that Moses did not chisel the commandments into the stone, but rather God himself wrote them with his own finger (cf. Exod 31:18; 34:1; Deut 9:10; 10:2). These stone tablets with the Ten Commandments were then placed in the ark of the covenant (which had not yet been made when the stone tablets were engraved; cf. Exod 25:16, 21; Deut 10:5; 1 Kings 8:9; Heb 9:4).

But why are the Ten Commandments so special that they would be spoken first by God directly to the people and alone written by God on stone tablets to be placed in the sanctuary? The Alexandrian Jewish philosopher Philo, a contemporary of Jesus, considered this question.

> Now we find that those which he gave in his own person and by his own mouth alone include both laws and heads summarizing particular laws, but those in which he spoke through the prophet all belong to the former class. (*On the Decalogue* 19)[4]

What Philo means is that all the laws in the Pentateuch can be categorized under the "heads" or "headings" provided by the Ten Commandments. This idea is not prominent in ancient Judaism—at least, it's not made explicit in many ancient Jewish writings—but perhaps it stands behind Jesus' response to the Rich Young Ruler; when he mentioned the laws, he started naming off the Ten Commandments (Luke

---

4. I've used the translation (by Colson for the Loeb Classical Library) found in Sarah Judith Pearce, "On the Decalogue," in *Outside the Bible: Ancient Jewish Writings Related to Scripture*, 3 vols., ed. Louis H. Feldman, James L. Kugel, and Lawrence H. Schiffman (Philadelphia: JPS, 2013), 1.989–1032, at 996.

18:19–20). At any rate, the idea that the Ten Commandments provide a sort of summary for the rest of the laws in the Pentateuch has been argued by some modern scholars, particularly in reference to the book of Deuteronomy, but also in reference to the remaining laws in Exodus.[5]

THE BOOK OF THE COVENANT

After God speaks the Ten Commandments to the people, Moses ascends the mountain again (Exod 20:21) and received further laws (20:22–23:33). This is still not the time that Moses spends 40 days on the mountain, which is upcoming, when he receives the instructions about the Tabernacle (24:18). In this instance, when Moses receives the various laws regarding Israelite behavior,[6] the text does not say how long it takes, but presumably it didn't take very long. After hearing all these laws, Moses again descends the mountain and reports the laws to the people.

> Then all the people responded with a single voice, "We will do everything that YHWH has commanded." And Moses wrote down all the words of YHWH. (24:3–4)

---

5. See Georg Braulik, "The Sequence of the Laws in Deuteronomy 12–26 and in the Decalogue," in *A Song of Power and the Power of Song: Essays on the Book of Deuteronomy*, ed. Duane L. Christensen (Winona Lake, IN: Eisenbrauns, 1993), 313–35. On the organization of the Book of the Covenant according to the Ten Commandments, see William H. C. Propp, *Exodus 19–40*, Anchor Bible (New York: Doubleday, 2006), 305–6.

6. For an outline of these laws, see Exploration 8.1.

> Then he took the Book of the Covenant and read it in the hearing of the people. And they said, "All that YHWH has spoken we will do, and we will be obedient." (24:7)

The text of Exodus itself gives the name "Book of the Covenant" to this group of laws: not the Ten Commandments, but all the other laws of Exod 20–23.[7]

In contrast to the Ten Commandments, which are pretty general, the laws of the Book of the Covenant get pretty specific: how to treat your slaves (21:2–11); what ought to happen if you're in a fight and someone gets hurt (21:18–19); or if you accidentally strike a pregnant woman (21:22–25); or if your ox hurts somebody (21:28–32). There are laws regulating when someone's property gets damaged (22:5–15), and premarital sex (22:16–17). There are laws against sorcery (22:18) and bestiality (22:19) and idolatry (22:20). There's a law against eating the carcass of an animal that was

---

7. A prominent idea in the study of the Book of the Covenant, but one we cannot here address, is that the structure of Exod 20–24 resembles ancient treaties, whether Hittite treaties or Assyrian treaties. For a brief account of this idea, see James L. Kugel, *How to Read the Bible: A Guide to Scripture, Then and Now* (New York: Free Press, 2007), 243–49. For a comparison of Deuteronomy to these ANE treaties, see Christopher B. Hays, *Hidden Riches: A Sourcebook for the Comparative Study of the Hebrew Bible and Ancient Near East* (Louisville: WJK, 2014), 161–89. There are some differences, such as the fact that "Gods in the ancient world did not issue laws; men did" (Kugel, *How to Read the Bible*, 242, with 721n6; cf. Hays, *Hidden Riches*, 139–40). There are also many similarities between the actual laws in the Book of the Covenant and the laws found on ancient Near Eastern monuments; see Hays, *Hidden Riches*, ch. 7; Kugel, *How to Read the Bible*, 270–74.

killed in the field (22:31). There's a law against perjury (23:1–3). There's a law against including yeast in a sacrificial offering (23:18). And, of course, there's a law against cooking a goat in the milk of its mother (23:19).

EXPLORATION 8.1

LAWS OF THE BOOK OF THE COVENANT

"...Moses approached the thick darkness in which God was present" (20:21)—and so Moses receives the laws...
- Worship
  - No idols (20:23)
  - Altar (20:24–26)
- Slaves (21:2–11; cf. 22:3)
- Capital crimes
  - Killing (with some exceptions, 21:12–14)
  - Violence against parents (21:15)
  - Kidnapping (21:16)
  - Cursing parents (21:17)
- Non-capital crimes
  - Injuring someone in a fight (21:18–19)
  - Injuring or killing a slave (21:20–21)
  - Causing a miscarriage (21:22)
- Lex talionis (21:23–25)
  - Exception: slaves (21:26–27)
- Goring ox (21:28–32)
- An open pit (21:33–34)
- Goring ox again (21:35–36)
- Stealing (22:1–4)

- Damaging someone else's property (22:5-15)
    - Animal eats in another's field—must repay with best of his own field (22:5)
    - Fire accidentally burns another's field—fully repay (22:6)
    - A entrusts money with B, but money is stolen (22:7-8)—
        - Thief must repay double
        - If thief is not caught, B must appear before God to see if he stole the money
    - Excursus: bringing disputes before God (22:9)
    - A entrusts animal with B (22:10-13)
        - Animal dies or is injured, no witnesses—B swears before Yhwh that he didn't cause the injury
        - Animal is stolen—B repays fully
        - Animal is attacked, carcass is evidence—no repayment
    - A loans animal to B, animal dies or is injured (22:14-15)—
        - A not present—B must pay fully
        - A present—no payment
- Premarital sex: man has sex with unmarried girl (22:16-17)—
    - Man must pay bride price
    - Man must marry girl unless her father refuses
- Sorceress must die (22:18)

- Bestiality—capital crime (22:19)
- Idolatry—capital crime (22:20)
- Immigrants, widows, orphans, the poor—God is their defender (22:21–27)
- Prohibition: cursing God or leaders (22:28)
- Offerings: produce, firstborn son, animals (22:29–31)
- Prohibition: eating carcass of animal killed in the field (22:31)
- Be honest witnesses in court (23:1–3)
- Treatment of another's animal (23:4–6)
- Honesty at court (23:6–8)
- Don't oppress immigrants (23:9; cf. 22:21)
- Farming rules: sabbatical year (23:10–11)
- Sabbath (23:12)
- Avoid pronouncing the names of foreign deities (23:13)
- Three pilgrimage festivals (23:14–17)
  - Festival of Unleavened Bread
  - Harvest Festival
  - Gathering Festival
- No yeast on a sacrifice (23:18)
- Don't leave fat of sacrifice until morning (23:18)
- Offer early produce at Yhwh's house (23:19)
- Don't boil a kid in its mother's milk (23:19)

Blessings (23:23–33)

These laws are of all different kinds. Some are worded like the Ten Commandments: "thou shalt" or "thou shalt not."

> You shall not permit a sorceress to live. (22:18)

> You shall not wrong a sojourner or oppress him. (22:21)

Some are case laws: if you should happen to get into a particular situation, this is what you should do about it.

> When men quarrel and one strikes the other with a stone or with his fist and the man does not die but takes to his bed, [19] then if the man rises again and walks outdoors with his staff, he who struck him shall be clear; only he shall pay for the loss of his time, and shall have him thoroughly healed. (21:18–19)

It's not exactly clear how these laws relate to "sin." The word "sin" comes up only once, in a warning against allowing the Canaanites to "make you sin against me" (23:33). I think it's safe to assume that breaking the Ten Commandments would constitute a sin, and being a sorceress would be a sin. But, presumably, if your ox hurts somebody, you haven't necessarily sinned, and you can avoid sinning as long as you follow the prescriptions in the Book of the Covenant (21:28–32). But in the case of a habitually troublesome ox, the outcome is death for the owner of the ox (21:29), unless the owner can pay a fine (to whom? 21:30). Nothing is mentioned in this case about making a sacrifice to atone for sin.[8] If we move beyond the Book of Exodus, similar (but different) questions arise. Surely none of us think that a woman commits some sort of "sin" when she has a baby, but she does contract an impurity that requires "atonement" (Lev 12).

These laws are also not incredibly burdensome; at least, I don't think so. I don't think it's an empty boast to say that I have never broken a single commandment in the Book of the Covenant.[9] I have never worshiped an idol (in the traditional sense), or mistreated my slave, or killed someone, or cursed my parents, or failed to control my ox, or failed to let my field go fallow in the seventh year. Well, I guess I have pronounced the names of foreign deities (23:13), but never to honor them or pray to them. I know you won't misunderstand me: I'm not saying I've lived a perfect life or that I've never sinned; I'm saying that these particular laws are not the ones I've struggled with, at least, if they are interpreted fairly literally. Certainly, the pronouncements of Jesus in Matthew 5 are much more "burdensome"—much more difficult to carry through—than the laws of the Book of the Covenant.

That point indicates what becomes obvious as you think carefully about these laws: the Book of the Covenant is not

---

8. I guess in some ways we have the same questions today: driving over the speed limit is against the law, and God expects us to obey civil laws, so is speeding a sin? But what if I pay the fine?

9. The Rich Young Ruler makes a similar claim (Luke 18:21); he doesn't seem to be weighed down by the requirements of the law. Neither do Zechariah and Elizabeth, who were "both righteous before God, walking blamelessly in all the commandments and statutes of the Lord" (Luke 1:6).

very comprehensive. It covers various areas of life, but it does not cover comprehensively any area of life. Rather than an all-encompassing law code, the Book of the Covenant illustrates certain behaviors and ways of thinking that the Israelites should embody. If the Ten Commandments are too broad to provide a detailed guide to life—i.e., what exactly does it mean to "kill" and how exactly do you define "adultery" and what exactly do you mean by "stealing"—the Book of the Covenant provides concrete examples of the kinds of things God has in mind. God will continue to reveal more laws in later books of the Pentateuch to cover other areas of life, but even once all 613 commandments were given,[10] not every possible circumstance in life was covered clearly, leaving room for later readers to offer their own interpretations, and come to different opinions.[11]

The Law as an Expression of God's Grace

For a fully biblical view of the law, it's important that we highlight what role it plays in the Old Testament. The law is viewed as a great blessing, the source of life.

> See, I have set before you today life and good, death and evil. [16] If you obey the commandments of YHWH your

---

10. This is the number of commandments in the Torah according to Jewish tradition; see Babylonian Talmud, tractate Makkot, 23b–24a.

11. For a good, brief account of later Jewish legal (halakic) interpretation, especially focusing on the time period of the New Testament, see James G. Crossley, *The New Testament and Jewish Law: A Guide for the Perplexed* (London: T&T Clark, 2010).

God that I command you today, by loving YHWH your God, by walking in his ways, and by keeping his commandments and his statutes and his rules, then you shall live and multiply, and YHWH your God will bless you in the land that you are entering to take possession of it. [17] But if your heart turns away, and you will not hear, but are drawn away to worship other gods and serve them, [18] I declare to you today, that you shall surely perish. You shall not live long in the land that you are going over the Jordan to enter and possess. [19] I call heaven and earth to witness against you today, that I have set before you life and death, blessing and curse. Therefore choose life, that you and your offspring may live, [20] loving YHWH your God, obeying his voice and holding fast to him, for he is your life and length of days, that you may dwell in the land that YHWH swore to your fathers, to Abraham, to Isaac, and to Jacob, to give them. (Deut 30:15–20)

And YHWH spoke to Moses, saying, [2] "Speak to the people of Israel and say to them, I am YHWH your God. [3] You shall not do as they do in the land of Egypt, where you lived, and you shall not do as they do in the land of Canaan, to which I am bringing you. You shall not walk in their statutes. [4] You shall follow my rules and keep my statutes and walk in them. I am YHWH your God. [5] You shall therefore keep my statutes and my rules; if a person does them, he shall live by them: I am YHWH. (Lev 18:1–5)

As we saw in the previous chapter, keeping the laws of God would distinguish Israel from the other nations, who would in turn marvel at the wonderful laws of the

Israelites (Deut 4:6). The psalmist rejoiced that Israel had been singled out to receive God's law.

> He declares his word to Jacob,
> his statutes and judgments to Israel.
> He has not done this for every nation;
> they do not know his judgments.
> Hallelujah!
> (Psalm 147:19–20)

Several psalms reflect on the wonders of God's law (cf. Psa 1:2; 19:7–11), none as remarkably or as lengthily as Psalm 119, all 176 verses of which are dedicated to praising God for his gift of Torah. I offer here just a few choice excerpts.

> Psalm 119
> 14, I have rejoiced in the way of thy testimonies
> 16, I will delight myself in thy statutes
> 24, Thy testimonies also are my delight and my counsellors
> 35, Make me to go in the path of thy commandments; for therein do I delight.
> 47, And I will delight myself in thy commandments, which I have loved.
> 70, I delight in thy law.
> 77, for thy law is my delight.
> 92, Unless thy law had been my delights, I should then have perished in mine affliction.
> 97, O how love I thy law! it is my meditation all the day.
> 103, How sweet are thy words unto my taste! yea, sweeter than honey to my mouth.

111, Thy testimonies have I taken as an heritage for ever: for they are the rejoicing of my heart.
113, thy law do I love.
127, Therefore I love thy commandments above gold; yea, above fine gold.
129, Thy testimonies are wonderful.
131, I opened my mouth, and panted: for I longed for thy commandments.
143, thy commandments are my delights.
159, I love thy precepts.
162, I rejoice at thy word.
163, thy law do I love.
165, Great peace have they which love thy law.
167, My soul hath kept thy testimonies; and I love them exceedingly.
174, thy law is my delight.

Even the minutiae of the laws could seem like a blessing, depending on one's point of view. In the words of James Kugel:

> Some of its commandments had the broadest scope (Lev. 19:17–18): others told you what to do when you chanced upon a bird's nest in the road (Deut. 22:6) or specified that you had to put a safety railing on the roof of your house (Deut. 22:8). There were rules about vows to God that you might utter in a moment of panic; what God had ordered you to do in case you contracted a then-common skin disease; rules about festivals and pilgrimages and fasting, menstruation and seminal emissions, rules and rules and rules, until it seemed like there was no area of life about which the Torah did not have *something* to say—and that, for Judaism, was the beauty of it. In doing each thing according to the way

that God had prescribed, a person could, as it were, turn life itself into a constant act of reaching out to God. Nothing was done for its own sake; everything was done to serve God.[12]

The Israelites recognized that the Law was not given so that by keeping it they might be saved, but rather it was given after they had already received salvation.

> When your son asks you in time to come, "What is the meaning of the testimonies and the statutes and the rules that YHWH our God has commanded you?" 21 then you shall say to your son, "We were Pharaoh's slaves in Egypt. And YHWH brought us out of Egypt with a mighty hand. 22 And YHWH showed signs and wonders, great and grievous, against Egypt and against Pharaoh and all his household, before our eyes. 23 And he brought us out from there, that he might bring us in and give us the land that he swore to give to our fathers. 24 And YHWH commanded us to do all these statutes, to fear YHWH our God, for our good always, that he might preserve us alive, as we are this day. 25 And it will be righteousness for us, if we are careful to do all this commandment before YHWH our God, as he has commanded us." (Deut 6:20–25)

The historical books of the Old Testament demonstrate that Israel frequently abandoned God and his ways. The prophets constantly call Israel back to the covenant that God had

---

12. Kugel, *How to Read the Bible*, 261.

made with her. Failure to observe God's law results in judgment, punishment, destruction.

The New Testament on Old Testament Law

Paul also saw the giving of the Law as a tremendous blessing.

> So what advantage has the Jew? Or what benefit is circumcision? Great in every respect! First, they were entrusted with the oracles of God. (Rom 3:1–2)

Paul certainly treated the Law as authoritative, at least, in some sense. He quoted it many times. But he argued that Gentiles should not be required to keep the commandments of the Torah, a move that created much controversy.

Exploration 8.2
Paul and the Law

Quotations (from Gen–Deut; 40x, half in Rom)
Rom 4:3 (Gen 15:6)
Rom 4:9 (Gen 15:6)
Rom 4:17 (Gen 17:5)
Rom 4:18 (Gen 17:5; Gen 15:5)
Rom 4:22 (Gen 15:6)
Rom 7:7 (Exod 20:17 // Deut 5:21)
Rom 9:7 (Gen 21:12)
Rom 9:9 (Gen 18:10, 14)
Rom 9:12 (Gen 25:23)

Rom 9:15 (Exod 33:19)
Rom 9:17 (Exod 9:16)
Rom 10:5 (Lev 18:5)
Rom 10:6 (Deut 9:4)
Rom 10:6–8 (Deut 30:12–14)
Rom 10:19 (Deut 32:21)
Rom 11:8 (Deut 29:4)
Rom 12:19 (Deut 32:35)
Rom 13:9 (Exod 20:13–17 // Deut 5:17–21)
Rom 13:9 (Lev 19:18)
Rom 15:10 (Deut 32:43)

1Cor 5:13 (Deut 17:7)
1Cor 6:16 (Gen 2:24)
1Cor 9:9 (Deut 25:4)
1Cor 10:7 (Exod 32:6)
1Cor 15:45 (Gen 2:7)

2Cor 6:16 (Lev 26:12)
2Cor 8:15 (Exod 16:18)
2Cor 13:1 (Deut 19:15)
Gal 3:6 (Gen 15:6)
Gal 3:8 (Gen 12:3; 18:18)
Gal 3:10 (Deut 27:26)
Gal 3:12 (Lev 18:5)
Gal 3:13 (Deut 21:23)
Gal 3:16 (Gen 12:7)
Gal 4:30 (Gen 21:10)
Gal 5:14 (Lev 19:18)

> Eph 5:31 (Gen 2:24)
> Eph 6:2–3 (Exod 20:12 // Deut 5:16)
>
> 1Tim 5:18 (Deut 25:4)
> 2Tim 2:19 (Num 16:5)

So, the basic question is this: Is the Law authoritative for Christians? And the answer must be "yes, but." The apostle Paul gives a full-throated "Yes!" and a full-throated "but!" This same answer is also given in Acts (ch. 15) and in Mark (ch. 7). The "Yes!" is also clear in the rest of the New Testament, the "but!" somewhat less clear.

Let's explore the "but" first. (This will have to be brief.) The "but" is most fully developed by Paul, who insists, "Yes, the Law is authoritative, but that doesn't mean Gentiles have to follow all of its ordinances in their literal sense."

Specifically, Gentiles should not be circumcised. Paul makes this argument most forcefully in Galatians, but also in Rom 4. But, according, to Paul, it's not just the circumcision is a matter of indifference, irrelevant to a person's standing with God; nay, much more, circumcision is damaging to the Gentile: "I, Paul, am telling you that if you get yourselves circumcised, Christ will not benefit you at all" (Gal 5:2). It is, perhaps, ironic that many twenty-first-century American Christian men have so limited Paul's prohibition to the first-century setting that they are circumcised and arrange for the circumcision of their newborn sons. (I wonder what Paul would say!) But I think the instinct is correct here. It's not about circumcision *per se*. The reason Paul was so opposed to circumcision was because of what it represented to certain people in Paul's own day—a path toward righteousness alternative to the path of faith in Jesus. "You who are trying to be justified by the law are alienated from Christ; you have fallen from grace" (v. 4). And I assume no modern American Christian is tempted toward this same view of circumcision; the procedure is not at all religious for American Christians, and therefore not religiously problematic as it was for Paul. After all, Paul is the one who said that some things are bad only if you think they're bad (Rom 14:14, 23).

It's another question altogether as to whether Paul would have counseled Jews to circumcise their sons, or whether Paul would have circumcised his own son.[13] I'm not sure that he ever addresses this question in his letters. He refused to circumcise Titus, but Titus wasn't a Jew (Gal 2:3). According to Acts, Paul did have Timothy circumcised (Acts 16:3); but Timothy's mother was Jewish, and so this was apparently the difference. But even here, Luke explains that Paul had Timothy circumcised "because of the Jews," apparently meaning that Timothy's ministry would be more effective if "to the Jews he became as a Jew" (cf. 1 Cor 9:20).[14]

---

13. See, e.g., New Testament scholar Larry Hurtado's discussion of this question at his blog, https://larryhurtado.wordpress.com/2014/03/25/would-paul-have-circumcised-his-son/.

14. It is not exactly clear, to me, at least, whether Timothy would have been considered a Jew on account of his mama, or a Gentile on account of his father. The traditional Jewish practice is to trace descent through the mother: someone is born a Jew if his/her mother is Jewish. But how far back does this idea go? The question is discussed by Shaye Cohen, who concludes that Timothy was not considered Jewish; see Shaye J. D. Cohen, "Was Timothy Jewish (Acts 16:1-3)? Patristic Exegesis, Rabbinic Law, and Matrilineal Descent," *Journal of Biblical Literature* 105 (1986): 251–68. (This essay has been reprinted in different collections, and a savvy googler can find it online.)

What else should Gentiles refrain from? I don't think Paul takes such a strong stance against any other practice, but he does tell Gentiles not to let anyone judge them in regard to the food they eat or the days they observe (Rom 14:1–6, 14–18; Col 2:16; 1 Tim 4:3; cf. Mark 7:19). And, of course, he never encourages his churches to make any sort of animal sacrifice—they would have to travel to the temple in Jerusalem, in any case, to sacrifice in accordance with the Torah (cf. Deut 12:5)—while Hebrews makes clear that atonement sacrifices are irrelevant in light of the sacrifice of Christ.

On the other hand, there is a way to understand circumcision such that it applies to Gentiles.

> So if an uncircumcised man keeps the law's requirements, will not his uncircumcision be counted as circumcision? [27] A man who is physically uncircumcised, but who keeps the law, will judge you who are a lawbreaker in spite of having the letter of the law and circumcision. [28] For a person is not a Jew who is one outwardly, and true circumcision is not something visible in the flesh. [29] On the contrary, a person is a Jew who is one inwardly, and circumcision is of the heart— by the Spirit, not the letter. (Rom 2:26–29)

There is an inward circumcision that marks out the people of God even in the absence of physical circumcision. Of course, Paul gets this idea straight out of the Torah (cf. Lev 26:41; Deut 10:16). Whether or not Paul would say that physical circumcision applies to anyone (certainly not Gentiles; maybe Jews?), he certainly says that this inward circumcision is required of everyone.[15] He is encouraging his readers to appropriate the commandment in a spiritual way. This kind of interpretation can be applied to other commandments. Hebrews 4 interprets the Sabbath as something that Christians look forward to enjoying. There are ways in which Christians engage in sacrifice (Rom 12:1–2; Heb 13:15). Paul sees himself as acting like a priest by offering up the Gentiles (Rom 15:16).

But now we are getting to the positive view of the law. Because if Gentile Christians are supposed to make sacrifices in some sense to God, then we can read in Leviticus about the types of things God wanted in his sacrifices, not for the purpose of reproducing those precise practices, but for learning about the types of sacrifices God approves (i.e., "without blemish and undefiled"), or learning about how Christ's death can be viewed as a sacrifice, pleasing to God. So, are the Levitical laws of sacrifice authoritative? Yes, but not in the sense that they are binding on us in their literal meaning, since their meaning, on the one hand, has been fulfilled (completed) by the sacrifice of Christ, and, on the other hand, is being fulfilled by our own acts of sacrifice. So also all of the laws, including the Ten Commandments and the Book of the Covenant, are authoritative for Christians today in the sense that they accurately tell us about our God, revealing to us his character.

> The goring-ox law, for instance, can warn us that those who commit negligent homicide are responsible for

---

15. On inward circumcision, see also Phil 3:2–8; Col 2:11–12; cf. Rom 4:9–12. In the Old Testament, see also Jer 4:4; 9:25–26.

their actions. In rural settings, this could still apply to a goring ox. In an urban context, it could apply to dangerous pit bulls. It could also apply to damage done by a driver who knows their car's brakes are faulty. The laws that keep Israel from acting like Canaanites in worship (the altar law and the law prohibiting cooking a young goat in its mother's milk) warn Christians about the danger of importing the practices of false religions into our own worship.[16]

Paul does actually once directly quote the Ten Commandments as binding on his Gentile readers.[17]

> Children, obey your parents in the Lord, for this is right.
> ² Honor your father and mother (this is the first commandment with a promise), ³ that it may go well with you and that you may live long in the land. (Eph 6:1–3; cf. Exod 20:12 // Deut 5:16)

This is not common, this direct quotation of a law from the Torah as immediately applicable to his audience. There are a few other instances, which we'll mention briefly.[18]

---

16. Tremper Longman, *How to Read Exodus* (Downers Grove, IL: IVP, 2009), 158.

17. Paul also says (1 Cor 14:34) that the practice of women keeping silent in churches is supported by the law, but he does not cite any specific text; see the brief discussion in Thompson, *Moral Formation*, 118.

18. See Richard B. Hayes, "The Role of Scripture in Paul's Ethics," in *The Conversion of the Imagination: Paul as Interpreter of Israel's Scripture* (Grand Rapid: Eerdmans, 2005), 143–62.

He certainly agrees with the Torah in many matters, such as sexual ethics. One might have expected him to quote one of the laws in the Pentateuch in 1 Cor 5, about the man sleeping with his father's wife (cf. Lev 18:6–8; 20:11), or in 1 Cor 6:15–17, about joining with a prostitute.[19] There are plenty of laws about fornication that might have applied in these situations, but Paul quotes none of them, even if his own sexual ethic was shaped by Leviticus and Deuteronomy, as it surely was. But he does quote the Torah, in both passages, just not the expected verse about sex. Instead, in 1 Cor 5:13, he quotes a law about expelling an evil person from God's congregation (Deut 17:7). And in 1 Cor 6:16, he quotes the statement at Gen 2:24 that Adam and Eve became one flesh. Another time he quotes a commandment from the Torah as relevant to Christians: "Do not muzzle an ox while it treads out grain" (1 Cor 9:9; cf. Deut 25:4). But Paul says it doesn't really apply in its literal sense but in a spiritualizing sense to Christian preachers (= oxen). (I wonder if Paul would say that it's really okay to muzzle an ox while its threshing. I would imagine he'd say that it's wrong to do so, but the application of the commandment should not be limited to animals. If that interpretation is correct, Paul's thoughts on the application of Scripture would be similar to what Jesus is doing in Matt 5:21–48.)

Yes, the law is authoritative, but it needs to be transformed into a law relevant to Christians, which means, often, a spiritualizing interpretation. But one law that doesn't really have to be transformed is "You shall love your

---

19. See Thompson, *Moral Formation*, 116–17.

neighbor as yourself" (Lev 19:18),[20] which is the fulfillment of "the whole law" (Gal 5:14; cf. Rom 13:9). This law is directly binding on Christians, and it provides the frame of reference by which to interpret all the other laws. Paul is probably echoing this sentiment a little later in Galatians when he encourages his readers to "bear one another's burdens, and so fulfill the law of Christ" (6:2). In between these two statements about "the whole law" and "the law of Christ," Paul has provided lists of sinful behaviors (5:19–21) and the fruit of the Spirit (5:22–26), so that Christians will know what fulfilling this law looks like on an everyday basis.[21]

Moreover, the storyline of the Torah is authoritative for us, in the sense that we should learn our identity as the people of God from the Torah. That much is clear in 1 Cor 10, when Paul admonishes his Gentile readers to reflect on "our fathers" who came out of Egypt (v. 1) and then, after narrating several events from Exodus and Numbers, says that "these things were written for our instruction" (v. 11).

But the law can become a "yoke of slavery" (Gal 5:1) if viewed in an improper way, as a source of righteousness apart from the righteousness of Christ. Christians are not "under law"—neither Jews nor Gentiles—but we are under

---

20. On the reception of this commandment in Second Temple Judaism, see Kengo Akiyama, *The Love of Neighbour in Ancient Judaism: The Reception of Leviticus 19:18 in the Hebrew Bible, the Septuagint, the Book of Jubilees, the Dead Sea Scrolls, and the New Testament* (Leiden: Brill, 2018).

21. See the discussion in Thompson, *Moral Formation*, 126–27.

grace (Rom 6:14). This type of teaching might lead to licentiousness, and Paul has been accused of this very thing (Rom 3:8), but Paul insists on the opposite: that those in whom the Spirit of Christ dwells can finally fulfill "the righteous requirement of the law" (Rom 8:4).

Now, there are other things to say about the New Testament's interpretation of the Torah, nor have we even come close to an exhaustive treatment of Paul's understanding of the point of the Torah. There is a passage (Gal 3:23–26) in which Paul talks about the Torah as a pedagogue to lead us to Christ, a pedagogue that would be only temporary (like all pedagogues). And Paul sometimes—rather frequently in Romans—describes a function of the Torah as increasing sin (Romans 3:20; 4:15; 5:13; 5:20; 7:5; 7:9–13; cf. Gal 3:19–22). He also says that the Torah was unable to accomplish the condemnation of sin because the Torah was weak through the flesh, and so God has accomplished this "through his own Son ... so that the just requirement of the law might be fulfilled in us, who walk not according to the flesh but according to the Spirit" (Rom 8:3–4).[22]

What does all this mean? I think Blackburn has it right.

> Paul saw as bondage the view that the law was the means by which we are justified before God. Yet, knowing that they are justified by believing in Christ, Paul goes on to exhort the people to do the very thing the law

---

22. For more on Paul's view of the law, see Rosner, *Paul and the Law*.

commanded [going on to quote Gal 5:13–14, which quotes Lev 19:18].[23]

Reception of the Old Testament Law in Christianity

Here we will be exceedingly brief.[24] The same set of issues have come up throughout Christian history. In the second century, Marcion rejected the entire Old Testament as the record of an inferior god who was not the same as the Father of Jesus Christ. This view was quickly labeled heresy, and Christian writers such as Justin Martyr and Irenaeus of Lyon insisted on the authority of the Old Testament, though not the direct binding authority of the law. Some of these second century writers said that God had never intended Jews to obey the literal meaning of the law (Epistle of Barnabas), while others said that God gave laws such as circumcision and Sabbath specifically because the Jews were sinful (Justin).[25]

Eventually, the idea developed that the Mosaic Law could be divided into three categories: moral, ceremonial, and judicial. This idea is already found in the thirteenth-century

---

23. W. Ross Blackburn, *The God Who Makes Himself Known: The Missionary Heart of the Book of Exodus* (Downers Grove, IL: IVP, 2012), 115.

24. For a somewhat less brief treatment, see Christopher J. H. Wright, *Old Testament Ethics for the People of God* (Downers Grove, IL: IVP, 2006), ch. 12.

25. For a survey of the relevant authors in the second century, see Ronald E. Heine, *Reading the Old Testament with the Ancient Church: Exploring the Formation of Early Christian Thought* (Grand Rapids: Baker, 2007), ch. 2.

author Thomas Aquinas (*Summa Theologica* 2.1.99).[26] John Calvin, in the sixteenth century, omitted the judicial part of the law from his discussion, but wrote about the moral and the ceremonial parts of the law (*Institutes* 2.7). The moral law is basically equivalent to the Ten Commandments, which Calvin expounds in the next chapter (2.8). Calvin does recognize that an aspect of the moral law was abrogated by Christ, specifically "its force to bind the conscience" (2.7.15). He continues: "The law not only teaches but forthrightly enforces what it commands. If it be not obeyed—indeed, if one in any respect fail in his duty—the law unleashes the thunderbolt of its curse. [...] To redeem us from this curse, I say, Christ was made a curse for us." In the next section (2.7.16), Calvin discusses the ceremonial law, beginning, "The ceremonies are a different matter: they have been abrogated not in effect but only in use." Christ has fulfilled these ceremonies. "Consequently Paul, to prove their observance not only superfluous but also harmful, teaches that they are shadows whose substance exists for us in Christ [Col. 2:17]."

And so the New Testament did away with the ceremonial law (ritual matters like sacrifices and such) and the judicial law (matters specific to Israel as a government), but the moral law (= the Ten Commandments) is still in force. This is the view codified in ch. 19 of the Westminster Confession of Faith from 1647.

---

26 https://dhspriory.org/thomas/summa/FS/FS099.html#FSQ99A5THEP1.

EXPLORATION 8.3
WESTMINSTER CONFESSION OF FAITH (1674)

CHAPTER XIX.

Of the Law of God.

[emphasis added]

God gave to Adam a law, as a covenant of works, by which He bound him and all his posterity to personal, entire, exact, and perpetual obedience, promised life upon the fulfilling, and threatened death upon the breach of it, and endued him with power and ability to keep it.

II. This law, after his fall, continued to be a perfect rule of righteousness; and, as such, was delivered by God upon Mount Sinai, in ten commandments, and written in two tables: the four first commandments containing our duty towards God; and the other six, our duty to man.

III. Beside this law, commonly called **moral**, God was pleased to give to the people of Israel, as a church under age, ceremonial laws, containing several typical ordinances, partly of worship, prefiguring Christ, His graces, actions, sufferings, and benefits; and partly, holding forth divers instructions of moral duties. **All which ceremonial laws are now abrogated, under the new testament.**

IV. To them also, as a body politic, He gave sundry **judicial laws, which expired together with the State of that people**; not obliging any other now, further than the general equity thereof may require.

V. **The moral law doth for ever bind all**, as well justified persons as others, to the obedience thereof; and that, not only in regard of the matter contained in it, but also in respect of the authority of God the Creator, who gave it. Neither doth Christ, in the Gospel, any way dissolve, but much strengthen this obligation.

VI. Although true believers be not under the law, as a covenant of works, to be thereby justified, or condemned; yet is it of great use to them, as well as to others; in that, as a rule of life informing them of the will of God, and their duty, it directs and binds them to walk accordingly; discovering also the sinful pollutions of their nature, hearts, and lives; so as, examining themselves thereby, they may come to further conviction of, humiliation for, and hatred against sin, together with a clearer sight of the need they have of Christ, and the perfection of His obedience. It is likewise of use to the regenerate, to restrain their corruptions, in that it forbids sin: and the threatenings of it serve to show what even their sins deserve; and what afflictions, in this life, they may expect for them, although freed from the curse thereof threatened in the law. The promises of it, in like manner, show them God's approbation of obedience, and what blessings they may expect upon the performance thereof: although not as due to them by the law as a covenant of works. So as, a man's doing good, and refraining from evil, because the law encourageth to the one, and deterreth from the other, is no evidence of his being under the law; and, not under grace.

> VII. Neither are the forementioned uses of the law contrary to the grace of the Gospel, but do sweetly comply with it; the Spirit of Christ subduing and enabling the will of man to do that freely, and cheerfully, which the will of God, revealed in the law, requireth to be done.

And it was this view that Alexander Campbell forcefully rejected in his Sermon on the Law (1816),[27] where he insisted that the Bible knows nothing of a division of the Mosaic Law into three parts, with one of those parts still binding.[28] He particularly objected to the use of this doctrine to establish the Christian practices of tithing and infant baptism.[29] This sermon, emphasizing what Campbell believed was the proper division between the Old Testament and the New Testament, is one of the primary documents of the American Restoration Movement, and some scholars have considered it a summary of the entire movement.[30] Campbell himself said in his comments introducing the sermon that the bitter reaction this sermon provoked

---

27. Alexander Campbell, "Sermon on the Law," *Millennial Harbinger*, Third Series, 3.9 (September 1846), 492–521, originally preached Sunday, September 1, 1816 (Campbell was 28 years old), at the annual meeting of the Redstone Baptist Association at the Cross Creek Church near Bethany, VA. A web search will lead to an online version.

28. Longman, *How to Read Exodus*, 158–59, regards this threefold categorization of law to be useful, though he recognizes that it is not found explicitly in the Bible. For the contrary position, see Wright, *Old Testament Ethics*, 288–89.

29. For these examples, see point 4 of Campbell's "Conclusions" in his sermon, p. 519 of the *Millennial Harbinger* version.

30. The essential reading on the sermon is Everett Ferguson, "Alexander Campbell's 'Sermon on the Law': A Historical and Theological Examination," *Restoration Quarterly* 29 (1987): 71–85.

compelled him to advocate the movement to call people back to the New Testament.[31]

Conclusion

The status of the Old Testament Law for Christians has been a contentious issue since the very beginning of Christianity. But what we cannot doubt is that every bit of the Bible, including the Law at Sinai, is "inspired by God and useful" (2 Tim 3:16). Our responsibility is to hold together the idea that righteousness cannot come through works of the law and the law leads us to Christ (Gal 3:23–26).

---

31. "It is, therefore, highly probable to my mind, that but for the persecution begun on the alleged heresy of this sermon, whether the present reformation had ever been advocated by me" (p. 492 in the *Millennial Harbinger* version of the sermon).

9

BLOOD OF THE COVENANT

Hence not even the first covenant was inaugurated without blood. [19] For when every commandment had been told to all the people by Moses in accordance with the law, he took the blood of calves and goats, with water and scarlet wool and hyssop, and sprinkled both the scroll itself and all the people, [20] saying, "This is the blood of the covenant that God has ordained for you." [21] And in the same way he sprinkled with the blood both the tent and all the vessels used in worship. [22] Indeed, under the law almost everything is purified with blood, and without the shedding of blood there is no forgiveness of sins. (Heb 9:18–22)

I have never slaughtered an animal. I guess the modern Western contexts in which one might do such a thing would be either on a farm or after hunting. I've never lived on a farm, and I've never put forth much effort toward hunting. I have no opposition to the idea of killing and cleaning an animal; it might be fun, certainly educational. I just have no experience with it. I can imagine it, and I guess I've seen videos of it. It's a bloody business.

I have lived a very sanitized existence, not least when it comes to blood. We are taught, for the most part, to avoid blood. If you get a cut, apply some neosporin and cover it up with a bandaid. Be sure to cook your meat well. Of course, sometimes our entertainment is filled with blood. For my part, I don't mind watching an action movie full of blood, but a doctor show makes me hide my eyes. I can't explain that. I used to give blood frequently, before I started traveling to places that render you ineligible to do so; whenever the needle went into my arm, I turned my head away and tried to think about something else. Some people in that situation don't mind at all; others faint.

I guess it's part of my modern, sanitized mindset that I have never considered blood to be a cleansing agent. I would never try to replace the soap in our squirt bottle with blood. It seems like it would stink and make your hands sticky. It's not considered a good thing to get blood on a shirt; usually you'll change clothes and either wash out the bloodied shirt or just throw it away. I certainly wouldn't wash my clothes in blood.

My, how times have changed. The religion of ancient Israel was a bloody religion, and the Bible does talk about blood as a cleansing agent. If an ancient Israelite encountered some impurity, the route toward purification almost always involved blood. As the writer of Hebrews noted, "under the law almost everything is purified with blood" (Heb

9:22).[1] Obviously, this line of thought has nothing to do with sanitation or hygiene; it's a different way of looking at what it means to be "clean" and "unclean." It's hard for us to get into this mindset, such that putting blood on people actually cleanses them. The closest thing I can think of is how I wash my dishes before putting them in the dishwasher. What's the point of putting clean dishes in the dishwasher? I don't know, I feel like it sort of purifies them. Maybe you know what I mean.

In Exodus 24, Moses splatters blood on the people of Israel, apparently to sanctify them, setting them apart as God's people. This action forms a part of a covenant ritual; Moses calls it "the blood of the covenant" (v. 8), words that Jesus will adopt and apply to himself.

Context

Moses has been on the mountain, at the "thick darkness where God was" (20:21), for some length of time—not the forty days and forty nights, which is still to come (24:18). God spoke the Ten Commandments directly to the people (20:1–19), and now Moses has received further laws (20:22–23:33). While still on the mountain, God tells Moses to gather some more people and come back up (24:1–2), apparently to receive further instruction (the tabernacle specifications, as it turns out). These additional people are

---

1. Cf. Lev 8:15, 30. A woman is rendered impure by her flow of blood, and the purification process involves a sacrifice (Lev 12). The ritual for cleansing the skin disease, as described in Lev 14, several times mentions blood.

Aaron and Aaron's sons Nadab and Abihu, along with seventy Israelite elders.[2] All these people—along with, we later learn (vv. 13–14), Hur and Joshua (both last mentioned in Exod 17:8–17)—should ascend the mountain in order to worship, while Moses ascends further toward God. Moses fulfills all these instructions in the second half of the chapter (starting in v. 9).

But first, Moses needs to report to the Israelites all the laws he has just received, and he needs to obtain assurance from the people that they are willing to obey.

> Moses came and told the people all the words of YHWH and all the ordinances; and all the people answered with one voice, and said, "All the words that YHWH has spoken we will do." (Exod 24:3)

So Moses writes down all the laws in a scroll, which is about to receive the name "the scroll (or book) of the covenant" (v.

---

2. Who are these seventy elders? Since Moses first returned to Egypt, he has been interacting with a group of Israelite elders (4:29), as God had instructed him (3:16), but their number is never given as seventy. In Exod 18, Moses' father-in-law, Jethro, advised him to appoint some judges to ease his burden, but neither in this chapter (18:17–26), nor in its retelling at Deut 1:9–18, do we read about seventy judges. At Num 11, when Moses again feels the weight of the burden of Israel upon himself alone, God tells him to assemble seventy elders so that God can "take some of the Spirit that is on you and put the Spirit on them" (vv. 16–17). But this story in Exod 24 is the first time we read about seventy elders. I suppose it is most natural to associate these elders with the judges appointed in Exod 18, who probably closely overlapped with the Israelite elders that Moses had first encountered upon his return to Egypt. Note Propp's comment on 24:1 that "The wording implies that there are more than seventy to choose from"; William H. C. Propp, *Exodus 19–40*, Anchor Bible (New York: Doubleday, 2006), 293.

7). After writing in the scroll, Moses builds an altar with twelve pillars that represent the twelve tribes of Israel (v. 4; cf. 1 Kings 18:31–32). Then he appoints some unidentified young men (= non-elders?)[3] to make burnt offerings and fellowship offerings (v. 6)—types of offerings that will be regulated by God's word in Leviticus.[4]

Now, notice what Moses does with the blood from the animals ("bulls," v. 5). Half of the blood he pours into bowls, and the other half he splatters on the altar that he has just made (v. 6). Later in Leviticus, applying to an altar the blood from sacrificial victims will become a regular part of a priest's job (e.g., Lev 1:5, 11; 3:2; etc.). But what is Moses going to do with the blood in the bowls? Usually, blood not applied to an altar is simply poured out at the base of the altar (Lev 1:15; 4:7, 18, 25, 30, 34; 5:9; 8:15; 9:9). But this time Moses saves the blood in bowls. He reads the scroll of the covenant that he has just written, and the people again affirm their willingness to keep these laws.

> Then he took the book of the covenant, and read it in the hearing of the people; and they said, "All that YHWH has spoken we will do, and we will be obedient." (Exod 24:7)

Then Moses makes use of those bowls full of blood.

---

3. The suggestion of Propp, *Exodus 19–40*, 294.
4. For the burnt offering, see Lev 1; for the fellowship offering (a.k.a. peace offering; a.k.a. well-being offering), see Lev 3.

> Moses took the blood, splattered it on the people, and said, "This is the blood of the covenant that YHWH has made with you concerning all these words." (Exod 24:8)

We will think about this ritual, and its strong resonance in the New Testament, in just a moment. The rest of Exod 24 shows the fulfillment of God's initial command to Moses to bring selected people up the mountain with him. When they all arrived,

> they saw the God of Israel. Beneath his feet was something like a pavement made of lapis lazuli, as clear as the sky itself. God did not harm the Israelite nobles; they saw him, and they ate and drank. (Exod 24:10–11)

This strange passage is never explained in the rest of Scripture. Whatever it might mean by "seeing God," one should take into account also Exod 33:20 ("You cannot see my face, for humans cannot see me and live") and the subsequent narrative in which Moses is permitted to see God's "back" (33:23). And there are plenty of other instances of God appearing to people, even sharing a meal with people, such as Gen 18, where the three visitors that eat with Abraham (v. 8) are identified as the Lord (v. 17) and two angels (19:1). What exactly did these mountain climbers in Exod 24 see? Later in the chapter, "the appearance of YHWH's glory to the Israelites was like a consuming fire on the mountaintop" (Exod 24:17). I take it that this verse refers to the Israelites at the foot of the mountain. I presume the mountain climbers also saw God as fiery, but they could see something that reminded them of "feet" (v. 10), perhaps simply a description of the bottom of the column of fire. Since only the "feet" are mentioned, it may be that these people are bowing down (cf. 24:1, "worship," i.e., "bow down").

This text assures us that even though these people were looking on the presence of God, they were not harmed, and even enjoyed a meal. "To eat before someone is to acknowledge his authority and beneficence, and conversely one's own dependence and vulnerability."[5] Elsewhere in the Bible, parties conclude covenant negotiations with a meal.[6]

Finally, Moses ascends further up the mountain alone—or, rather, with Joshua, at least part of the way (24:12-13; cf. 32:17). He leaves Aaron and Hur in charge (v. 14), though Hur is never mentioned again and Aaron appears to be a rather weak leader (32:1-6, 21-24). Moses leaves them in order to receive "the stone tablets" on which God has written some things (v. 12). Later, we learn that there are two stone tablets (31:18; 32:15), and that the Ten Commandments are inscribed on them (34:28; Deut 4:13; 10:4). But what will take more than a month on the mountain (24:18) is for God to reveal to Moses the plans for the tabernacle and its furnishings (chs. 25-31).

---

5. Propp, *Exodus 19-40*, 297, citing as examples 1 Kings 1:25; Ezek 44:3. Propp continues (p. 298): "As suzerain, God does not eat in his subjects' presence."

6. Gen 26:28-31 (Isaac and Abimelech); 31:44-54 (Jacob and Laban); Josh 9:11-15 (the Israelites and Gibeonites); 2 Sam 3:20-21 (David and Abner, Saul's chief military officer). These passages are cited by Propp, *Exodus 19-40*, 297.

Covenant

The word "covenant" (Heb.: *berit*) appears 287x in the Hebrew Bible, 82x in the Pentateuch,[7] and 13x in Exodus. Besides the two appearances in Exod 24:7–8 ("book of the covenant"; "blood of the covenant"), the word appears in the following contexts in Exodus.

- recalling the covenant with Abraham, Isaac, and Jacob (2:24; 6:4–5)
- covenant with Israel (19:5; 34:10, 27)
- prohibition of covenant with Canaanite nations (23:32; 34:12, 15)
- Sabbath is an eternal covenant (31:16)
- the covenant written on two tablets (34:28)

Sometimes covenants are enacted between humans,[8] but in the Bible a covenant is usually between God and people. It is "a solemn commitment guaranteeing promises or obligations undertaken by one or both covenanting parties.[9]

This covenant between God and Israel follows the wonderful act of salvation that God has already accomplished on Israel's behalf, and so God identifies himself as "YHWH your God, who brought you out of the land of Egypt, out of

---

[7]. It is more frequent in Genesis (mostly ch. 9 and ch. 17) and Deuteronomy, each with 27x occurrences.

[8]. Gen 14:13; 21:27, 32; 26:28; 31:44; Exod 23:32; 34:12; Deut 7:2.

[9]. Paul R. Williamson, "Covenant," in *Dictionary of the Old Testament: Pentateuch*, ed. T. Desmond Alexander and David W. Baker (Downers Grove, IL: IVP, 2003), 139–55, at 139.

the place of slavery" (20:2). The covenant that God makes with Israel shares many similarities (especially structural similarities) with other ancient Near Eastern treaties.[10] From that way of looking at it, God is the powerful king who delivers a people from a foreign oppressor and in return demands honor and loyalty. In human treaties, the great king usually demanded tribute payments; God demands obedience and sacrifice.[11] Israel does not become God's people at Sinai, since the beginning of Exodus shows that Israel already belongs to God (cf. 3:7). "The covenant at Sinai is a vocational covenant within the context of the Abrahamic covenant [...]. The vocational covenant is defined in Exodus 19:5-6: Israel is to be a priestly kingdom and a holy nation."[12]

This ritual in Exod 24 appears to be part of the process by which God establishes his covenant with the nation of Israel. There is a sacrifice (v. 5), as in at least some other covenant

---

10. "The seminal insight of twentieth-century biblical scholarship [...] is that the biblical Covenant is more than a general contract [...]. It is specifically a *political* treaty between a suzerain (Yahweh) and his vassal (Israel)"; Propp, *Exodus 19–40*, 34. Many scholarly works examine the relevant parallels. For an example of an ancient Near Eastern treaty and an excellent discussion of this genre's parallels with the Bible (specifically Deuteronomy), see Christopher B. Hays, *Hidden Riches: A Sourcebook for the Comparative Study of the Hebrew Bible and Ancient Near East* (Louisville: WJK, 2014), ch. 9; another valuable discussion (with a specific comparison to Exodus) in James K. Hoffmeier, *Ancient Israel in Sinai: The Evidence for the Authenticity of the Wilderness Tradition* (Oxford: Oxford University Press, 2005), 183–92.

11. "The people's regular offerings are nothing less than the periodic tribute owed to their contractual Overlord, whose benevolence is contingent on Israel's fidelity"; Propp, *Exodus 19–40*, 33.

12. Terence E. Fretheim, "Exodus, Book of," in *Dictionary of the Old Testament: Pentateuch*, ed. T. Desmond Alexander and David W. Baker (Downers Grove, IL: IVP, 2003), 249–58, at 255.

ceremonies (Gen 8:20–21; cf. 15:9–10). There is a meal, which we have already seen characterizes some covenant rituals. And there is a unique element: Moses splattering blood on the people.

Blood on People

The Old Testament describes three ceremonies involving the ritual application of blood to a human person.[13] First is this story in Exod 24 in which Moses splatters blood on the people of Israel. Second, Moses anoints Aaron and his sons with blood when he consecrates them to their priestly office.

> And you shall kill the ram and take part of its blood and put it on the tip of the right ear of Aaron and on the tips of the right ears of his sons, and on the thumbs of their right hands and on the great toes of their right feet, and throw the rest of the blood against the sides of the altar. [21] Then you shall take part of the blood that is on the altar, and of the anointing oil, and sprinkle it on Aaron and his garments, and on his sons and his sons' garments with him. He and his garments shall be holy, and his sons and his sons' garments with him. (Exod 29:20–21; cf. Lev 8:23–24)

---

13. Richard E. Averbeck connects all three of these ceremonies: "For obvious reasons, the ritual of splashing blood around on the people as an act of consecration for the whole nation (Ex 24:8) became more specific when only one Israelite was involved (Lev 14:14)"; see his "Tabernacle," in *Dictionary of the Old Testament: Pentateuch*, ed. T. Desmond Alexander and David W. Baker (Downers Grove, IL: IVP, 2003), 807–27, at 809.

Third, those with the skin disease described in Lev 14 (traditionally, "leprosy") must participate in an elaborate cleansing ritual that lasts more than a week (14:1–20), part of which involves sprinkling blood on the diseased man in two different ceremonies (v. 7, and then a week later, v. 14). Whereas we would probably think of blood as a defiling agent—and, in some ways, so did the Israelites (e.g., Lev 12)—in these instances, blood not only purifies (renders clean) in the case of the diseased man, but also consecrates (renders holy) in the case of priestly ordination.[14]

In the case of the ritual described in Exodus 24, it's not exactly clear what the application of blood symbolizes, but it is clearly symbolic.

> This act is heavily freighted with symbolism. Exodus 24 describes a rite of passage whereby Israel enters into vassalage under Yahweh.[15]

Propp proposes several potential meanings, all of which might be valid. Among these suggestions are the following. Splattering blood on the people …

- …made them God's family (cf. Exod 4:22). Here we might think of a "blood brothers" ritual.
- …suggested a threat: if you do not keep the covenant, you will bring harm upon yourself. Think about the

---

14. On these concepts, see John E. Hartley, "Holy and Holiness, Clean and Unclean," in *Dictionary of the Old Testament: Pentateuch*, ed. T. Desmond Alexander and David W. Baker (Downers Grove, IL: IVP, 2003), 420–31.

15. Propp, *Exodus 19–40*, 308. See also Williamson, "Covenant," 151.

- symbolism of the halved animals in the covenant ceremony in Gen 15 (and note the word "covenant" in v. 18).
- ...sanctified the people, making them a "royal priesthood, a holy nation" (Exod 19:6).

Moses calls this blood "the blood of the covenant," which doesn't really help us narrow down the meaning, and as I said, all of these suggestions may be valid simultaneously. This splattering blood on the nation is never repeated in the Old Testament, but the language is later heard on the lips of Jesus.

Jesus and Moses

Before Moses died, he assured the Israelites that "YHWH your God will raise up for you a prophet like me from among your own brothers" (Deut 18:15), but the book of Deuteronomy ends, sometime after the death of Moses, with the assertion that "no prophet has arisen again in Israel like Moses" (34:10). The prophet like Moses was still to come. This idea was surprisingly little mentioned in later Jewish literature, but some Qumran texts do anticipate the prophet like Moses. For example:

> They shall govern themselves using the original precepts by which the men of the *Yahad* [= community]

began to be instructed, doing so until there come the Prophet and the Messiahs of Aaron and Israel.[16]

The Old Testament prophets also frequently describe the future salvation of God in terms of another and even better exodus.[17]

> I will perform miracles for them as in the days of your exodus from the land of Egypt. (Micah 7:15)

> The days are surely coming, says YHWH, when I will raise up for David a righteous Branch, and he shall reign as king and deal wisely, and shall execute justice and righteousness in the land. [6] In his days Judah will be saved and Israel will live in safety. And this is the name by which he will be called: "YHWH is our righteousness." [7] Therefore, the days are surely coming, says YHWH, when it shall no longer be said, "As YHWH lives who brought the people of Israel up out of the land of Egypt," [8] but "As YHWH lives who brought out and led the offspring of the house of Israel out of the land of the north and out of all the lands where he had driven

---

16. The Rule of the Community (1QS) 9.10–11, trans. Michael Wise, Martin Abegg Jr., and Edward Cook, *The Dead Sea Scrolls: A New Translation*, rev. ed. (San Francisco: HarperSanFrancisco, 2005), 130–31. The other passage is the Testimonia Collection (4QTest) 5–8, available in Wise, Abegg, and Cook, p. 259. This latter Qumran text quotes Deut 18:18–19 within a collection of other scriptural quotations, apparently all bound together by their common messianic themes. On the idea of a prophet to come, see the discussion of Richard Bauckham, *The Testimony of the Beloved Disciple: Narrative, History, and Theology in the Gospel of John* (Grand Rapids: Baker, 2007), 212–25.

17. See Hos 2:14–15; Isa 43:15–19; for further references, see Pitre, *Jesus and the Last Supper*, 59n22.

them." Then they shall live in their own land. (Jer 23:5–8)

Combining these notions of a prophet like Moses and a new exodus, some Jews anticipated a coming deliverer who would work wonders and bring destruction against the enemies of God's people. These ideas are closely tied to the concept of a messiah—at least, the outcome is largely the same: redemption—but it's a different way of looking at it, a different set of associations.

While post-biblical Jewish texts (at least, the ones we have) do not reference the pophet like Moses very often, the New Testament does refer to the coming Prophet several times.

> This is the testimony given by John when the Jews sent priests and Levites from Jerusalem to ask him, "Who are you?" [20] He confessed and did not deny it, but confessed, "I am not the Messiah." [21] And they asked him, "What then? Are you Elijah?" He said, "I am not." "Are you the prophet?" He answered, "No." (John 1:19–21)

> When the people saw the sign that he had done, they began to say, "This is indeed the prophet who is to come into the world." (John 6:14)

> When they heard these words, some in the crowd said, "This is really the prophet." (John 7:40)

Peter quotes Moses' prophecy about the coming prophet (Acts 3:22–23), as does Stephen (7:37). Of course, they see

Jesus as the fulfillment of Moses' prediction. Like Moses, Jesus accomplishes salvation for God's people and establishes a covenant by means of blood.[18]

THE COVENANT IN JESUS' BLOOD

At the Last Supper, Jesus says this about the cup.

> For this is my blood of the covenant, which is poured out for many for the forgiveness of sins. (Matt 26:28)

> He said to them, "This is my blood of the covenant, which is poured out for many." (Mark 14:24)

> And he did the same with the cup after supper, saying, "This cup that is poured out for you is the new covenant in my blood." (Luke 22:20)

> In the same way he took the cup also, after supper, saying, "This cup is the new covenant in my blood. Do this, as often as you drink it, in remembrance of me." (1 Cor 11:25)

Clearly, the wording in Matthew and Mark hearken back to Moses' statement at Exod 24:8, but even the slightly different wording of Luke and Paul—emphasizing the newness of

---

18. For further connections between Jesus and Moses, see Pitre, *Jesus and the Last Supper*, 54–55, who lists five: "finger of God"; 12/70 disciples; "this evil generation"; feeding thousands in the wilderness; blood of the covenant. But for cautions on relating Jesus' prophetic ministry exclusively to Deut 18, see N. T. Wright, *Jesus and the Victory of God* (Minneapolis: Fortress, 1996), 163.

the covenant and certainly evoking Jer 31:31—also reflects the ritual of Exod 24. (Note that the word "blood" does not appear in the new covenant prophecy of Jer 31.) And Jesus says his blood is "poured out," just as in the case of a sacrifice (Exod 29:12; Lev 4:7; etc.).

Crucifixion is not, actually, a bloody form of execution, not like the guillotine, for instance. Jesus himself may have bled from the flogging he received beforehand (Matt 27:26; Mark 15:15; John 19:1), but the gory details that might interest us are not mentioned. On the cross, a soldier pierced Jesus' side, so that blood and water came forth (John 19:34). But other than that single reference, there is no mention of blood in the Passion narratives.

So references to Jesus' blood in the New Testament are probably not reflections of his actual death but metaphorical representations of Jesus as a sacrificial victim. Just to say it again, when the New Testament writers talk about the blood of Jesus, they are speaking metaphorically about Jesus as if he were a sacrificial animal.[19] Sometimes they make this association explicit.

> ... whom God put forward as a sacrifice of atonement by his blood, effective through faith. (Rom 3:25)

> ... he entered once for all into the Holy Place, not with the blood of goats and calves, but with his own blood, thus obtaining eternal redemption. (Heb 9:12)

---

19. Acts 20:28; Rom 5:9; Eph 1:7; 2:13; Col 1:20; Heb 9:14; 10:19, 29; 12:24; 13:12, 20; 1 John 1:7; Rev 1:5. The same sort of language is used for Stephen in Acts 22:20.

> ... the precious blood of Christ, like that of a lamb without defect or blemish. (1 Pet 1:19)

> You are worthy to take the scroll and to open its seals, for you were slaughtered and by your blood you ransomed for God saints from every tribe and language and people and nation. (Rev 5:9)

All that to say that references to Jesus pouring out his blood are not to be taken literally, but they are expressions of the symbolic world of sacrifice.[20] Yes, Jesus is thinking ahead to his Crucifixion when he encourages his disciples to drink the cup that is his poured-out blood, but the reason he articulates it in those terms is to represent his death as a sacrifice. He is looking back to Moses, ushering in a covenant through his own sacrificial act just as Moses enacted a covenant through sacrifice.

Note, finally, that the Last Supper, as a meal, evokes the meal that the elders and priests enjoyed in the presence of God as part of the covenant ratification ritual (Exod 24:11).

And if Jesus' re-establishes the covenant ceremony first enacted by Moses—although, now the covenant ceremony happens not just once for all time but "as often as you eat this bread and drink this cup" (1 Cor 11:26)—on whom is the blood of the covenant sprinkled?

> Those who have been chosen and destined by God the Father and sanctified by the Spirit to be obedient to

---

20. The expression "poured out for many" in the Last Supper speech also resonates with the Suffering Servant of Isaiah (53:12), who was himself depicted as a sacrificial lamb (53:7).

Jesus Christ and to be sprinkled with his blood. (1 Pet 1:2)[21]

Like the covenant blood in Exod 24, the people of God are sanctified by the blood of Jesus, but also they receive warning.

How much worse punishment do you think will be deserved by those who have spurned the Son of God, profaned the blood of the covenant by which they were sanctified, and outraged the Spirit of grace? (Heb 10:29)[22]

---

21. For Jesus' blood as "sprinkled," see also Heb 12:24.
22. At 13:20, Hebrews refers to the blood of Jesus as the "blood of the eternal covenant."

10

God's Dwelling Place

God desires to be present among his people.[1] It's a pretty good guess—and a pretty common one—that that desire is the point of everything, that the main reason for God's creating the universe was so that God's love, which defines his character (1 John 4:8), could have a worthy object: humans, made in his image. We see an echo of this desire in the Garden of Eden, when God walked in the garden in the cool of the day, looking for the person he had made (Gen 3:8-9). Christians worship a God who is Trinity, who experiences community within himself. God's creation of humans is an expression (outgrowth) of the community inherent within the divine nature. Humans image God in part by fulfilling their own purpose and communing with God.

The Bible is the story about how God seeks to be present among his people. It doesn't take long at the beginning of

---

1. See G. K. Beale and Mitchell Kim, *God Dwells among Us: Expanding Eden to the Ends of the Earth* (Downers Grove, IL: IVP, 2014); and the fuller treatment in G. K. Beale, *The Temple and the Church's Mission: A Biblical Theology of the Dwelling Place of God* (Downers Grove, IL: IVP, 2004).

the story for the community between humans and God to be ruptured (Gen 3), but the end of the story shows that community is eventually restored.

> Then I heard a loud voice from the throne: Behold, the tabernacle of God is with people, and he will live [or "tabernacle"] with them, and they will be his people, and God himself will be with them and will be their God. (Rev 21:3)

Along the way, the theme of God's presence among his people recurs again and again. The epitome is Jesus, who is the presence of God in a human body, whose entire purpose in life was to reconcile God with humans.

> If I go away and prepare a place for you, I will come again and take you to myself, so that where I am you may be also. (John 14:3)

Before and after the Gospels, the Bible shows us variations on this theme, and much of the imagery revolves around the Tabernacle or Temple, just as it does in Rev 21:3, quoted above. The Tabernacle/Temple is the earthly home of God. Of course, this whole discussion is involved in symbolism, because God doesn't really live at any particular location.

> Heaven is my throne, and earth is my footstool.
> Where could you possibly build a house for me?
> And where would my resting place be? (Isa 66:1)

But God has chosen to make his name dwell in a particular location (cf. Deut 12:5). The Tabernacle/Temple symbolizes his presence among his people.

> I will consecrate the tent of meeting and the altar; Aaron also and his sons I will consecrate, to serve me as priests. [45] I will dwell among the Israelites, and I will be their God. [46] And they shall know that I am YHWH their God, who brought them out of the land of Egypt that I might dwell among them; I am YHWH their God. (Exod 29:44–46)

The Tabernacle was set up in the middle of the Israelite camp, with all the tribes encamped around it (Num 2–3). Again, this location suggests God's desire to be present among his people. But God is holy, and people typically are not, so there are certain rules associated with the Tabernacle in order to protect people from the dangerous holiness of their God.

Context

Immediately after the covenant ratification ritual in Exod 24, Moses (and Joshua) ascends further up Mt. Sinai in order to receive "the stone tablets with the law and commandments that I [= God] have written for their [= Israelites] instruction" (24:12). Then this happened:

> Then Moses went up on the mountain, and the cloud covered the mountain. [16] The glory of YHWH settled on Mount Sinai, and the cloud covered it for six days;

on the seventh day he called to Moses out of the cloud. ¹⁷ Now the appearance of the glory of YHWH was like a devouring fire on the top of the mountain in the sight of the people of Israel. ¹⁸ Moses entered the cloud, and went up on the mountain. Moses was on the mountain for forty days and forty nights.

Obviously, if it took 40 days, God did more than just hand Moses the two stone tablets. It was at this time that he gave fairly detailed plans about how to build the Tabernacle and all its furnishings. I say the plans are *fairly* detailed, but there's actually not quite enough detail to reconstruct the Tabernacle with complete confidence.[2] For instance, we don't know exactly how the sections of curtains around the Tabernacle were joined together. The text never tells us any dimensions for the bronze wash basin (30:17–21). But there are enough details to get a pretty good idea of what it all looked like. We also know about some other desert tent shrines in the ancient Near East, which help us to understand the Tabernacle a little better.[3]

The Tabernacle was completed and set up about a year after the exodus (Exod 40:2, 17; cf. Num 7). God had inspired the workmen Bezalel and Oholiab for the job (31:1–

---

2. Perhaps that's the very reason Exodus does not provide more detailed plans, i.e., to prevent us from building our own Tabernacle; this is the suggestion of William H. C. Propp, *Exodus 19–40*, Anchor Bible (New York: Doubleday, 2006), 497.

3. Benjamin D. Sommer, *The Bodies of God and the World of Ancient Israel* (Cambridge: Cambridge University Press, 2009), 93–94.

11). But where did the Israelites get all the gold and other material needed for the Tabernacle and its furnishings? The only possible answer provided by the text is that they had taken it from the Egyptians.

> The Israelites acted on Moses' word and asked the Egyptians for silver and gold items and for clothing. [36] And YHWH gave the people such favor with the Egyptians that they gave them what they requested. In this way they plundered the Egyptians. (12:35–36; cf. 3:21–22; 11:2–3)

God provided the plans for the Tabernacle (25:8, and see below), the materials, and the skill.

We actually get the Tabernacle material twice in Exodus. The instructions for building the Tabernacle and its furnishings come in chs. 25–31. Then there are three chapters dealing with the Golden Calf sin and its aftermath (chs. 32–34). The Book of Exodus concludes with chapters covering the construction of the Tabernacle and its furnishings (chs. 35–40), essentially repeating much of the material in chs. 25–31. This sustained treatment of the Tabernacle in Exodus means that there is more material in the Pentateuch (probably the entire Old Testament) about the Tabernacle than there is about any other single theme.

INSTRUCTION	CONSTRUCTION
Ark of the Covenant (25:10–22)	37:1–9
Table (25:23–30)	37:10–16
Lampstand (25:31–40)	37:17–24

Tabernacle (ch. 26)	36:8–38
Altar of Burnt Offering (27:1–8)	38:1–8
Court and Its Hangings (27:9–19)	38:9–20
Oil for the Lamp (27:20–21)	
Priestly Clothing (28:1–6)	39:1
Ephod (28:6–14)	39:2–7
Breastplate (28:15–30)	39:8–21
Other Priestly Clothing (28:31–43)	39:22–31
Consecration of Priests (29:1–37)	(Lev 8–9)
Daily Offerings (29:38–46)	
Altar of Incense (30:1–10)	37:25–28
Ransom in a Census (30:11–16)	
Bronze Basin (30:17–21)	
Anointing Oil and Incense (30:22–38)	37:29
Bezalel and Oholiab (31:1–11)	
Sabbath Law (31:12–17)	
Two Tablets Written By God (31:18)	

TERMINOLOGY

What we call the Tabernacle actually goes by three different names in the Bible.[4]

- Sanctuary, *miqdash* (מקדש), used only 16x in the Pentateuch (Exod 25:8; Lev 12:4; Num 3:28).

---

4. Of course, source critics of the Pentateuch attribute some of these different terms to different sources; see the interesting discussion in this regard in Sommer, *Bodies of God*, ch. 4.

- Tabernacle or dwelling place, *mishkan* (משכן), emphasizing the "presence and immanence of the Lord suggested by the fact that he would 'dwell in their [Israel's] midst' [Exod 25:8]."[5] Used 58x in Exodus and 42x in Numbers. This word does not necessarily refer to a temporary structure.[6]
- Tent of meeting, *ohel mōēd* (אהל מועד), used frequently in Exodus (34x), Leviticus (43x) and Numbers (56x), and only 13x in the rest of the Old Testament.

Appearance

The Tabernacle was a large tent—or, at least, it was large relative to the tents most of us own, family camping tents. It was about 30 feet long and 10 feet wide, with the opening on one of the short sides.[7] The opening faced east. The Tabernacle had two rooms, one smaller than the other. The

---

5. Richard E. Averbeck, "Tabernacle," in *Dictionary of the Old Testament: Pentateuch*, ed. T. Desmond Alexander and David W. Baker (Downers Grove, IL: IVP, 2003), 807–27, at 809.

6. Sommer, *Bodies of God*, 96–97.

7. These figures assume that a cubit is 18 inches, and that the sections of the Tabernacle overlapped a little bit. If they didn't overlap but each section butted up against the next one, then the structure would be a little bigger, about 45 feet long and 15 feet wide. On the dimensions of the Tabernacle, see Richard Elliott Friedman, *Who Wrote the Bible?* (New York: Simon and Schuster, 1987), 174–87. Friedman's view is accepted by James K. Hoffmeier, *Ancient Israel in Sinai: The Evidence for the Authenticity of the Wilderness Tradition* (Oxford: Oxford University Press, 2005), 198–99.

smaller room, called the Holy of Holies (= Most Holy Place), took up about a third of the Tabernacle, at the back, opposite the entrance. The two rooms were divided by a curtain (Exod 26:31–33). Around the Tabernacle was a kind of fence made of curtains that created a courtyard, measuring about 150 feet by 75 feet, 7 ½ feet high (Exod 27:18). In this courtyard, the priest performed much of his work, because the altar of burnt offering was there.

You can easily find online some great drawings of the Tabernacle. You can also find some nice videos on YouTube.

Furniture

The courtyard contained two items:

- The large bronze altar for burnt offerings, 7 ½ feet wide (square) and 4 ½ feet high, with "horns" on the corners.
- The wash basin, i.e., the laver, in the middle between the Tabernacle and the bronze altar.

In the large room of the Tabernacle, i.e., the Holy Place, there were three items:

- The Menorah, i.e., candelabra, with seven branches, somewhat resembling a tree.
- The Table of Showbread, on which bread was placed weekly (Lev 24:5–9). There should be twelve loaves,

arranged in two rows (or stacks?) on the table (probably representing the tribes of Israel). Each week the priests ate the old bread.
- The golden altar of incense.

The most important piece of furniture in the Tabernacle was the ark of the covenant, which was the only thing in the smaller room, the Holy of Holies. (We'll talk about the ark in the next chapter.)

This is all based on the text of Exodus, but the New Testament Epistle to the Hebrews says it a little differently.

> Now even the first covenant had regulations for worship and an earthly sanctuary. ² For a tent was constructed, the first one, in which were the lampstand, the table, and the bread of the Presence; this is called the Holy Place. ³ Behind the second curtain was a tent called the Holy of Holies, ⁴ having the golden altar of incense and the ark of the covenant overlaid on all sides with gold, in which there were a golden urn holding the manna, and Aaron's rod that budded, and the tablets of the covenant; ⁵ above it were the cherubim of glory overshadowing the mercy seat. Of these things we cannot speak now in detail. (Heb 9:1–5)

The author of Hebrews seems to say that the altar of incense was in the Holy of Holies (v. 4). I think, though, that this cannot be right, and that what Hebrews says is true regarding the *effects* of the altar of incense—i.e., the smoke created by the altar entered the Holy of Holies and covered the ark

(Lev 16:12–13)—rather than the physical location of the altar.[8]

I say this not just because of the way Exodus represents the location of the altar but also because of the function of the altar. But first, the location: "And you shall put it in front of the veil that is above the ark of the testimony, in front of the mercy seat that is above the testimony, where I will meet with you" (30:6). "In front of the veil" (לפני הפרכת) is ambiguous enough that the altar could be inside the Holy of Holies or outside of it, though Jewish tradition almost unanimously locates the incense altar outside of the Holy of Holies.[9] That is certainly the implication in the instructions for breaking down the Tabernacle in Numbers 4, which first mentions the ark of the covenant (v. 5), and then mentions

---

8. This issue was flagged by Martin Luther in his Lectures on Hebrews. He suggests that there was a third altar within the Holy of Holies; see *Lectures on Hebrews*, trans. Walter A. Hansen, Luther's Works 29 (Saint Louis: Concordia, 1968), 204–5. On the other hand, Wayne Jackson basically agrees with my explanation; see his article "The Altar of Incense: Where Was It Located?" at christiancourier.com.

9. On the ambiguity of the language, see Harold W. Attridge, *Hebrews*, Hermeneia (Minneapolis: Fortress, 1993), 234–35; Luke Timothy Johnson, *Hebrews: A Commentary*, New Testament Library (Louisville: WJK, 2006), 219–20. Jewish works locating the incense altar outside the Holy of Holies include Philo, *Who is Heir?* 226; *Life of Moses* 2.94, 101; Josephus, *Jewish War* 5.218; *Antiquities of the Jews* 3.147, 198; Mishnah, tractate *Tamid* 1.4; 3.1, 6, 9; 6.1. An alternative tradition locating the altar of incense within the Holy of Holies may be represented by 2 Maccabees 2:4–8; 2 Baruch 6:7. The text of Hebrews was thought to be problematic in antiquity, as evidenced by Codex Vaticanus (a fourth-century manuscript of the Greek Bible), which "corrects" Hebrews so that the golden altar of incense appears in v. 2 among the furnishings of the Holy Place rather than v. 4.

the table of the bread of the presence (v. 7), the menorah (v. 9), and the golden altar of incense (v. 11). If the golden altar were in the Holy of Holies, you would expect it to be mentioned along with the ark of the covenant.

But the function of the altar is really the clincher: "Aaron shall offer fragrant incense on it; every morning when he dresses the lamps he shall offer it" (Exod 30:7). How could Aaron burn incense on this altar every day if it were located in the Holy of Holies, the room he was to enter but once every year (Lev 16:2–3; Heb 9:7)?

Symbolism

What does all this mean? Why is God so concerned about these details for the Tabernacle and its furnishings? Ancient people asked these questions and developed symbolic interpretations of the Tabernacle. Josephus and Philo explained that the Tabernacle symbolized various things about the cosmos.

> It happened that such an arrangement of the Tent was also an imitation of the nature of the universe.[10]

Josephus explains (this time, speaking of the Temple rather than the Tabernacle):

---

10. Josephus, *Antiquities of the Jews* 3.123; trans. Louis H. Feldman, *Flavius Josephus: Judean Antiquities 1–4* (Leiden: Brill, 2000), 263. Josephus explains the symbolism briefly at §§ 181–83. See also Philo, *Questions on Exodus* 2.51–106; *Life of Moses* 2.81–108; *Who is Heir?* 221–29.

The mixture of materials had a clear mystic meaning, typifying all creation: it seemed that scarlet symbolized fire, linen the earth, blue the air, and purple the sea. In two cases the resemblance was one of colour; in the linen and purple it was a question of origin, as the first comes from the earth, the second from the sea. Worked in the tapestry was the whole vista of the heavens except for the signs of the Zodiac. Passing through the gate one entered the ground-floor chamber of the Sanctuary, 90 feet high, 90 long, and 30 wide. But the length was again divided. In the first part, partitioned off at 60 feet, were three most wonderful, world-famous works of art, a lampstand, a table, and an altar of incense. The seven lamps branching off from the lampstand symbolized the planets, the twelve loaves on the table the Zodiac circle and the year. The altar of incense, by the thirteen spices from sea and land, inhabited and uninhabited, with which it was kept supplied, signified that all things are from God and for God.[11]

Some of this symbolism may be a little fanciful, but the basic idea has been argued more recently by scholars. That is, the idea that the Tabernacle represents the "cosmos in miniature" is well-accepted today.[12] For instance, the curtains of the Tabernacle are described as "blue, purple, and scarlet yarn, with a design of cherubim worked into them" (Exod 26:1). Being in a room surrounded by such curtains would

---

11. Josephus, *Jewish War* 5.213–18; trans. G. A. Williamson, in Josephus, *The Jewish War*, rev. ed. (London: Penguin, 1981), 304.
12. Averbeck, "Tabernacle," 816–18.

suggest, on the one hand, the sky, and, on the other hand (but similarly), the throne room of God. The notion of entering into the presence of God derives also from the materials of the Tabernacle's construction; the metals, for instance, increase in value (from bronze to gold) as one progresses in the Tabernacle complex toward the Holy of Holies.[13]

There are also several resonances between the Tabernacle and the Garden of Eden, as if the one was designed with the other in mind. The shape of the Menorah is reminiscent of the Tree of Life. Both Eden and the Tabernacle functioned as a place for humans and God to commune. Like the Tabernacle, the Garden had an opening on the east (cf. Gen 3:24). Like in the Tabernacle, a Cherub guarded the way to God's habitation (again, Gen 3:24). Adam was supposed to "work" and "keep" the garden (Gen 2:15), just as the priests were to do with the Tabernacle (Num 3:7–8).[14]

What Happened to the Tabernacle?

Upon entrance into the Promised Land, the Israelites set up the Tabernacle at Shiloh (Josh 18:1), 30 miles north of Jerusalem. That's where Samuel was raised. It was from Shiloh that the ark of the covenant was taken into battle and then

---

13. See Menahem Haran, *Temples and Temple Service in Ancient Israel* (Oxford: Oxford University Press, 1978), 158–59.
14. For such correspondences, see Kyle R. Greenwood, "Old Testament Reverberations of Genesis 1–2," in *Since the Beginning: Interpreting Genesis 1 and 2 through the Ages*, ed. Kyle R. Greenwood (Grand Rapids: Baker, 2018), 1–22, at 17–18.

captured by the Philistines (1 Sam 4). The ark never returned to the Tabernacle, as far as we know. When the Philistines sent the ark back, it first went to Beth-shemesh and then to Kiriath-jearim (1 Sam 6), where it stayed for a while. Eventually, David moved the ark from Kiriath-jearim (a.k.a., Baale-judah) and took it to Jerusalem (2 Sam 6), to a new tent that David had devised (2 Sam 6:17; cf. 7:6). Meanwhile, Shiloh had been destroyed and was no longer the home of the Tabernacle (cf. Jer 7:12–15). The Chronicler reports that in David's day, the Tabernacle was located at Gibeon (1 Chron 16:39; 21:29), as it would be in Solomon's time, also (2 Chron 1:1–5).

What happened to the Tabernacle after that is a matter of speculation. Of course, Solomon was the one who built the temple, effectively replacing the Tabernacle. Perhaps the Tabernacle fell into neglect and decay? Perhaps it was ritually destroyed? The Bible does not say. But some scholars have found evidence that the Tabernacle was actually incorporated into the Temple.[15] At the dedication of the Temple...

---

15. The idea is associated with Richard Elliott Friedman, "Tabernacle," in *Anchor Bible Dictionary*, ed. David Noel Freedman, 6 vols. (New York: Doubleday, 1992), 6.292–300; Friedman, "The Tabernacle in the Temple," *Biblical Archaeologist* 43 (1980): 241–48. For criticism of Friedman's view, see Victor Avigdor Hurowitz, "The Form and Fate of the Tabernacle: Reflections on a Recent Proposal," *Jewish Quarterly Review* 86 (1995): 127–51; Averbeck, "Tabernacle," 813–14. Supporting Friedman's proposal is Hoffmeier, *Ancient Israel in Sinai*, 198–99. A modified version of Friedman's proposal—that only the Holy of Holies was moved into the Temple—is offered by Michael S. Heiser, *The Unseen Realm: Recovering the Spiritual Worldview of the Bible* (Bellingham, WA: Lexham, 2015), 224–26.

> The priests and the Levites brought the ark of YHWH, the tent of meeting, and the holy utensils that were in the tent. (1 Kings 8:4; cf. 2 Chron 24:6; 29:3–7)

I'm not sure, but I consider it possible that the Tabernacle, or the Holy of Holies, was incorporated into the Temple.

THE HEAVENLY TABERNACLE

> You must make it according to all that I show you—the pattern (תבנית, *tavnît*) of the tabernacle as well as the pattern of all its furnishings. (Exod 25:9)

> Be careful to make them according to the pattern (תבנית, *tavnît*) you have been shown on the mountain. (25:40)

> You are to set up the tabernacle according to the plan (משפט, *mishpat*) for it that you have been shown on the mountain. (26:30)

> Construct the altar with boards so that it is hollow. They are to make it just as it was shown to you on the mountain. (27:8)

> This is the way the lampstand was made: it was a hammered work of gold, hammered from its base to its flower petals. The lampstand was made according to the pattern (מראה, *mareh*) YHWH had shown Moses. (Num 8:4)

> Our ancestors had the tabernacle of the testimony in the wilderness, just as he who spoke with Moses commanded him to make it according to the pattern (τύπος, *typos*) he had seen. (Acts 7:44)
>
> These serve as a copy and shadow of the heavenly things, as Moses was warned when he was about to complete the tabernacle. For God said, Be careful that you make everything according to the pattern (τύπος, *typos*) that was shown to you on the mountain [Exod 25:40]. (Heb 8:5)
>
> Therefore, it was necessary for the copies of the things in the heavens to be purified with these sacrifices, but the heavenly things themselves to be purified with better sacrifices than these. ²⁴ For Christ did not enter a sanctuary made with hands, only a model (ἀντίτυπος, *antitypos*) of the true one, but into heaven itself, so that he might now appear in the presence of God for us. (9:23–24)

The text of Exodus says that the Tabernacle is reproducing a blueprint or pattern that God has shown to Moses (cf. 1 Chron 28:19). It may even be that the Tabernacle is a copy of a heavenly reality, as if the Tabernacle is an imitation of God's throne room. That is exactly the way many ancient interpreters understood these verses, and it's the way that the writer of Hebrews reflected on the significance of

Christ's sacrifice in comparison to the rituals of the Tabernacle.[16] While the priests served faithfully in the Tabernacle, they were only imitating a truer reality that existed in heaven, a reality to which they could not possibly have access. But their priesthood was itself an imitation of Christ's eternal priesthood "according to the order of Melchizedek," and only this true, spiritual high priest can enter the true Holy of Holies in heaven and accomplish everlasting atonement. The work of the priests in the Tabernacle were pointing toward the work of Christ, which is not an imitation or copy of anything.

CHRIST, THE PRESENCE OF GOD

The theme of Christ as the true Temple/Tabernacle is especially prominent in John. At the very beginning of the Gospel, readers learn that "the Word became flesh and dwelt among us" (John 1:14), where the term "dwelt" translates a Greek word (σκηνόω, *skēnóō*) related to the Greek word for "tent." Christ "tented" or "tabernacled" among us. Just as the Tabernacle represented the presence of God among his people, so also Christ—in a more perfect way—represents that same thing.

In the next chapter, Jesus cleansed the Temple (2:13–17). Those who beheld this action demanded a sign from him, and he said, that he would rebuild "this temple" when others

---

16. See the discussion in Johnson, *Hebrews*, 227–32.

had destroyed it (2:19). Of course, those listening failed to understand that "he was speaking about the temple of his body" (2:21).

This same theme probably also explains the confusing verse in John 7:37–38, which should probably be translated:

> Let anyone who is thirsty come to me, and let the one who believes in me drink. As the Scripture has said, Out of his belly shall flow rivers of living water.

No Scripture says exactly these words, but Zechariah 14:7–8 and Ezekiel 47:1–2 do talk about a river flowing from the temple, a river that gives life to all around. Probably Jesus is alluding to these prophecies of the temple, and he is connecting the prophecies to himself. Essentially, he is saying, "I am the temple, and just as has been prophesied, out of me shall flow rivers of living water." (That is, "his belly" refers to Christ and not to the believer.)[17] Christ, as the temple of God, communicates God's presence and spirit to those who come to him.

Church as Temple

In Christ, believers also become repositories of God's Spirit, little temples in this world representing the major temple that is Christ. And so individual Christians should avoid impurity, such as the defilement of prostitution, because "your

---

17. For this interpretation, see Richard B. Hays, *Echoes of Scripture in the Gospels* (Waco: Baylor University Press, 2016), 314–16.

body is a temple of the Holy Spirit" (1 Cor 6:18–19). But the church as a whole can also be thought of as God's temple, so that dissension within the church becomes a very serious matter: "If anyone destroyed God's temple, God will destroy him, for God's temple is holy, and that is what you are" (1 Cor 3:17).

But just because we are God's temple does not mean that we are what we ought to be. Rather, we are growing into the temple.

> So then you are no longer strangers and aliens, but you are citizens with the saints and also members of the household of God, [20] built upon the foundation of the apostles and prophets, with Christ Jesus himself as the cornerstone. [21] In him the whole structure is joined together and grows into a holy temple in the Lord; [22] in whom you also are built together spiritually into a dwelling place for God. (Eph 2:19–22)

> Come to him, a living stone, though rejected by mortals yet chosen and precious in God's sight, and [5] like living stones, let yourselves be built into a spiritual house, to be a holy priesthood, to offer spiritual sacrifices acceptable to God through Jesus Christ. (1 Pet 2:4–5)

Conclusion

God has always desired to be present among his people, and that's what the Tabernacle signifies. Christ brought God's presence to us in a more complete way, and now by the

Spirit we experience that presence in Christ. And we look forward to a time when we will be present with God in the new heaven and new earth, where John the Seer "did not see a temple in it, because the Lord God the Almighty and the Lamb are its temple" (Rev 21:22).

11

Ark of the Covenant

> When Moses went into the tent of meeting to speak with YHWH, he would hear the voice speaking to him from above the mercy seat that was on the ark of the covenant from between the two cherubim; thus it spoke to him. (Num 7:89)

The most important piece of furniture in the Tabernacle was the ark of the covenant. Calling it a piece of furniture might seem a little odd, since it's not something you'd sit on or set your plate and drink on. It wasn't furniture for people but for God. It sometimes seems to be God's throne, and sometimes it seems to be called his footstool. Whichever of those images is correct—and probably they are both correct at different times—the ark represented the presence of God. That much is clear from the passage quoted above.

But the ark served another important function. Once a year, on the Day of Atonement (Yom Kippur), the priest would sprinkle blood on the ark to make atonement for himself and for God's people. The ark—and particularly the lid of the ark, called the mercy seat—was the place of atonement, an idea that would find an important echo in the New Testament.

Context

The context is the same as in the previous chapter on the Tabernacle. When Moses ascended the mountain for his 40-day stay (Exod 24:18) in order to learn about the plans for the Tabernacle, the first thing God tells him about is the ark of the covenant (25:10–22). The ark is the first piece of Tabernacle furniture built by Bezalel (37:1–9).

Terminology

What is an ark? Do we ever use this word without allusion to the Bible? I'm not sure that we do. In other words, the only times I can recall that the word "ark" is used in English are in reference to Noah's ark or to the ark of the covenant. These seem to be two completely unrelated objects; why are they labeled with the same word?

The Hebrew words are different. Noah's ark is a *tēvat* (תֵּבַת); Moses' ark is an *arōn* (אֲרוֹן). The word *tēvat* appears in the Bible only 28x, almost always in reference to Noah's ark (Gen 6–9), but twice it refers to the papyrus basket in which baby Moses floated on the Nile (Exod 2:3, 5).[1] The word *arōn* appears more than 200x in the Bible, almost always in reference to the ark of the covenant. But a couple of

---

1. Here the LXX has θῖβις, *thibis*, "basket."

times *arōn* refers to something else: the coffin in which Joseph was buried (Gen 50:26)[2]; a treasure chest (2 Kings 12:9–10).[3]

Both of these Hebrew words were translated into Greek (the Septuagint, LXX) with the word κιβωτός, *kibōtos*, "box,"[4] and the Latin Vulgate has the word *arca*, "box," for both terms.

On top of the ark of the covenant was a lid that had a special name and function (Exod 25:17). Usually in English we have called this lid the "mercy seat." The Hebrew word is *kappōret* (כַּפֹּרֶת), and there is debate about what exactly it means.[5] On the one hand, the function of this object (i.e., a cover for the ark) and a related term in Arabic suggests the translation "cover" or "lid." On the other hand, the Hebrew root of our word *kappōret* usually has something to do with atonement or reconciliation, as in Yom Kippur = Day of Atonement. So, maybe "atonement lid" would be best? At any rate, you can probably see where the translation "mercy seat" came from.

In Greek (LXX), this *kappōret* became a ἱλαστήριον, *hilastērion*, which again has something to do with atonement. The Latin Vulgate has *propitiatorium*, "place of propitiation." The first English translation of the full Bible was made by John Wycliffe and his associates from the Latin Vulgate

---

2. Here the LXX has σορός, *soros*, "coffin."
3. Here the LXX has κιβωτός, *kibōtos*, "box."
4. Josephus uses different Greek words; Louis H. Feldman, *Flavius Josephus: Judean Antiquities 1–4* (Leiden: Brill, 2000), 29n186, commenting on *Jewish Antiquities* 1.77 (Noah's ark).
5. See William H. C. Propp, *Exodus 19–40*, Anchor Bible (New York: Doubleday, 2006), 385–86.

in the late fourteenth century, and they just adopted the Latin term, "propiciatorie." The second major English translation, by William Tyndale directly from the Hebrew (1530), coined the term "merciseate," no doubt in reliance on Martin Luther's translation *Gnadenstuhl*, "grace chair," published a few years prior (1524).

On top of the mercy seat were two *cherubim* (Exod 25:18). This Hebrew word has come into English, so there is no need to survey the history of translations. (The LXX and Vulgate, like the English, simply use the Hebrew term.) Unfortunately, our English word "cherub" gives the wrong impression of the sort of creatures *cherubim* were. Ezekiel gives a description of *cherubim*, calling them "living creatures"(1:4–11)—but he uses the word *cherubim* for them at 10:20—and they definitely are not chubby babies. They are composite creatures with body parts that we associate with different animals (in the same way that a faun is a composite creature, a cross between a human and a goat; or a centaur, a cross between a human and a horse). Ancient Near Eastern temples and palaces featured statues of these types of creatures, used as guardians (similar to gargoyles).[6] To get this idea across, one scholar has taken to calling them griffins, but he doesn't mean the classic griffin, the winged lion with a falcon head, because it's not clear exactly what the biblical cherub looked like, except that it was a combination creature, like the griffin.[7] Cherubim appear mostly as decorations in the Bible—the golden statues on top of the

---

6. You can find pictures online, such as at lmcarthur.weebly.com/ancient-near-east-2.html.

7 Propp, *Exodus 19–40*, 386.

ark, and woven into the curtains of the Tabernacle (Exod 26:1)—but also as guardians of Paradise (Gen 3:24; Ezek 28:14–16).

Appearance

What did the ark look like? You can listen to Indiana Jones explain, but you shouldn't trust everything he says.[8] As the name "ark" implies, it was essentially a box. The dimensions given in the Bible are 2 ½ cubits by 1 ½ cubits, and 1 ½ cubits tall (Exod 25:10). Assuming the cubit is 18 inches, the box would be nearly four feet long (45 inches), a little more than two feet wide (27 inches), and a little over two feet tall (27 inches).

The box is made out of wood and overlaid with gold inside and out. There are four golden rings on the bottom of the ark into which poles should fit for carrying the ark. The dimensions of the poles are not given, but they should also be made of wood and overlaid with gold. The mercy seat fits right on top of the ark, with the same dimensions: 45 inches by 27 inches. But the mercy seat is not made of wood overlaid with gold; it is made only of gold (v. 17), as are the cherubim on top (v. 18). The wood had to be a particular type of wood, called by the Hebrew word *shittim* (שטים, pronounced shih-teem). Apparently, this is some sort of Acacia wood.[9] "There are many species of acacia, most of which are thorny bushes or shrubs, but a few have trunks from

---

8. Go to YouTube and search "Raiders of the Lost Ark Talk with Army Intel."
9. Go to Wikipedia and look up "Vachellia seyal."

which timber could be cut. It is a very hard and durable wood that is also lightweight."[10] Propp describes the ark as "a gold-plated wooden box [...] with a solid gold lid surrounded by two golden Griffins."[11] Again, you can easily find online pictures of an ark that looks reasonably accurate, except that most of them have human-like angels on top instead of *cherubim* the way the Bible describes them.

The ark of the covenant was not completely unprecedented. Other cultures had similar objects. Some that are often cited are the Egyptian sacred bark (where "bark" means "boat") and the Anubis Shrine from the grave of Tutankhamun.[12] It is interesting that there are these Egyptian parallels to the ark, given that the Israelites had recently emerged from Egypt.[13]

What Was the Ark?

Some scholars talk about the ark—or the *cherubim* on top of the ark—as the throne of God.[14] The following biblical

---

10. Averbeck, "Tabernacle," in *Dictionary of the Old Testament: Pentateuch*, 807–27, at 814.

11. Propp, *Exodus 19–40*, 515.

12. On this (uncommon today) meaning of the word "bark," go to Wikipedia and look up "barque." On the Egyptian sacred bark, just google it. Same for the Anubis Shrine.

13. On Egyptian connections, see Scott B. Noegel, "The Egyptian Origin of the Ark of the Covenant," in *Israel's Exodus in Transdisciplinary Perspective: Text, Archaeology, Culture, and Geoscience* (New York: Springer, 2015), 223–42.

14. John Day, "Whatever Happened to the Ark of the Covenant?" in *Temple and Worship in Biblical Israel: Proceedings of the Oxford Old Testament Seminar*, ed. John Day (New York: T&T Clark, 2007), 250–70, at 263. Propp, *Exodus 19–40*, argues that the *cherubim* are not the throne but rather that they hold the (invisible) throne.

passages may support this interpretation.

> So the people sent to Shiloh, and brought from there the ark of the covenant of YHWH of hosts, who is enthroned on the *cherubim.* The two sons of Eli, Hophni and Phinehas, were there with the ark of the covenant of God. (1 Sam 4:4)

> David and all the people with him set out and went from Baale-judah, to bring up from there the ark of God, which is called by the name of YHWH of hosts who is enthroned on the *cherubim.* (2 Sam 6:2)

On the other hand, the ark also seems to be identified with the footstool of God, in which case perhaps the Israelites imagined that he was enthroned in heaven.[15] There are several verses that support the ark-as-footstool view.

> Then King David rose to his feet and said: "Hear me, my brothers and my people. I had planned to build a house of rest for the ark of the covenant of YHWH, for the footstool of our God; and I made preparations for building." (1 Chron 28:2)

> Let us go to his dwelling place; let us worship at his footstool. Rise up, YHWH, and go to your resting place, you and the ark of your might. (Psa 132.7–8)

---

15. G. K. Beale, *The Temple and the Church's Mission: A Biblical Theology of the Dwelling Place of God* (Downers Grove, IL: IVP, 2004), 35.

But at Isa 66:1, while heaven is God's throne, the earth (and not the ark) is his footstool, so that passage probably has no bearing on how Israelites thought about the ark. So, maybe when the ark is thought of as God's footstool we shouldn't think of heaven as his throne but rather the cherubim. Maybe he sits on the wings of the *cherubim* and rests his feet on the mercy seat. Psalm 99 might attest this idea.

> YHWH is king; let the peoples tremble! He sits enthroned upon the cherubim; let the earth quake! (Psa 99:1)

> Extol YHWH our God; worship at his footstool. Holy is he! (Psa 99:5)

Another scholar combines these notions in a different way, suggesting that in the Tabernacle, the ark was considered God's throne, but later in Solomon's temple, the huge temple *cherubim* (15 feet tall; 1 Kings 6:23) served as God's throne so that the ark became the footstool.[16]

WHAT WAS IN THE ARK?

That's an easy one. Hebrews tells us.

> Behind the second curtain was a tent called the Holy of Holies. [4] In it stood the golden altar of incense and the ark of the covenant overlaid on all sides with gold, in

---

16. Michael S. Heiser, *The Unseen Realm: Recovering the Supernatural Worldview of the Bible* (Bellingham, WA: Lexham, 2015), 175, 225.

which there were a golden urn holding the manna, and Aaron's rod that budded, and the tablets of the covenant; ⁵ above it were the cherubim of glory overshadowing the mercy seat. (Heb 9:3–4)

According to Hebrews, there were three items in the ark: the two tablets of the law, a golden jar of manna, and Aaron's rod. But the Old Testament is not explicit on the ark's inclusion of these three things. In fact, it's pretty clear in one verse that the ark held only the two stone tablets.

Nothing was in the ark except the two stone tablets that Moses had put there at Horeb, where YHWH made a covenant with the Israelites when they came out of the land of Egypt. (1 Kings 8:9)

This verse is from the chapter in which Solomon dedicates the temple. Perhaps by this time the manna and the rod had been removed, or disintegrated, or whatever. But earlier we're not exactly told that they were in the ark of the covenant itself. The Old Testament is explicit only about the two stone tablets. In the original instructions for building the ark, God says:

Put the tables of the testimony that I will give you into the ark. (25:16)

Set the mercy seat on top of the ark and put the tablets of the testimony that I will give you into the ark. (25:21; cf. Deut 10:2; 2 Chron 5:10)

A jar of manna (Exod 16:33-34)[17] and Aaron's budding staff (Num 17:1-11) were supposed to be in the Holy of Holies, but these texts do not explicitly say that these items should be placed in the ark. But Jewish tradition does mention additional items in the ark: a Torah scroll, or silver columns, or the broken pieces of the first stone tablets (Exod 32:19).[18]

At any rate, the presence of the stone tablets in the ark is the reason that it is called "the ark of the covenant" (i.e., the covenant box; Num 10:33) or "the ark of the testimony" (Exod 25:22).

Did the Ark Lead Israel into Battle?

Sometimes. Or, at least, a couple times. This is the use of the ark that Indiana Jones emphasizes, and it's the reason that the Nazis are looking for the ark. Marcus Brody claims, "The Bible speaks of the ark leveling mountains and laying waste to entire regions. An army which carries the ark before it is invincible."[19] Well ... the Bible says no such thing. There's nothing in the Bible of anyone or anything leveling mountains, except in apocalyptic visions of the future, and the closest thing to the Bible talking about the ark causing the

---

17. Like Hebrews, Philo (*On the Preliminary Studies* 100) also says that this jar was golden.
18. See the Babylonian Talmud, tractate *Bava Bathra* 14a. Interestingly, Indiana Jones also thinks that those broken pieces from the first stone tablets were carried in the ark. On that idea, see also tractate *Berakot* 8b.
19. This comment is at the end of the same clip mentioned above; go to YouTube and search "Indiana Jones Talk with Army Intel."

waste of a region is when the Israelites carry the ark around Jericho and the walls come tumbling down (Josh 6). The Bible makes it very clear that even an army which carries the ark is not invincible (cf. 1 Sam 4). And there is nothing in the Bible about the ark melting people's faces.[20]

As far as I can tell, the Bible mentions the ark going into battle with the Israelites only twice: at the battle of Jericho (Josh 6) and in the disastrous battle against the Philistines, in which the ark was captured (1 Sam 4). There is also perhaps the implication that the ark should go into battle, at least in battles for the conquest of Canaan. After the Israelites rebelled against God and Moses by refusing to enter the Promised Land, the Israelites then reverse course and make a foolish attempt to do what they should have done in the first place.

> But they presumed to go up to the heights of the hill country, even though the ark of the covenant of YHWH, and Moses, had not left the camp. (Num 14:44)

Again, this verse seems to imply that the Israelites needed to bring the ark into their battle. But later on we hear almost nothing of this. For instance, we never get any record of David taking the ark into battle. This was not the primary purpose of the ark.

---

20. I know you want to see that clip; go to YouTube and search, "Raiders of the Lost Ark, Opening the Ark."

Divine Presence and Atonement

The main purpose of the ark was to represent the presence of God. That's why the symbolism of the ark is significant: it was something like the throne or the footstool of God. When you walked into the Holy of Holies—which, of course, you'd never do, but you could hear about it—you would imagine the invisible divine presence enthroned above the ark. Or, maybe not exactly invisible.

> I am present in the cloud above the mercy seat. (Lev 16:2)

Whereas other temples featured idols of their gods, the Israelite sanctuary featured a throne/footstool, but no image of the deity. But you could be confident that God was there because he said he would be.

Other verses testify to God's presence at the ark. The instructions for the ark include this purpose statement:

> There I will meet with you, and from above the mercy seat, from between the two cherubim that are on the ark of the covenant, I will deliver to you all my commands for the Israelites. (Exod 25:22)

When the ark would move, it signified that God was on the move.

> Whenever the ark set out, Moses would say, "Arise, YHWH, let your enemies be scattered, and your foes flee before you." ³⁶ And whenever it came to rest, he

would say, "Return, YHWH of the ten thousand thousands of Israel." (Num 10:35–36)

The presence of the Lord is what made the waters of the Jordan dry up.

> When the soles of the feet of the priests who bear the ark of YHWH, the Lord of all the earth, rest in the waters of the Jordan, the waters of the Jordan flowing from above shall be cut off; they shall stand in a single heap. (Josh 3:13)

It was because the ark represented God's presence that the Israelites wanted to take it into battle against the Philistines.

> When the troops came to the camp, the elders of Israel said, "Why has YHWH put us to rout today before the Philistines? Let us bring the ark of the covenant of YHWH here from Shiloh, so that he may come among us and save us from the power of our enemies." [4] So the people sent to Shiloh, and brought from there the ark of the covenant of YHWH of hosts, who is enthroned on the cherubim. The two sons of Eli, Hophni and Phinehas, were there with the ark of the covenant of God. (1 Sam 4:3–4)

So the ark represents God's presence, and for that very reason it was a centerpiece of the annual cleansing ritual that the high priest would perform on the Day of Atonement (Lev 16).

> He shall take a censer full of coals of fire from the altar before YHWH, and two handfuls of crushed sweet incense, and he shall bring it inside the curtain ¹³ and put the incense on the fire before YHWH, that the cloud of the incense may cover the mercy seat that is upon the covenant, or he will die. ¹⁴ He shall take some of the blood of the bull, and sprinkle it with his finger on the front of the mercy seat, and before the mercy seat he shall sprinkle the blood with his finger seven times. ¹⁵ He shall slaughter the goat of the sin offering that is for the people and bring its blood inside the curtain, and do with its blood as he did with the blood of the bull, sprinkling it upon the mercy seat and before the mercy seat. ¹⁶ Thus he shall make atonement for the sanctuary, because of the uncleannesses of the people of Israel, and because of their transgressions, all their sins; and so he shall do for the tent of meeting, which remains with them in the midst of their uncleannesses. (Lev 16:12–16)

Note that the high priest—in this action of sprinkling blood on the mercy seat—is making atonement for the sanctuary (v. 16). In the next few verses we learn that he also needs to atone for the altar (vv. 18–20).[21] Of course, he also must atone for his own sin and the sin of the people (v. 17). But here we can see that the sin of the people not only renders them impure but also infects the holy objects in their midst, so that these objects must be ritually cleansed.

---

21. This is probably the bronze altar of burnt offering; see Jacob Milgrom, *Leviticus 1–16*, AB 3 (New York: Doubleday, 1991), 1089.

Yom Kippur (the Day of Atonement) is not the only day of the year in which a cleansing ritual is performed. There is also a sin offering, described in Lev 4, for unintentional sins committed by various sorts of people. When a ruler or individual sins unintentionally, the priest can take some of the blood of the sin offering and apply it to the altar of burnt offering, pouring out the rest of the blood at the base of the altar (Lev 4:25, 30). If the high priest sins unintentionally, or the whole congregation of Israel, the high priest would sprinkle some of the blood of the sin offering before the curtain (vv. 6, 17), apply some of the blood to the altar of incense (vv. 7, 18), and pour out the rest of the blood at the base of the bronze altar (vv. 7, 18).

The Tabernacle contained different areas with varying levels of holiness. The holiest place on earth was the inner sanctuary of the Tabernacle, the Holy of Holies, where the ark of the covenant was located. Essentially, the presence of God above the *cherubim* radiated holiness outward, so that the closer you got to the ark, the holier was the location, and the more dangerous. But the sin of Israel rendered all spaces impure, threatening the presence of God in their midst. These holy spaces needed to be ritually cleansed to ensure that God would continue to dwell in the midst of Israel. Throughout the year, the various ritual objects of the Tabernacle would need to be cleansed ritually through the sin offering, but on one day a year, the high priest would enter the Holy of Holies and cleanse the mercy seat, the very location of God's presence.

Whereas the unintentional sins of the people defile the (outer) altar of burnt offering, and the unintentional sins of the high priest and the congregation defile the tent of meeting (including the inner altar of incense and the curtain), the high-handed sins of the people (for example, of the kind portrayed in Ezekiel 8) generate an impurity that penetrates all the way to the inner sanctuary that houses the ark and the [*kappōret*], the very place where God comes to be present to Israel. Since such impurity cannot be removed through the regular sin offering, it is crucial that it be removed on the annual Day of Atonement (Lev. 16:16).[22]

If Israel did not remove the impurity caused by their sin, the ultimate danger would be that God could not dwell in their midst anymore. This scenario is played out in the book of Ezekiel. When the prophet is transported spiritually to Jerusalem from his exilic home in Babylon (chs. 8–11), he witnesses the glory of God, riding on the *cherubim*, abandoning the temple because of the people's sins (ch. 10), eventually going to reside on a mountain outside the city (11:22–23), leaving Jerusalem to the impending destruction by the Babylonians in 586 BC.

---

22. Stephen Hultgren, "*Hilastērion* (Rom. 3:25) and the Union of Divine Justice and Mercy. Part I: The Convergence of Temple and Martyrdom Theologies," *Journal of Theological Studies* 70 (2019): 69–109, at 77–78.

What Happened to the Ark?[23]

Another Indiana Jones reference: there's actually no evidence that the ark now resides in a warehouse somewhere in America.[24]

According to everybody, there was no ark in the Second Temple, the one built by Zerubbabel and others after the Babylonian exile, when the Jews returned to Judah under the rule of the Persians (Ezra 6:14–15).[25] Josephus describes the Temple in the first century:

> The innermost recess measured twenty cubits and was screened in like manner from the outer portion by a veil. In this stood nothing whatever: unapproachable, inviolable, invisible to all, it was called the Holy of Holy.[26]

The Roman historian Tacitus, a contemporary of Josephus writing at the end of the first century, had also heard that the Holy of Holies was empty.

> The first Roman to subdue the Jews and set foot in their temple by right of conquest was Gnaeus Pompey [63 BC]: thereafter it was a matter of common knowledge

---

23. See Day, "Whatever Happened to the Ark of the Covenant."
24. Search YouTube for "Raiders of the Lost Ark Top Secret."
25. Despite the absence of the ark from the Second Temple, Hultgren ("Hilastērion," 71n9) says that a blood ritual still took place on Yom Kippur.
26. Josephus, *Jewish Antiquities* 5.219; translation by H. St. J. Thackeray in Josephus, *The Jewish War, Books V–VII*, Loeb Classical Library (Cambridge: MA: Harvard University Press, 1928), 69.

that there were no representations of the gods within, but that the place was empty and the secret shrine contained nothing.[27]

The ark disappeared sometime around the exile, or before, but there are several possibilities about what happened to it. After the ark was transported to Jerusalem by David (2 Sam 6)—when it resided in the tent constructed by David (v. 17)—and then moved into the new Temple constructed by Solomon (1 Kings 8), we lose track of the ark.

Samaritans believe the ark is hidden somewhere on Mt. Gerizim (cf. Josephus, *Antiquities* 18.85),[28] while Ethiopian Christians believe that the ark was transferred to Ethiopia during the time of Solomon and that it is still there, in the Church of Our Lady Mary of Zion, in the city of Axum.[29]

There are several times that the Temple was raided of its treasures. In these accounts, the ark is never mentioned, but it's not outside the realm of possibility that the ark was taken during one of these raids. For instance, during the reign of

---

27. Tacitus, *Histories* 5.9; translation by Clifford H. Moore in Tacitus, *The Histories, Books IV–V*, Loeb Classical Library (Cambridge, MA: Harvard University Press, 1931), 191.

28. Day, "Whatever Happened to the Ark of the Covenant," 250–51.

29. The Wikipedia page on "the Church of Our Lady Mary of Zion" mentions this legend. The Church is also mentioned as one of the main tourist attractions in the Wikipedia article on Axum. For more on the legend of the ark in Ethiopia, see the *National Geographic* article "In Search of the Real Queen of Sheba," by Stanley Stewart (Dec. 3, 2018), available online; and the *Los Angeles Times* article "Documentary: Does Trail to Ark of Covenant End Behind Aksum Curtain?" by Michael A. Hiltzik (June 9, 1992), available online.

Rehoboam, son of Solomon, Pharaoh Shishak / Shoshenq I invaded Judah.[30]

> In the fifth year of King Rehoboam, King Shishak of Egypt came up against Jerusalem; [26] he took away the treasures of the house of YHWH and the treasures of the king's house; he took everything. He also took away all the shields of gold that Solomon had made; [27] so King Rehoboam made shields of bronze instead, and committed them to the hands of the officers of the guard, who kept the door of the king's house. (1 Kings 14:25–27)

The idea that Shishak / Shoshenq took the ark is the one that turned out to be correct in *Raiders of the Lost Ark*—which is why Indiana Jones had to go to Egypt to find the ark. (See again Indiana's explanation to the Army, but note that Marcus Brody gets the date wrong by about 60 years; Shishak would have invaded Judah about 920 BC, not 980.) Nevertheless, the evidence for the ark's continuing presence in Jerusalem until the exile means that Shishak probably did not take the ark.

> The poles were so long that the ends of the poles were seen from the holy place in front of the inner sanctuary; but they could not be seen from outside; they are there to this day. (1 Kings 8:8)

---

30. Wikipedia has an article on "Shoshenq."

Whenever 1 Kings was written, the temple still stood and the poles of the ark could still be seen from outside the Holy of Holies. We don't know exactly when "to this day" refers, but it must be long after the time of Solomon—probably late in the Judean kingdom, not long before the exile.

Jeremiah also provides evidence that the ark continued in the Temple until just before the exile.

> And when you have multiplied and increased in the land, in those days, says YHWH, they shall no longer say, "The ark of the covenant of YHWH." It shall not come to mind, or be remembered, or missed; nor shall another one be made. (Jer 3:16)

The ark may have been carried away by the Babylonians at the time of the exile, as with other temple vessels, but the ark is not mentioned in our records,[31] and the return of the temple vessels in Ezra 1:7–11 does not mention the ark.

A popular view among the Rabbis is that King Josiah hid the ark somewhere on the Temple Mount in order to prevent its destruction by the Babylonians (whose conquest of Jerusalem he foresaw).[32] Another ancient view is that Jere-

---

31. See 2 Kings 24:13; 2 Chron 36:10, referring to 597; and 2 Kings 25:13–17; 2 Chron 36:18; Jer 52:17–23, referring to 586 BC
32. Babylonian Talmud, tractate *Yoma* 52b, 53b–54a; and tractate *Horayot* 12a.

miah hid the ark. One version of this view is found in 2 Maccabees.³³

> It was also in the same document that the prophet, having received an oracle, ordered that the tent and the ark should follow with him, and that he went out to the mountain where Moses had gone up and had seen the inheritance of God. ⁵ Jeremiah came and found a cave-dwelling, and he brought there the tent and the ark and the altar of incense; then he sealed up the entrance. ⁶ Some of those who followed him came up intending to mark the way, but could not find it. ⁷ When Jeremiah learned of it, he rebuked them and declared: "The place shall remain unknown until God gathers his people together again and shows his mercy. ⁸ Then the Lord will disclose these things, and the glory of the Lord and the cloud will appear, as they were shown in the case of Moses, and as Solomon asked that the place should be specially consecrated." (2 Maccabees 2:4–8)

This is all just legend. Probably the ark burned in the Temple (2 Kings 25). "The evidence strongly suggests that the ark disappeared about the time of the exile and the most likely explanation is that it was simply destroyed along with the Temple in 586 BCE."³⁴ We seem to have evidence of this

---

33. See also the Jewish historian Eupolemus (mid-second century BC), as preserved by Eusebius, *Preparation for the Gospel* 9.39.5; probably the easiest way to access this fragment (Greek and English) is in the collection by Carl R. Holladay, *Fragments from Hellenistic Jewish Authors*, vol. 1: *Historians* (Chico, CA: Scholars Press, 1983), 133–35, where Holladay classifies it as "fragment four." See also *The Lives of the Prophets* 2.11–13.

34. Day, "Whatever Happened to the Ark of the Covenant," 265.

explanation in Lamentations 2:1. In this lament about the destruction of Jerusalem by the Babylonians, we read:

> How the Lord in his anger has humiliated daughter Zion! He has thrown down from heaven to earth the splendor of Israel; he has not remembered his footstool in the day of his anger.

Remember that the ark is sometimes called God's footstool.

In Ezekiel's vision of a restored Temple (Ezek 40–48), there is no mention of the ark of the covenant. But in John's vision of the heavenly temple, he sees "the ark of his covenant" (Rev 11:19).

Jesus and the Mercy Seat

The ark is not mentioned in the New Testament very much. It does show up in that vision of the heavenly temple in Revelation (11:19), and the writer of Hebrews mentions the ark (9:3–5). Those are the only New Testament appearances of the word *kibōtos* in reference to the ark of the covenant. (The other appearances of this word refer to Noah's ark.)

There is, though, one important New Testament reference to the mercy seat.

> But now, apart from law, the righteousness of God has been disclosed, and is attested by the law and the prophets, [22] the righteousness of God through faith in Jesus Christ for all who believe. For there is no distinction, [23] since all have sinned and fall short of the glory of God; [24] they are now justified by his grace as a gift,

through the redemption that is in Christ Jesus, ²⁵ whom God put forward as a *hilastērion* by his blood, effective through faith. He did this to show his righteousness, because in his divine forbearance he had passed over the sins previously committed; ²⁶ it was to prove at the present time that he himself is righteous and that he justifies the one who has faith in Jesus. (Rom 3:21–26)

There has been a lot of discussion about what Paul meant with this word *hilastērion* in Rom 3:25.³⁵ It is sometimes translated "propitiation" or "expiation" or "atoning sacrifice." It's important to notice that this is the same Greek word that the Septuagint used for the mercy seat, and this Old Testament use surely influenced Paul's choice of words. As Hultgren says, "If Paul did not intend such an allusion, his writing would be at least potentially misleading."³⁶

To get to the point: just as the mercy seat was at the center of the cleansing ritual on the Day of Atonement, to purify the people and the Tabernacle so that God could continue to dwell among his people, so now God has put forward his Son as the mercy seat, and the blood sprinkled on this mercy seat is the Son's own blood, by which he purifies from sin all who would have faith in him.

> If we walk in the light as he himself is in the light, we have fellowship with one another, and the blood of Jesus his Son cleanses us from all sin. (1 John 1:7)

---

35. Here is an entire doctoral dissertation on the topic: https://www.repository.cam.ac.uk/handle/1810/251694.

36. Hultgren, "Hilastērion," 71.

12

MOSES' SHINING FACE

When Pope Julius II was 62 years old, he turned his thoughts toward death—more specifically, where his corpse would be entombed. As the reigning Pope, he could afford the greatest artist in the world to commemorate him; since his papacy occurred in the early sixteenth century, Michelangelo was available. The great Italian sculptor planned a magnificent tomb in St. Peter's Basilica with 40 statues. But he was able to progress only a little way in this design by the time the Pope died in 1513, eight years after commissioning his tomb. As it turned out, Michelangelo completed the project on a much-reduced scale in 1545, when he himself was around 60 years old. The Tomb of Pope Julius II has never held the body of Julius II, who is now, as planned, buried in St. Peter's Basilica, while his Tomb created by Michelangelo is in the nearby church building San Pietro in Vincoli (Saint Peter in Chains).

The claim to fame of the church building and of Julius' tomb is one particular statue produced by Michelangelo around the time of the pope's death or shortly thereafter. Michelangelo's marble *Moses*—only slightly less famous than his *David*—shows the great lawgiver sitting, apparently ready to judge the people, holding the two tables of the Law. Unlike in the case of the *David*, we don't have to wonder where Moses' clothes went (he's fully dressed), but the statue does present an equally curious element: the two little horns protruding from his head. Why?

Figure 7. Michelangelo. *Moses*. c. 1513–1515. Westerdam. [https://creativecommons.org/ licenses/by-sa/4.0)].

The reason for those horns has to do with an ambiguous Hebrew word and the history of its translation. And it all concerns a passage in Exodus that the apostle Paul highlights as foreshadowing—but also contrasting with—his own ministry of the gospel.

The passage in Exodus, however, is usually translated—in most modern languages, anyway—without any mention of horns. Instead of sprouting horns, Moses' face shines.

> Moses came down from Mount Sinai. As he came down from the mountain with the two tablets of the covenant in his hand, Moses did not know that the skin of his face shone because he had been talking with God. [30] When Aaron and all the Israelites saw Moses, the skin of his face was shining, and they were afraid to come near him. [31] But Moses called to them; and Aaron and all the leaders of the congregation returned to him, and Moses spoke with them. [32] Afterward all the Israelites came near, and he gave them in commandment all that YHWH had spoken with him on Mount Sinai. [33] When Moses had finished speaking with them, he put a veil on his face; [34] but whenever Moses went in before YHWH to speak with him, he would take the veil off, until he came out; and when he came out, and told the Israelites what he had been commanded, [35] the Israelites would see the face of Moses, that the skin of his face was shining; and Moses would put the veil on his face again, until he went in to speak with him. (Exod 34:29–35)

We will look at where the tradition of Moses' horns come from in a little bit, and we will want to see how this passage shows up in the New Testament, but first let's see where this story fits into the book of Exodus.

Context

A lot has happened in the storyline of Exodus since the material covered in the previous chapter. After entering into covenant with God, the Israelites hastened to transgress the very first laws of that covenant by worshiping an idol, a golden calf (Exod 32:1–6). As the story is presented in Exodus, this sin so enraged the Lord that he threatened to destroy the entire nation and start anew with Moses (32:10), but Moses interceded for the people so that "YHWH relented concerning the disaster he had said he would bring on his people" (v. 14).[1] But still, the covenant was broken, and Moses shattered the stone tablets of the covenant (v. 19).

All hope is not lost. Moses will still lead the people to the Promised Land, but whether or not the Lord will accompany them is up for debate: he proposes to send an angel in his place (33:1–3). Moses again protests, and the Lord again relents (33:12–17). Moses asks to see God's glory (33:18), and God consents, in a manner of speaking (vv. 19–23). The Lord then reveals himself to Moses as gracious and compassionate (34:5–7) and renews the covenant (34:10).

---

1. For a brilliant analysis of this episode, see Gary A. Anderson, "The Impassibility of God: Moses, Jonah, and the Theo-Drama of Intercessory Prayer," in *Christian Doctrine and the Old Testament: Theology in the Service of Biblical Exegesis* (Grand Rapids: Baker, 2017), 23–38.

All of this material is well-known and theologically profound, certainly worthy of more penetrating study. But—strange to say—none of this material comes up very prominently in the New Testament. The revelation of God to Moses (particularly the description of the Lord at 34:6–7) reappears several times in the Old Testament (e.g., Joel 2:13; Jonah 4:2), and the Lord's character as revealed in this passage is the same as his character as revealed by Jesus Christ, but the New Testament never seems to reflect specifically on Exod 34:6–7. The golden calf was the great sin of Israel (cf. Psa 106:19), destined to be repeated and amplified centuries later by Jeroboam the son of Nebat (cf. 1 Kings 12:28). And the golden calf episode is quoted once in the New Testament (1 Cor 10:7; cf. Exod 32:6) and mentioned by Stephen (Acts 7:39–41). But it's hard to find that even this famous episode exerted much influence in the New Testament. Since our focus here is on the impact of Exodus on the New Testament and Christian theology, we leave aside even such important passages as these in order to concentrate on material in Exodus that does feature prominently in the New Testament. And that is the case for the next story in the book.

After another forty-day period with the Lord on the mountain (34:28; cf. 24:18), Moses approached the people with the new tablets of the law in his hands. But this time his face looked different, and he intermittently donned a veil to conceal his altered appearance (34:29–35).

The Face of Moses

Moses glowed—or, the skin of his face was radiant—after he had been with the Lord. Why would that be? The obvious answer is that God is light (cf. 1 John 1:5), and he is presented this way in the book of Exodus. We first encounter God in this book as a burning bush. The major theophany at Sinai shows God coming down on the mountain "in fire" (Exod 19:18). Later: "The appearance of YHWH's glory to the Israelites was like a consuming fire on the mountaintop" (24:17). There are other, similar descriptions in the Bible (cf. Ezek 1:27–28; Psa 104:2). This passage about Moses glowing because he had been with the Lord must mean something like the Lord's glory had infused Moses' body—or, at least, his face, i.e., the exposed part of the body—with glorious light. I'm thinking of this process as sort of like a glow-in-the-dark frisbee that I have; it won't glow in the dark unless you put it under a light for several minutes so that it can charge up.

One of the ancient Aramaic biblical translations (Targum) renders Exod 34:29:

> At the time that Moses came down from Mount Sinai, with the two tables of the testimony in Moses' hand as he came down from the mountain, Moses did not know that the splendor of the features of his face shone because of the splendor of the glory of the shekinah [=

presence] of the Lord at the time that he spoke with him.²

This captures the point: it's the splendor of the Lord that sort of rubs off on Moses and causes his own resplendent skin.

The people are scared when they see Moses—even Aaron (v. 30). So he covers himself with a veil whenever he is not serving as God's mouthpiece. He removes the veil when he speaks to the Lord (v. 34) and when he speaks to the people on the Lord's behalf (vv. 33, 34–35). Otherwise, he uses the veil to conceal the glow.

It is worth noting the parallel between Exod 34:29 and the earlier account at 32:15. As Walter Moberly points out: "Each time Moses descends with the tablets in his hand. But whereas the first time he was confronted by sin and apostasy, now he is met with awe and reverence. A right relation between Yahweh, Moses, and the people has been restored."³

The Horns of Moses?

The Hebrew verb translated "shine" in Exod 34 is *qaran* (קרן), which appears only four times in the Hebrew Bible,

---

2. Targum Pseudo-Jonathan, translated in *Targum Neofiti 1: Exodus and Targum Pseudo-Jonathan: Exodus*, trans. Martin McNamara and Michael Maher, Aramaic Bible (Collegeville, MN: Liturgical Press, 1994), 260.

3. R. W. L. Moberly, *At the Mountain of God: Story and Theology in Exodus 32–34*, JSOT Sup 22 (Sheffield: JSOT Press, 1983), 106.

three of which are in this passage (vv. 29, 30, 35). The other time is at Psalm 69:31.

> This will please YHWH more than an ox or a bull with horns and hoofs.

The words "with horns" translate our verb *qaran*. There is also a related noun, *qeren* (קֶרֶן), which appears 76x in the Hebrew Bible, and means "horn" everywhere.[4] This is the word used for the horns of a ram (Gen 22:13) or the horns of oxen (Psa 22:21) or the horns of the altar (Exod 29:12). Sometimes "horn" is a metaphor for power (cf. 2 Sam 22:3). So, everywhere we know what *qaran* or *qeren* mean, they have something to do with horns. "Linguistically, therefore, the evidence in favour of the verb meaning 'to be horned' is overwhelming."[5]

Moses grew horns.

Nevertheless, "the context demands the sense of 'shine',"[6] and that is almost always the way the passage has been translated. You can sort of see how the two meanings could be related, if we think of beams of light emanating from Moses like horns. The medieval Jewish commentator Rashi understood the passage in this way: "The verb *karan* is related to the word *keren*, 'horn.' For the light radiated

---

4. A possible exception is Habakkuk 3:4, where the meaning is debated.
5. Moberly, *At the Mountain*, 210n205.
6. Moberly, *At the Mountain*, 108.

from his face in hornlike rays."[7]

Most ancient translations reflect the view that *qaran* means "shine." The Septuagint translates it:

> Moyses did not know that the appearance of the skin of his face (ἡ ὄψις τοῦ χρωτὸς τοῦ προσώπου αὐτοῦ) was charged with glory (δεδόξασται) while he was speaking to him. (NETS)

We have already seen one of the Aramaic translations that also translates in terms of "shining."

But there are two preserved ancient translations that use "horns" for Moses. The earlier one is from the Jewish Greek translator named Aquila, who lived in the second century AD. We actually do not have his translation anymore (it was not transmitted to modern times), but his translation of this phrase is reported by the Latin Christian writer Jerome, who lived in the fourth and fifth centuries. In Jerome's *Commentary on Amos*, he says that Aquila had translated the clause, "and Moses was not aware that the appearance of his face was horned."[8] Aquila was an extraordinarily literal biblical

---

7. Translated in Michael Carasik, *The Commentators' Bible: The JPS Miqra'ot Gedolot, Exodus* (Philadelphia: JPS, 2005), 310. On the same page, Rashbam says "Anyone who, because the verb *karan* sounds like *keren*, the word for 'horn,' takes it to mean that Moses had horns is nothing but a fool."

8. Jerome is commenting on Amos 6:13. Translation in Thomas P. Scheck, ed., *Jerome: Commentaries on the Twelve Prophets*, 2 vols., Ancient Christian Texts (Downers Grove, IL: IVP, 2016–2017), 2.371. Jerome reports Aquila's translation in Latin: *et Moyses nesciebat quia cornuta erat species vultus eius*. Aquila would have actually written in Greek.

translator, so it is no surprise that he chose to preserve in his translation the association of the Hebrew word with "horns." That translation choice does not necessarily mean that Aquila thought Moses actually had horns; he may have interpreted the passage metaphorically, or even in the way that Rashi interpreted it: hornlike beams of light.

That is likely how Jerome interpreted the passage. In the Latin Vulgate translation that Jerome produced in the early fifth century, Exod 34:29 is translated in a manner close to Aquila's version (*et ignorabat quod cornuta esset facies sua*). The Vulgate served as the basis for the Roman Catholic English translation called the Douay-Rheims Bible (1609/10), translated a year or two before the King James Version, and this Catholic translation renders the passage, "and he knew not that his face was horned." But there is a marginal note explaining the meaning[9]: "So his face appeared to the beholders, by reason of the glistering beames of his countenance shining gloriously, after his conversation with God fourtie dayes." Probably this note correctly interprets Jerome's own thoughts; though he translated the passage as saying that Moses had horns, he probably interpreted the language as signifying the way the light appeared to people. Jerome does say in his *Commentary on Ezekiel*: "forty days later the unworthy common people did not see the face of Moses, with their darkened eyes, because the face of Moses

---

9. You can find this on Google Books. Search for "Holy Bible Faithfully Translated into English (1634)." See the note on p. 246, note e.

was glorified, or, as is found in the Hebrew, horned."[10] Jerome seems to understand "horned" as a way of saying "glorified."

The first major English translation of the Bible was translated from the Latin Vulgate by John Wycliffe and his associates in the fourteenth century. Exodus 34:29 is rendered:

> And whanne Moises cam doun fro the hil of Synai, he helde twei tablis of witnessyng, and he wiste not that his face was horned of the felouschipe of Goddis word.

But William Tyndale's sixteenth century translation directly from the Hebrew text gives the more familiar wording:

> And Moses came doune from mount Sinai and the .ij. tables of witnesse in his hande, and yet he wyst not that the skynne of his face shone with beames of his comenynge with him.

So the medieval artists who depict Moses with horns come by this image honestly: they read it in their Bible. The earliest artistic representations of a horned Moses, according to Ruth Mellinkoff,[11] are illustrations in an eleventh-

---

10. This is a comment on Ezek 40:5–13; translation in Thomas P. Scheck, *St. Jerome: Commentary on Ezekiel*, Ancient Christian Writers 71 (New York: Newman, 2017), 451–52.

11. Ruth Mellinkoff, *The Horned Moses in Medieval Art and Thought* (Berkeley: University of California Press, 1970).

century biblical manuscript, the *Paraphrase of the Pentateuch and Joshua* by Aelfric of Eynsham (Canterbury).[12]

Figure 8. *Moses Receives the Tablets.* Old English Illustrated Hexateuch. 11th Century. Used by permission.

This artistic tradition leads directly to the most famous such depiction: Michelangelo's sculpture. Perhaps we should also interpret the marble horns arising from Moses' head as representing Moses' glory.

Moberly urges us to ask the next question: if the Hebrew verb *qaran* must have something to do with horns, but the

---

12. For information and images of this manuscript, see www.bl.uk/collection-items/anglo-saxon-justice-in-the-old-english-hexateuch. The relevant image of the horned Moses is the last one presented, image 31.

passage in Exodus clearly encourages us to take these "horns" metaphorically or symbolically as indicating light beams, why does the story not employ a more usual Hebrew word for "shining" (such as אור)? Moberly answers the question by suggesting a reference to the very beginning of this section of Exodus, the account of the golden calf (32:1-6). If we interpret the golden calf as an attempt to replace the absent Moses as a mediator for God, then the use of the word *qaran*, "to have horns," to refer to Moses' shining face would exalt Moses as the true mediator of the Lord, more radiant even than the golden cow. "The writer makes the point that Moses was to the people what they wanted the calf to be—a leader and mediator of the divine presence."[13]

REMOVING THE VEIL BY THE SPIRIT

There are some strong echoes of Exod 34:29–35 in certain passages of the New Testament, particularly the accounts of Jesus' Transfiguration.[14] After all, there is a mountain, there is a glowing face, and there is Moses himself. But the Transfiguration passages do not explicitly reflect on Exod 34.

Paul does. He doesn't exactly quote the passage, but he is definitely thinking about it and applying its imagery to his

---

13. Moberly, *At the Mountain*, 109.
14. Matt 17:1–8; Mark 9:2–8; Luke 9:28–36. On this theme, see Dale C. Allison, *The New Moses: A Matthean Typology* (Minneapolis: Fortress, 1993).

own current situation in 2 Corinthians 3.[15] It's a difficult passage, difficulty well-described by Richard Hays.

> Unfortunately, 2 Corinthians 3, though squeezed and prodded by generations of interpreters, has remained one of the more inscrutable reflections of a man who had already gained the reputation among his near-contemporaries for writing letters that were "hard to understand" (2 Peter 3:16). It is hard to escape the impression that, to this day, when 2 Corinthians 3 is read a veil lies over our minds.[16]

We won't even try to solve the problems here, or make suggestions for what everything means. Our concern is with how the apostle thought about Exodus, and how he saw in the story of Moses' glowing face something relevant to his own time.

The context of the passage in 2 Corinthians has to do with a dispute between Paul and some other traveling missionaries whom Paul labels "super-apostles" (2 Cor 11:5). (We have to speculate on the context, since Paul doesn't explain it, but the following makes sense of what he writes and

---

15. For what follows, I rely heavily on Richard B. Hays, "A Letter from Christ," in *Echoes of Scripture in the Letters of Paul* (New Haven: Yale University Press, 1989), 122–53. See also N. T. Wright, "Reflected Glory: 2 Corinthians 3," in *The Climax of Covenant: Christ and the Law in Pauline Theology* (London: T&T Clark, 1991), 175–92; and most recently Christopher D. Land, "It's Not Like Moses Veiled So That the Israelites Didn't Stare: a Hypothesis Regarding Paul's Understanding of Exodus 34," in *Paul and Scripture*, ed. Stanley E. Porter and Christopher D. Land (Leiden: Brill, 2019), 263–302.

16. Hays, "Letter from Christ," 123.

enjoys widespread agreement among students of this letter.) Apparently, these super-apostles had presented to the Corinthians some letters of recommendation from respected individuals validating their claims as Christian teachers, and they perhaps called into question Paul's own ministry partly because he had no such letters. Paul protests (2 Cor 3:1–3): he does have letters—the Corinthians themselves, and that is all the validation he needs. God's Spirit had used Paul's ministry to form this new people in Corinth. Paul does not rely on something written down for validation, but he relies on the Spirit (3:4–6).

At this point, Paul has already started thinking of Moses, as we can tell from the reference to the "tablets of stone" in v. 3 and the reference to Jeremiah's new covenant in v. 6 (cf. Jer 31:31–34), which is of course *new* in respect to the previous covenant enacted through Moses. Paul mentions Moses in the next sentence, and stays with him through the rest of the chapter.

> Now if the ministry of death, chiseled in letters on stone tablets, came in glory so that the people of Israel could not gaze at Moses' face because of the glory of his face, a glory now set aside, [8] how much more will the ministry of the Spirit come in glory? [9] For if there was glory in the ministry of condemnation, much more does the ministry of justification abound in glory! [10] Indeed, what once had glory has lost its glory because of the greater glory; [11] for if what was set aside came through glory, much more has the permanent come in glory! (2 Cor 3:7–11)

The main things we want to think about here are the significance of Moses' shining face ("glory") and the significance of the veil. First, the face: Paul legitimates his ministry in comparison with that of Moses by mentioning the shining face of Moses, representing the glory of the Sinai covenant. In other words, Paul reads Exod 34 as indicating that the Sinai covenant with Israel was glorious, so much so that even the human intermediary glowed. Nevertheless, Paul insists, this glory that Moses enjoyed was only temporary. Paul says several times that the glory was "fading" or—better—"transitory, impermanent" (vv. 7, 11, 13, 14). That is not to say that Moses' face was losing its glow, but rather that what was once thought to be glorious has been outshined by the greater glory of the new mediator.

The ministry of Moses is called a "ministry of death" (v. 7) not because obedience to the law brought death but because disobedience brought death.

> [For Paul] The problem with this old covenant is precisely that it is (only) written, lacking the power to effect the obedience that it demands. Since it has no power to transform the readers, it can only stand as a witness to their condemnation. That is why Paul remarks aphoristically, "The script [= that which is merely written] kills, but the Spirit gives life" (cf. Rom. 7:6–8:4).[17]

Hays paraphrases 2 Cor 3:7 in this way:

---

17. Hays, "Letter from Christ," 131.

> But if the ministry of death, chiseled in stone script, came with such glory that the sons of Israel were not able to gaze upon the face of Moses because of the glory of his face (a glory now nullified in Christ), how much more will the ministry of the Spirit come with glory.[18]

Because this old covenant was so very glorious, the Israelites could not bear to look at it, so that Moses was compelled to hide this glory with a veil.

> Since, then, we have such a hope, we act with great boldness, [13] not like Moses, who put a veil over his face to keep the people of Israel from gazing at the goal of the thing being nullified. [14] But their minds were hardened. Indeed, to this very day, when they hear the reading of the old covenant, that same veil is still there, since only in Christ is it set aside. [15] Indeed, to this very day whenever Moses is read, a veil lies over their minds; [16] but when one turns to the Lord, the veil is removed. [17] Now the Lord is the Spirit, and where the Spirit of the Lord is, there is freedom. [18] And all of us, with unveiled faces, seeing the glory of the Lord as though reflected in a mirror, are being transformed into the same image from one degree of glory to another; for this comes from the Lord, the Spirit. (2 Cor 3:12–18)

Notice something about this passage: v. 13 as translated above talks about the "goal of the thing being nullified," whereas this verse is often rendered as if it were talking about the end or cessation of the old covenant. The Greek

---

18. Hays, "Letter from Christ," 135.

word here is *telos* (τέλος), which can mean "cessation," but more normally means "goal." So, probably Paul means that the "goal" or "purpose" of the old covenant was to reveal the glory of God, which glory is Christ himself. While the old covenant is nullified by the coming of a new one, the goal of this old covenant is thereby fulfilled (i.e., by the coming of the new covenant).

But that interpretation of *telos* would mean that Moses put the veil on his face in order to hide the true intent of the law. Can we accept that view? Here, we need to recognize that Paul is using this passage in Exodus as a metaphor or symbol for his own ministry, so we should not press the details too far. Of course, Paul did not mean that Moses wanted to hide the true intent of the law from the people. Rather, the need for the veil arose from the hardness of the people, from their inability to look at the glory reflected in Moses' face.

But now Moses with his veil becomes a symbol for the experience of every Christian, because when he turned to the Lord, Moses removed the veil (Exod 34:34). So also we—"when one turns to the Lord, the veil is removed" (2 Cor 3:16). Just as Moses reflected the glory of God, so also we—each one of us, since all of us enjoy close communion with God, and not just one of our leaders—so also we reflect the glory of God (v. 18). Just as Moses was transformed in the presence of the Lord, so also we.

Hays paraphrases this whole concluding paragraph of the chapter.

The veil on Moses' face hid from Israel the glory of God, which Moses beheld at Sinai, a glory that transfigured him. Israel could not bear looking at the transfigured person and concentrated instead on the script that he gave them. That text, too, bears witness (in a more indirect or filtered manner) to the glory, to the person transfigured in the image of God, who is the true aim of the old covenant. For those who are fixated on the text as an end in itself, however, the text remains veiled. But those who turn to the Lord are enabled to see through the text to its *telos*, its true aim. For them, the veil is removed, so that they, like Moses, are transfigured by the glory of God into the image of Jesus Christ, to whom Moses and the Law had always, in veiled fashion, pointed.[19]

May we all, like Moses, project the glory of God from our communion with him.

---

19. Hays, "Letter from Christ," 137.

13

The Divine Cloud

In August of 2017, I took my wife and kids to my parents' home in western Kentucky to witness what was being billed as the Great American Eclipse. The problem with witnessing a solar eclipse is that you can't actually look at it, or you're not supposed to—looking at the sun damages your eyes, even if the sun is being blocked by the moon. Not to worry: my mom had bought the special eclipse sunglasses for the whole family, and an uncle had put together one of those cardboard box things for capturing the shadow of the eclipse (called a pinhole projector, the internet tells me). We made the four-hour drive to witness this event that lasted about a minute and a half, an event we couldn't even really look at directly. Oh well, it was really about being with family, and saying, "I was there." I'm bringing up the eclipse because it's something like how the Bible describes looking at God.

What does God look like? To go back to Michelangelo for a moment (from the previous chapter), the great Renaissance artist gave us a classic depiction of God on the ceiling of the Sistine Chapel: old man in the sky, flowing white beard.

Figure 9. Michelangelo. *The Creation of Adam.* c. 1511.

The Bible never mentions a beard, but there are various references to God's hands (e.g., Jer 18:6) and feet (e.g., 2 Sam 22:10) and head (e.g., Isa 59:17) and eyes (e.g., Gen 6:8).[1] This way of representing God as some sort of heavenly human not only makes sense to us because we know what humans look like but it also coheres with the way other ancient cultures depicted their gods, such as Baal or Marduk or Zeus.[2] There are a few biblical theophanies, particularly in Genesis, in which God appears as a human being: in the

---

1. See the biblical texts compiled by Andreas Wagner, *God's Body: The Anthropomorphic God in the Old Testament* (London: T&T Clark, 2019), 20–22.

2. Wikipedia has pictures of each of these gods.

story of the three visitors to Abraham (Gen 18), and perhaps in the strange story of the divine being that wrestles Jacob (Gen 32:24–32). And then there's Jesus, but we'll get to him later.

On the other hand, it was Xenophanes of Colophon in the fifth-century BC that said: "If cows and horses or lions had hands, or could draw with their hands and make things as men can, horses would have drawn horse-like gods, cows cow-like gods, and each species would have made the gods' bodies just like their own."[3]

God's Glory

More often, the Bible represents God's appearance as something quite different from a normal human being, something even deadly to behold. When Moses asks to see God's "glory" (i.e., apparently, his "face"),[4] God demurs.

> You cannot see my face, for humans cannot see me and live. (Exod 33:20)

---

3. Translation in Robin Waterfield, *The First Philosophers: Presocratics and Sophists*, Oxford World's Classics (Oxford: Oxford University Press, 2000), 27. This fragment from Xenophanes is preserved in Clement of Alexandria, *Stromata* 5.109.3.

4. Cf. Exod 33:18, where "glory" is apparently equivalent to the presence of God mentioned earlier in the passage. On this passage, see Benjamin D. Sommer, *The Bodies of God and the World of Ancient Israel*, 60. Note that the Hebrew word sometimes translated "presence" in Exod 33:14 is the very same word usually translated "face" at v. 20.

Why is that? Presumably because the direct sight of God is dangerous for humans. This is where the eclipse analogy becomes useful, especially once you remember (as we also noted briefly in the previous chapter) that God is often depicted, particularly in Exodus, as a bright light, like fire. Recall again the theophany at Sinai.[5]

> Now Mount Sinai was wrapped in smoke because YHWH had descended on it in fire. (Exod 19:18)

Now this "fire" is some sort of divine fire, not regular, earthly fire.[6] While the Bible says that it's dangerous to look at God, it never indicates that it's dangerous to get too close to God because of the heat he emits. Presumably there's not much heat involved; it's a fiery-looking light. This is probably why the burning bush was not consumed; it wasn't really on fire, it just looked like it. As Benjamin Sommer has commented: "A blazing body of God has located itself inside the bush, but that divine blaze is self-sustaining. The bush is not providing fuel for the fire-like substance that is God's pres-

---

5. Further references to God's fiery appearance are in Moses' speech in Deut 4:12, 15, 24, 33, 36, where Moses couples this description with the repeated assertion that the Israelites saw "no form" of God on the mountain (4:12, 15, 16). See also Deut 5:4, 22–26; 9:3; Heb 12:29. Such language sometimes also characterized the gods of ancient Mesopotamia; see Sommer, *The Bodies of God and the World of Ancient Israel*, 20–21.

6. See Sommer's helpful description of God's *kabod* ("glory") at *The Bodies of God and the World of Ancient Israel*, 60–62, 68.

ence; it is merely sharing space with that presence, so that to Moses' eye the bush appears to be on fire even as it does not burn."[7]

This fiery appearance of God is also called God's "glory" (Hebrew: *kavod* or *kabod*).[8]

> Now the appearance of the glory of YHWH was like a devouring fire on the top of the mountain in the sight of the people of Israel. (Exod 24:16)

And since it was like a dangerously bright fire, it needed to be covered for the protection of others.

> And as Aaron spoke to the whole congregation of the Israelites, they looked toward the wilderness, and the glory of YHWH appeared in the cloud. (Exod 16:10)

Moses wanted to see God's "face," that is, his "glory," the full essence of God without any protection. And some people

---

7. Sommer, *Bodies of God*, 71. I realize that Exod 3:2 says that it's an "angel of YHWH" in the bush, but then YHWH himself goes on to have a conversation with Moses. Apparently, this "angel" of the Lord is some sort of manifestation (or embodiment) of the Lord and can speak as if he himself is God (cf. Gen 16:7–13; 22:11–18; etc.), because he is. See Sommer, *Bodies of God*, 41–42, cited in Chapter Two above (note 11).

8. This word does not always mean the same thing (Sommer, *Bodies of God*, 61). Sometimes it refers to God's fiery essence, and sometimes it simply means something like "honor" or whatever, something more like what it means usually in English (e.g., Psa 57:11).

want to look at a solar eclipse without any sunglasses. Bad idea. That's why God won't permit it (33:20–23).[9]

> **EXPLORATION 13.1**
> **APPEARANCES OF GOD IN EXODUS (AND BEYOND)**
>
> Exodus 13:21–22
> And YHWH went before them by day in a pillar of cloud, to lead them the way, and by night in a pillar of fire, to give them light; to go by day and night. [22]He took not away the pillar of the cloud by day, nor the pillar of fire by night, from before the people.
>
> Exodus 14:19–20
> And the angel of God, which went before the camp of Israel, removed and went behind them; and the pillar of cloud went from before their face, and stood behind them: [20]And it came between the camp of the Egyptians and the camp of Israel; and it was a cloud and darkness to them, but it gave light by night to these: so that the one came not near the other all the night.
>
> Exodus 14:24
> And it came to pass, that in the morning watch YHWH looked unto the host of the Egyptians through the pillar

---

9. For a different way of putting all these references together, see Menahem Haran, "The Shining of Moses' Face: A Case Study in Biblical and Ancient Near Eastern Iconography," in *In the Shelter of Elyon: Essays on Ancient Palestinian Life and Literature in Honor of G. W. Ahlström*, JSOT Sup 31, ed. W. Boyd Barrick and John R. Spencer (Sheffield: JSOT Press, 1984), 159–73, esp. 167.

of fire and of the cloud, and troubled the host of the Egyptians.

Exodus 16:7
and in the morning you will see the glory of YHWH.

Exodus 16:9–10
Then Moses said to Aaron, "Say to the whole Israelite community, 'Come near to YHWH, because he's heard your complaints.'" ¹⁰As Aaron spoke to the whole Israelite community, they turned to look toward the desert, and just then the glory of YHWH appeared in the cloud (וְהִנֵּה כְּבוֹד יְהוָה נִרְאָה בֶּעָנָן).

Exodus 16:33–34
Moses said to Aaron, "Take a jar, and put one full omer of manna in it. Then set it in YHWH's presence (לִפְנֵי יְהוָה), where it should be kept safe for future generations. ³⁴Aaron did as YHWII commanded Moses, and he put it in front of the covenant document (לִפְנֵי הָעֵדֻת) for safekeeping.

Exodus 17:5–6
YHWH said to Moses ... ⁶I'll be standing there in front of you on the rock at Horeb (הִנְנִי עֹמֵד לְפָנֶיךָ שָּׁם עַל־הַצּוּר בְּחֹרֵב).

Exodus 18:12
Aaron came with all of Israel's elders to eat a meal with Moses' father-in-law in God's presence (לִפְנֵי הָאֱלֹהִים).

Exodus 19:9
And YHWH said to Moses, "Behold, I am coming to you in a thick cloud, that the people may hear when I speak with you, and may also believe you forever."

Exodus 19:16–18
On the morning of the third day there were thunders and lightnings and **a thick cloud** on the mountain and a very loud trumpet blast, so that all the people in the camp trembled. [17] Then Moses brought the people out of the camp to meet God, and they took their stand at the foot of the mountain. [18] Now Mount Sinai was wrapped **in smoke because YHWH had descended on it in fire**. The **smoke** of it went up like the smoke of a kiln, and the whole mountain trembled greatly.

Exodus 20:21
And the people stood afar off, and Moses drew near unto the thick darkness where God was.

Exodus 23:20–22
I'm about to send an angel in front of you to guard you on your way and to bring you to the place that I've made ready. [21] Pay attention to him and do as he says. Don't rebel against him. He won't forgive the things you do wrong because my name is in him. [22] But if you listen carefully to what he says and do all that I say, then I'll be an enemy to your enemies and fight those fighting you.

Exodus 24:9–11
Then Moses and Aaron, Nadab and Abihu, and seventy elders of Israel went up, [10] and they saw Israel's God (וַיִּרְאוּ אֵת אֱלֹהֵי יִשְׂרָאֵל). Under God's feet there was what looked like a floor of lapis-lazuli tiles, dazzlingly pure like the sky. [11] God didn't harm the Israelite leaders, though they looked at God (וַיֶּחֱזוּ אֶת־הָאֱלֹהִים), and they ate and drank.

Exodus 29:42–46
It shall be a regular burnt offering throughout your generations at the entrance of the tent of meeting before YHWH, where I will meet with you, to speak to you there. [43] There I will meet with the people of Israel, and it shall be sanctified by my glory. [44] I will consecrate the tent of meeting and the altar. Aaron also and his sons I will consecrate to serve me as priests. [45] I will dwell among the people of Israel and will be their God. [46] And they shall know that I am YHWH their God, who brought them out of the land of Egypt that I might dwell among them. I am YHWH their God.

Exodus 32:34–35
But now go, lead the people to the place about which I have spoken to you; behold, my angel shall go before you. Nevertheless, in the day when I visit, I will visit their sin upon them." [35] Then YHWH sent a plague on the people, because they made the calf, the one that Aaron made.

Exodus 33:1–3

YHWH said to Moses, "Depart; go up from here, you and the people whom you have brought up out of the land of Egypt, to the land of which I swore to Abraham, Isaac, and Jacob, saying, 'To your offspring I will give it.' ² I will send an angel before you, and I will drive out the Canaanites, the Amorites, the Hittites, the Perizzites, the Hivites, and the Jebusites. ³ Go up to a land flowing with milk and honey; but I will not go up among you, lest I consume you on the way, for you are a stiff-necked people."

Exodus 33:7–11

Now Moses used to take the tent and pitch it outside the camp, far off from the camp, and he called it the tent of meeting. And everyone who sought Yhwh would go out to the tent of meeting, which was outside the camp. ⁸ Whenever Moses went out to the tent, all the people would rise up, and each would stand at his tent door, and watch Moses until he had gone into the tent. ⁹ When Moses entered the tent, **the pillar of cloud** would descend and stand at the entrance of the tent, and **YHWH would speak with Moses**. ¹⁰ And when all the people saw **the pillar of cloud** standing at the entrance of the tent, all the people would rise up and worship, each at his tent door. ¹¹ Thus YHWH used to speak to Moses **face to face**, as a man speaks to his friend. When Moses turned again into the camp, his assistant Joshua the son of Nun, a young man, would not depart from the tent.

Exodus 33:12–16

Moses said to YHWH, "See, you say to me, 'Bring up this people,' but you have not let me know **whom you will send with me**. Yet you have said, 'I know you by name, and you have also found favor in my sight.' [13] Now therefore, if I have found favor in your sight, please **show me now your ways, that I may know you** in order to find favor in your sight. Consider too that this nation is your people." [14] And he said, "**My presence (or face,** פָּנַי**)** will go with you, and I will give you rest." [15] And he said to him, "If **your presence (or face,** פָּנֶיךָ**)** will not go with me, do not bring us up from here. [16] For how shall it be known that I have found favor in your sight, I and your people? Is it not in **your going with us**, so that we are distinct, I and your people, from every other people on the face of the earth?"

Exodus 33:17–23

And YHWH said to Moses, "This very thing that you have spoken I will do, for you have found favor in my sight, and I know you by name." [18] Moses said, "Please show me your glory (כְּבֹדֶךָ)."

[19] And he said, "I will make all my goodness (טוּבִי) pass before you and will proclaim before you my name YHWH. And I will be gracious to whom I will be gracious, and will show mercy on whom I will show mercy. [20] But," he said, "you cannot see my face (פָּנַי), for man shall not see me and live (כִּי לֹא־יִרְאַנִי הָאָדָם וָחָי)."
[21] And YHWH said, "Behold, there is a place by me where

you shall stand on the rock, ²² and while my glory (כְּבֹדִי) passes by I will put you in a cleft of the rock, and I will cover you with my hand until I have passed by. ²³ Then I will take away my hand, and you shall see my back (אֲחֹרָי), but my face (פָּנַי) shall not be seen."

Exodus 34:5–9
YHWH descended in the cloud and stood with him there, and proclaimed the name YHWH. ⁶ And YHWH passed before him and proclaimed, "YHWH, YHWH, a God merciful and gracious, slow to anger, and abounding in steadfast love and faithfulness, ⁷ keeping steadfast love for thousands, forgiving iniquity and transgression and sin, but who will by no means clear the guilty, visiting the iniquity of the fathers on the children and the children's children, to the third and the fourth generation." ⁸ And Moses quickly bowed his head toward the earth and worshiped. ⁹ And he said, "If now I have found favor in your sight, O Lord (אֲדֹנָי, *adonai*), please let the Lord (אֲדֹנָי, *adonai*) go in the midst of us, for it is a stiff-necked people, and pardon our iniquity and our sin, and take us for your inheritance."

Exodus 40:34–38
Then the cloud covered the tent of meeting, and the glory of YHWH filled the tabernacle. ³⁵ And Moses was not able to enter the tent of meeting because the cloud settled on it, and the glory of YHWH filled the tabernacle.
³⁶ Throughout all their journeys, whenever the cloud was

taken up from over the tabernacle, the people of Israel would set out. ³⁷ But if the cloud was not taken up, then they did not set out till the day that it was taken up. ³⁸ For the cloud of YHWH was on the tabernacle by day, and fire was in it by night, in the sight of all the house of Israel throughout all their journeys.

Numbers 9:15–23
On the day the tabernacle was set up, the cloud covered the tabernacle, the tent of the covenant; and from evening until morning it was over the tabernacle, having the appearance of fire. ¹⁶ It was always so: the cloud covered it by day and the appearance of fire by night. ¹⁷ Whenever the cloud lifted from over the tent, then the Israelites would set out; and in the place where the cloud settled down, there the Israelites would camp. ¹⁸ At the command of YHWH the Israelites would set out, and at the command of YHWH they would camp. As long as the cloud rested over the tabernacle, they would remain in camp. ¹⁹ Even when the cloud continued over the tabernacle many days, the Israelites would keep the charge of YHWH, and would not set out. ²⁰ Sometimes the cloud would remain a few days over the tabernacle, and according to the command of YHWH they would remain in camp; then according to the command of YHWH they would set out. ²¹ Sometimes the cloud would remain from evening until morning; and when the cloud lifted in the morning, they would set out, or if it continued for a day and a night, when the cloud lifted they would set out. ²² Whether it was two days, or a month, or a longer

time, that the cloud continued over the tabernacle, resting upon it, the Israelites would remain in camp and would not set out; but when it lifted they would set out. ²³ At the command of YHWH they would camp, and at the command of YHWH they would set out. They kept the charge of YHWH, at the command of YHWH by Moses.

Numbers 10:11–13
In the second year, in the second month, on the twentieth day of the month, the cloud lifted from over the tabernacle of the covenant. ¹² Then the Israelites set out by stages from the wilderness of Sinai, and the cloud settled down in the wilderness of Paran. ¹³ They set out for the first time at the command of YHWH by Moses.

Numbers 10:34
…the cloud of YHWH being over them by day when they set out from the camp.

Numbers 11:25
Then YHWH came down in the cloud and spoke to him, and took some of the spirit that was on him and put it on the seventy elders; and when the spirit rested upon them, they prophesied. But they did not do so again.

Numbers 12:5
Then YHWH came down in a pillar of cloud, and stood at the entrance of the tent, and called Aaron and Miriam; and they both came forward.

> Numbers 12:8
> With him I speak face to face—clearly, not in riddles; and he beholds the form (תְּמוּנָה, *temunah*) of YHWH.[10]
>
> Numbers 14:14
> (Moses speaking to the Lord) ... and they [= the Egyptians] will tell the inhabitants of this land [i.e., Canaan]. They have heard that you, O YHWH, are in the midst of this people; for you, O YHWH, are seen face to face, and your cloud stands over them and you go in front of them, in a pillar of cloud by day and in a pillar of fire by night.
>
> Numbers 16:42
> And when the congregation had assembled against them, Moses and Aaron turned toward the tent of meeting; the cloud had covered it and the glory of YHWH appeared.

The person in the Bible who gets the best look at God's glory is actually a prophet from much later in Israel's history: Ezekiel, who lived during the exile. While sitting in Babylon, Ezekiel "saw visions of God" (Ezek 1:1). This is what he saw:

> Upward from what appeared like the loins I saw something like gleaming amber, something that looked like fire enclosed all around; and downward from what

---

10. The word *temunah* appears only 10x in the Hebrew Bible. Exod 20:4 (against idolatry); Num 12:8; Deut 4:12, 15 (you saw no form); Deut 4:16, 23, 25; 5:8 (against idolatry). And Psa 17:15; Job 4:16.

looked like the loins I saw something that looked like fire, and there was a splendor all around. ²⁸ Like the bow in a cloud on a rainy day, such was the appearance of the splendor all around. This was the appearance of the likeness of the glory of YHWH. (Ezek 1:27–28)

Ezekiel receives the special privilege of beholding "the appearance of the likeness of the glory of YHWH" when "the heavens were opened" (1:1). I take his description in verse 28 to mean that he didn't see YHWH's glory itself, just the likeness of the glory.[11] At any rate, usually God's glory is too much for humans to look at, too dangerous. But it takes up residence among the Israelites in the Tabernacle.

God's Glory Cloud in His Dwelling Place

There is more about the Tabernacle in the book of Exodus (even in the Pentateuch) than about any other single topic, and the whole point of this long description is for God's bright and dangerous glory to take up residence among his people. That's why Israel was supposed to build this tent.

> I will meet with the Israelites there, and it shall be sanctified by my glory. (Exod 29:43)

Once the Tabernacle is constructed, that's exactly what happens.

---

11. Sommer, *Bodies of God*, 68, thinks that Ezekiel "saw the *kabod* directly and clearly." He goes on to argue that "likeness" is not the right translation of the Hebrew word *demut*, but rather "form."

> Then the cloud covered the tent of meeting, and the glory of YHWH filled the tabernacle. [35] And Moses was not able to enter the tent of meeting because the cloud settled on it, and the glory of YHWH filled the tabernacle. [36] Throughout all their journeys, whenever the cloud was taken up from over the tabernacle, the people of Israel would set out. [37] But if the cloud was not taken up, then they did not set out till the day that it was taken up. [38] For the cloud of YHWH was on the tabernacle by day, and fire was in it by night, in the sight of all the house of Israel throughout all their journeys. (Exod 40:34–38)

The Tabernacle was sanctified by God's glory. It was the earthly abode of God's fiery essence. That's why, on the Day of Atonement, the high priest needed to burn incense before entering the Holy of Holies. He needed to create a barrier between himself and God so that he could enter into the presence of God without suffering harm.[12]

> And he shall take a censer full of coals of fire from the altar before YHWH, and two handfuls of sweet incense beaten small, and he shall bring it inside the veil [13] and put the incense on the fire before YHWH, that the cloud of the incense may cover the mercy seat that is over the testimony, so that he does not die. (Lev 16:12–13)

---

12. For this interpretation of the purpose of burning incense, see Sommer, *Bodies of God*, 68.

Remember that the ark of the covenant, or the mercy seat specifically, is the throne/footstool of the Lord.

Once Solomon built the Temple, the same thing happened. When the priests carried in the ark, God's glory filled his new home.

> And when the priests came out of the Holy Place, a cloud filled the house of YHWH, [11] so that the priests could not stand to minister because of the cloud, for the glory of YHWH filled the house of YHWH. (1 Kings 8:10–11)

You may recall from our discussion of the ark of the covenant that we lose track of God's throne/footstool around the time of the exile, and it was probably destroyed when the Babylonians burned the Temple (2 Kings 25:9). At any rate, there was no ark of the covenant in the Second Temple, the one built after the exile (cf. Ezra 6:14–16). Even worse, there is no record of God's glory cloud entering the Second Temple as it had the Tabernacle and Solomon's Temple. According to Jewish tradition, the Second Temple lacked the presence of God.

> ... in five things the first Sanctuary differed from the second: in the ark, the ark-cover, the cherubim [these three all count as one thing], the fire, the *Shekhinah*, the Holy Spirit, and the urim and thummim.[13]

---

13. Babylonian Talmud, tractate *Yoma* 21b.

It's the *Shekhinah* that we're talking about. *Shekhinah* (look it up on Wikipedia) is a Hebrew word that means "dwelling" and refers to God's presence dwelling among his people. But according to this Jewish tradition, the Second Temple did not house the *Shekhinah* as the First Temple had.

Jesus and the Glory Cloud

The beginning of John's Gospel—or, really, the Gospel as a whole—resonates with this conception of God, that is, God as light, God's glory, God's cloud. Of course, there are also deep echoes of Gen 1, since John wants to clarify at the beginning of his telling of Jesus that this same human being was actually "with God" even at creation, or, rather, before creation, and that he himself is the agent of creation. Genesis 1 says that God created all things by speaking (e.g., "Let there be light"), or, as Psalm 33:6 puts it, "By the word of YHWH the heavens were made." John wants us to understand that Jesus is that Word.

But Jesus is also the light. Even as John reflects on Gen 1 and brings some of its concepts to bear on his account of Jesus, he also now begins thinking of God's glorious light in the Old Testament. That manifestation of God as fiery light, that embodiment of God in the Old Testament—John sees that fiery light as, in a sense, an embodiment of God's Word (Jesus) before the Embodiment of God's Word, the Incarnation.

> The true light that gives light to everyone was coming into the world. (1:9)
>
> The Word became flesh and dwelt among us. We observed his glory, the glory of the one and only Son from the Father, full of grace and truth. (1:14)
>
> No one has ever seen God. The one and only Son, who is himself God is at the Father's side—he has revealed him. (1:18)

It is Jesus who embodies God's glory, who reveals God, who is God's light. John uses the term "glory" (Greek *doxa*) 19x, more than any other Gospel. Oftentimes, the word "glory" just means "honor," as in: "How can you believe if you accept glory from one another?" (5:44).[14] But other times it seems to mean something different. For instance:

> And so they could not believe, because Isaiah also said, [40] "He has blinded their eyes and hardened their heart, so that they might not look with their eyes, and understand with their heart and turn—and I would heal them." [41] Isaiah said this because he saw his glory and spoke about him. (John 12:39–41)

Here, John is explaining why many Jews rejected Jesus even though he performed so many signs attesting that he came from God. John says that this rejection corresponds to the message of Isaiah, and he quotes Isa 6:9–10 ("blinded their eyes and hardened their heart"). And then John says that the

---

14. See also John 7:18; 8:50, 54; 9:24.

reason Isaiah uttered this prophecy is because "he saw his glory and spoke about him," referring to Jesus. Isaiah saw the glory of Jesus and spoke about him. When did he do that?

Well, let's look at the chapter in Isaiah that John is quoting, Isaiah 6. That's the chapter in which Isaiah has a vision of...

> the Lord [*adonai*] seated on a high and lofty throne, and the hem of his robe filled the temple. ² Seraphim were standing above him; they each had six wings: with two they covered their faces, with two they covered their feet, and with two they flew. ³ And one called to another: Holy, holy, holy is YHWH of Armies; his glory fills the whole earth. ⁴ The foundations of the doorways shook at the sound of their voices, and the temple was filled with smoke. ⁵ Then I said: Woe is me for I am ruined because I am a man of unclean lips and live among a people of unclean lips, and because my eyes have seen the King, YHWH of Armies. (Isa 6:2–5)

This passage evokes images we've encountered in Exodus: God's glory, the smoke, the danger of seeing God. But note that John interprets this passage as a revelation of Jesus; Isaiah prophesied the words of Isa 6:9–10 because "he saw his glory," that is, the glory of Jesus. In John's mind, this manifestation of God's glory to Isaiah is a vision of the preincarnate Christ. Jesus embodies the glory of God.

Let's also look briefly at Paul's experience of God's glory, both in Acts and in his letters.[15] On the road to Damascus, Paul had a vision of the heavenly Jesus.

> Now as he was going along and approaching Damascus, suddenly a light from heaven flashed around him. [4] He fell to the ground and heard a voice saying to him, "Saul, Saul, why do you persecute me?" (Acts 9:3–4)

The bright light blinded Paul (v. 8). Paul retold this story twice in Acts, once to a crowd of Jews in Jerusalem (22:1–21), and once to King Agrippa (26:1–23).

> While I was on my way and approaching Damascus, about noon a great light from heaven suddenly shone about me. [7] I fell to the ground and heard a voice saying to me, 'Saul, Saul, why are you persecuting me?' [8] I answered, 'Who are you, Lord?' Then he said to me, 'I am Jesus of Nazareth whom you are persecuting.' [9] Now those who were with me saw the light but did not hear the voice of the one who was speaking to me. ... [11] Since I could not see because of the brightness [*doxa*, glory] of that light, those who were with me took my hand and led me to Damascus. (Acts 22:6–9, 11)

> At midday along the road, your Excellency, I saw a light from heaven, brighter than the sun, shining around me and my companions. (Acts 26:13)

---

15. On this topic, see David B. Capes, *Old Testament Yahweh Texts in Paul's Christology*, 174–77.

In none of these accounts does Paul actually see Jesus. He hears Jesus, but all he sees is a bright, glorious light, brighter than the sun. (Matthew describes the transfigured Jesus this way: "his face shone like the sun; his clothes became as white as the light" [Matt 17:2].) Maybe we should say that Paul did see Jesus, who appeared as the glory of God. (See Luke's version of the Transfiguration: "they saw his glory" [Luke 9:32].)

In his letters, Paul sometimes connects Jesus with God's glory in a way that suggests he may have in mind the Old Testament depictions of God's glory that we have noticed. That is especially true in the sequel to the passage we looked at in the previous chapter about Moses' shining face.

> In their case the god of this world has blinded the minds of the unbelievers, to keep them from seeing the light of the gospel of the glory of Christ, who is the image of God. [5] For we do not proclaim ourselves; we proclaim Jesus Christ as Lord and ourselves as your slaves for Jesus' sake. [6] For it is the God who said, "Let light shine out of darkness," who has shone in our hearts to give the light of the knowledge of the glory of God in the face of Jesus Christ. (2 Cor 4:4–6)

But perhaps even more amazing than the glory of God becoming human and dwelling among us, God also allows us to participate in his glory.[16]

---

16. Compare the Eastern Orthodox doctrine of "theosis." Google will help you learn about it, and there is a good article on Wikipedia. Or see Timothy Ware, *The Orthodox Church: An Introduction to Eastern Christianity*, 3d ed. (London: Penguin, 2015), 225–31.

But our citizenship is in heaven, and it is from there that we are expecting a Savior, the Lord Jesus Christ. [21] He will transform the body of our humiliation that it may be conformed to the body of his glory, by the power that also enables him to make all things subject to himself. (Phil 3:20–21)

And all of us, with unveiled faces, seeing the glory of the Lord as though reflected in a mirror, are being transformed into the same image from one degree of glory to another; for this comes from the Lord, the Spirit. (2 Cor 3:18)

APPENDIX
QUESTIONS FOR REFLECTION

1. Moses Through the Lens of the New Testament

1. Stephen's speech in Acts 7 spends more time on Moses than on any other character (vv. 17–44). What point does Stephen want to make about Moses?

2. Read Exodus chs. 1–3 and compare it with Stephen's speech. What elements of Moses' life mentioned by Stephen are not directly mentioned in the text of Exodus?

3. What are the highlights of Moses' career that the author of Hebrews mentions (11:23–29)? What does he leave out?

4. What kind of person is Moses, according to Hebrews?

5. What similarities do you see between the portrait of Moses in Hebrews and in Stephen's speech?

2. God's Name

1. In the account of the burning bush (Exodus 3), God reveals his name to Moses. What is the name of God and what is its significance?

2. What does God reveal about his name in Exodus 6:2–8? Look at this passage in different translations.

3. What is unusual about the angel in Exodus 23:20–23?

4. What do you think Jesus is saying in John 8:58? Why do people want to stone him?

5. According to Philippians 2:9, what does God give to Jesus?

3. Pharaoh's Hard Heart

1. Read through the account of the Ten Plagues, especially Exodus 7–11. Who is responsible for Pharaoh's hard heart?

2. When the text says that God hardened Pharaoh's heart, what do you think it means?

3. What was the purpose for which God hardened Pharaoh's heart?

4. Paul quotes a verse about Pharaoh's hard heart at Romans 9:17. What point does Paul want to make from the example of Pharaoh?

5. Do you think that God's hardening Pharaoh's heart contradicts the idea that God "desires all men to be saved and to come to a knowledge of the truth" (1 Tim 2:4)?

4. Passover

1. Read Exodus 12. What were the Israelites commanded to eat on Passover? Why?

2. In Exodus 12–13, find all the times that the Israelites are supposed to explain the significance of the rituals to their children. What are they supposed to say to their children?

3. The instructions for Passover are also found in Deuteronomy 16:1–8. Do you notice any differences in this set of instructions from what you find in Exodus? See also Exodus 23:14–17; Leviticus 23:4–8.

4. Mark 14 makes clear that the Last Supper is a Passover meal. What is the significance of Jesus' holding this meal at Passover?

5. Read John's account of the Crucifixion (John 19:16–37). How does John make explicit the connection between Jesus and the Passover lamb? See also John 1:29.

5. Bread from Heaven

1. Why do you think that God will not allow the Israelites to store up manna for multiple days in Exodus 16?

2. Exodus 16 contains the first commandment in the Bible regarding the Sabbath day, which will later become the fourth of the Ten Commandments (Exod 20:8–11). Why do you think God wants Israel to observe the Sabbath already in Exodus 16?

3. In what way do the events of Exodus 16 make it clear that "it was the LORD who brought you out of the land of Egypt" (v. 6)? What does this expression mean?

4. Jesus preaches on manna in John 6:22–59. What point is he making?

5. How does Paul use the story of the giving of the manna to develop a principle for Christian giving? See 2 Corinthians 8:15 (cf. Exod 16:18).

6. Water from a Rock

1. Exodus 17:1–7 is the first "water from a rock" story in Scripture. Why do you think the Lord responds to the people's complaining in the way that he does? Why does he provide water in this way rather than, say, making it rain? What lesson does Psalm 95:8–9 draw from this episode?

2. The second "water from a rock" story is at Numbers 20:1–13. What differences do you see between these two stories?

3. Paul brings up the ancient Israelites when admonishing the Corinthians in 1 Corinthians 10:1–13. What point does Paul want the Corinthians to derive from these stories of the ancient Israelites?

4. What does Paul mean when he says that the "rock was Christ" (1 Cor 10:4)?

7. A Kingdom of Priests

1. When the people of Israel arrive at Sinai in Exodus 19, God describes them as his own possession, as a kingdom of priests, and as a holy nation. What implications do you think these terms have for Israel's role as God's people?

2. What does God mean by calling Israel a "kingdom of priests"? Later a particular group of Israelites are designated as "priests" (Exod 28:1), so in what sense is the whole nation a kingdom of priests?

3. Do you see a relationship between this passage from Exodus and God's promises to Abraham in Genesis 12:1–3? Is the "priestly" role of Israel related somehow to the idea that Abraham's descendants ("seed") would bring blessing to the nations?

4. When Peter references this passage from Exodus in 1 Peter 2:4–9, what point is the apostle trying to make? How does he want his readers to see themselves?

5. Does this concept of priesthood have any implications for the way Christians ought to behave? Does it have any consequences for how Christians relate to the world? Or to God?

8. The Law at Sinai

1. The Ten Commandments are listed twice in the Bible, in Exodus 20 and Deuteronomy 5. Do you notice any differences between these two lists?

2. God spoke the Ten Commandments directly to the people of Israel. What was the reaction of the people? (Exod 20:18–21)

3. The apostle Paul claimed that "love is the fulfillment of the law" (Rom 13:10). What did he mean by this statement?

4. What does Paul say is the purpose of the law in Galatians 3:19–26?

5. Do you think Paul's statement in 2 Timothy 3:16 applies to the law at Sinai? In what ways might the law still be valuable for Christians?

9. Blood of the Covenant

1. Moses comes down from the mountain in Exodus 24 and tells the people about all the laws he has just received from the LORD. What is the response of the people?

2. What are the elements of the ceremony that takes place in Exodus 24?

3. Why does Moses splatter blood on the people? For something similar, see Exodus 29:15–21.

4. What significance do you think it has that Jesus uses the language "blood of the covenant" while instituting the Lord's Supper (Mark 14:22–25)? Is he consciously invoking Exodus 24?

5. Can you think of other similarities between the life of Jesus and the life of Moses, perhaps things that Jesus does or says that are reminiscent of Moses?

10. God's Dwelling Place

1. Exodus 25–31 gives instructions for the Tabernacle and its furnishings, while chapters 35–40 narrate their construction. Summarize the instructions for what the curtains will look like (26:1–6). Do you think there's any reason behind this look for the curtains?

2. Several times God tells Moses to construct the Tabernacle according to the pattern (25:9, 40; 26:30; 27:8). What pattern is God talking about?

3. What is the point that the author of Hebrews wants to make about the Tabernacle in Hebrews 8:1–6?

4. What does John mean by speaking about Jesus' body as a temple (John 2:21)?

5. How does Paul use the image of God's dwelling place to give significance to the church? See, for example, Ephesians 2:21–22.

11. Ark of the Covenant

1. The instructions for the ark of the covenant are in Exodus 25:10–22. What is the relationship between the ark and the mercy seat?

2. Read Leviticus 16 on the Day of Atonement. What would the priest do to the mercy seat on the Day of Atonement?

3. Go to YouTube and search for "Indiana Jones Talk with Army Intel." How many things does Dr. Jones get wrong about the ark?

4. At Romans 3:25, Paul calls Jesus a "propitiation," but this word could also be translated "mercy seat" (it's the same word in Greek). Do you think that Paul had the mercy seat

in mind in this passage? What connections do you see between Jesus and the mercy seat?

5. What does John say about the ark in Revelation 11:19? What significance does this verse have?

12. Moses' Shining Face

1. Why do you think Moses' skin shone after being on the mountain (Exod 34:29–35)?

2. Why would Moses put a veil over his face?

3. See the picture of Michelangelo's statue of Moses on p. 258. Why does Moses have horns?

4. What significance does Paul get from this account of Moses' shining face (2 Cor 3:7–11)?

5. How does Moses' veil help Paul to explain the newness of Christ (2 Cor 3:12–18)?

13. The Divine Cloud

1. What do you think is the relationship between God and the cloud that leads the Israelites? Is God in the cloud? Is the cloud God? Is the cloud an aspect of God? See Exodus 13:21–22; 14:19–20, 24; 16:9–10; 33:7–11; etc.

2. What do you think is meant by the phrase "the glory of the Lord" in passages such as Exodus 16:7–10; 29:43; 33:18–22; 40:34–38. What relationship do you think the glory has to the cloud?

3. In the wake of the golden calf fiasco (Exod 32), God threatens not to accompany Israel on its journey. Read Exodus 32–33. What are the different ways that God talks about his presence?

4. What significance do you see in what the cloud does when the Tabernacle is set up (Exod 40:34–38)? See also 1 Kings 8:10–11 in the case of the Temple.

5. In John 1:1–18, do you see any echoes of this way of talking about God's presence?

GLOSSARY

Adonai. "Lord." This Hebrew word has long been used by many Jews as a substitute for God's name, because they do not want to pronounce YHWH.

Apocrypha. In biblical studies, this term often refers to the books present in the Bible of Roman Catholics or Greek Orthodox that are not present in the Bible of Protestants. These books include Tobit, Judith, the books of Maccabees (there are four total), Wisdom of Solomon, and Sirach (a.k.a. Ecclesiasticus, a.k.a. Wisdom of Ben Sira).

Codex Vaticanus. A fourth-century AD manuscript of the Greek Bible, i.e., the Septuagint and the New Testament. It is housed today in the Vatican Library.

Dead Sea Scrolls. These scrolls were discovered in the 1940s and 1950s in caves near a settlement called Qumran, on the northwest shore of the Dead Sea, about 20 miles east of Jerusalem.

Feast of Unleavened Bread. A spring festival that begins with Passover. See Exod 23:15; Lev 23:5–8; Deut 16:1–8.

Festival of Harvest. A summer feast day later known (in Greek) as Pentecost. Also known in the Bible as the Feast of Weeks. See Exod 23:16; Lev 23:15–21; Deut 16:9–12.

Hebrew Scripture. The Hebrew Bible. The Old Testament.

LXX. This is an abbreviation for Septuagint, the Greek translation of the Old Testament. The word "Septuagint" comes from the Latin *septuaginta*, "seventy," and refers to the legend of the translation of the Old Testament into Greek by seventy(-two) Jewish sages. The abbreviation LXX is the Roman numeral for seventy.

Masoretes. These medieval Jewish scribes often based in the Israeli town of Tiberias produced an edition of the Hebrew Bible that we call the Masoretic Text, which today forms the basis for most English translations of the Old Testament.

Mishnah. This rabbinic document is usually dated to around AD 200, though it contains some traditions going back long before that time, some perhaps from the time of Jesus or before. It is arranged as a group of sixty-three tractates. To find something in the Mishnah, you first have to open it to the right tractate, just like when you want to find something in the Bible you first have to open to the right book. Each tractate is divided into chapters and small paragraphs (called mishnahs, but you can also think of each paragraph as like a verse).

Pseudepigrapha. In biblical studies, this term refers to ancient Jewish literature that is usually not included in any Bible, as the Apocrypha are. Probably the most prominent pseudepigrapha are the books known as *1 Enoch* and *Jubilees* (both of these books are actually included in the Ethiopian Bible), but there are also many others.

Qumran community. This is the community responsible for the Dead Sea Scrolls.

Rabbinic Literature. The Jewish Rabbis produced literature in Hebrew and Aramaic starting in the second or third century AD. The earliest rabbinic literature is the Mishnah and Tosefta (see the glossary entries on those items), while the Talmud is from a few centuries later, perhaps the sixth century. Rabbinic Literature also includes the Targumim, Midrashim, and other works.

Second Temple Period. This is a period of Jewish history during which the second temple existed. King Solomon built the first temple, which was destroyed by Nebuchadnezzar in 586 BC at the beginning of the Babylonian exile of Judah. When Cyrus, king of the Persians, conquered Babylon (539 BC), he allowed the Jews to return to Judah (Ezra 1:1–4), and some Jews did return to Judah and rebuilt the temple in Jerusalem (cf. Ezra 6:13–15). This was the second temple, and it was reestablished in about 516 BC. Eventually the Romans destroyed this second temple in AD 70.

Septuagint. See LXX above.

Shekhinah. This Hebrew word meaning "dwelling" is used in rabbinic literature (not the Bible) to refer to the presence of God, as in the glory cloud by which God manifests his presence in the book of Exodus (cf. Exod 13:21).

Shema. This Hebrew word meaning "hear" is the traditional Jewish name for a series of biblical passages, the first of which is Deut 6:4–9, which begins: "Hear [*shema*], O Israel, YHWH your God is one YHWH." Jews traditionally recite the Shema every day, morning and evening.

Targum Onqelos. A Targum is an Aramaic translation of the Old Testament. There are several different targums (or targumim) for different parts of the Bible, and sometimes these targums are named after their reputed translator. Targum Onqelos is one of the more literal targums for the Pentateuch.

Tetragrammaton. This Greek term meaning "four-letter word" refers to the four-letter name of God, YHWH.

Torah. This Hebrew term meaning "instruction" or, sometimes, "law," is the traditional Jewish designation for the first five books of the Bible, the Torah of Moses (i.e., the Pentateuch).

Tosefta. This is an early rabbinic collection of material, a little later than the time of the Mishnah. It is arranged more-or-less in the same manner as the Mishnah.

Vulgate. This Latin translation of the Bible was (for the most part) produced by Jerome during the years AD 390–405.

YHWH. This is an English rendering of God's name as revealed to Moses at the burning bush (Exod 3:14). Hebrew has traditionally not been written with vowels, so that is why people often leave the vowels out of this word. See chapter two on "God's Name" for further explanation.

Yom Kippur. This is the Hebrew term translated "Day of Atonement," a day of fasting, rest, reflection, and atonement, observed in the autumn. See Lev 16; 23:26–32.

BIBLIOGRAPHY

Akiyama, Kengo. *The Love of Neighbor in Ancient Judaism: The Reception of Leviticus 19:18 in the Hebrew Bible, the Septuagint, the Book of Jubilees, the Dead Sea Scrolls, and the New Testament.* Leiden: Brill, 2018.

Albrektson, Bertil. "On the Syntax of אהיה אשר אהיה in Exodus 3:14." Pages 15–28 in *Words and Meanings: Essays Presented to David Winton Thomas.* Edited by Peter R. Ackroyd and Barnabas Lindars. Cambridge: Cambridge University Press, 1968.

Allison, Dale C. *The New Moses: A Matthean Typology.* Minneapolis: Fortress, 1993.

Anderson, Gary A. "The Impassibility of God: Moses, Jonah, and the Theo-Drama of Intercessory Prayer." Pages 23–38 in *Christian Doctrine and the Old Testament: Theology in the Service of Biblical Exegesis.* Grand Rapids: Baker, 2017.

Aquinas, Thomas. *Summa Theologica of Saint Thomas Aquinas.* 21 vols. New York: Benziger Brothers, 1912-25.

Attridge, Harold W. *Hebrews.* Hermeneia. Minneapolis: Fortress, 1993.

Augustine. *Confessions and Enchiridion.* The Library of Christian Classics 7. Edited and translated by Albert C. Outler. Philadelphia: Westminster Press, 1955.

———. "On the Predestination of the Saints." Pages 218–70 in *Saint Augustine: Four Anti-Pelagian Writings*. Fathers of the Church 86. Washington, DC: Catholic University of America Press, 1992.

———. *On Rebuke and Grace*. In vol. 5 of The *Nicene and Post-Nicene Fathers*, Series 1. 14 vols. Edited by Philip Schaff. Buffalo, NY: Christian Literature Publishing Co., 1886–1889.

Averbeck, Richard E. "Tabernacle." Pages 807–27 in *Dictionary of the Old Testament: Pentateuch*. Edited by T. Desmond Alexander and David W. Baker. Downers Grove, IL: InterVarsity, 2003.

The Babylonian Talmud. 30 vols. Edited by Isidore Epstein. New York: Traditional Press, 1979.

Bauckham, Richard. *Jesus and the God of Israel: God Crucified and Other Studies on the New Testament Christology of Divine Identity*. Grand Rapids: Eerdmans, 2008.

———. *The Testimony of the Beloved Disciple: Narrative, History and Theology in the Gospel of John*. Grand Rapids: Baker, 2007

Beale, G. K. *The Temple and the Church's Mission: A Biblical Theology of the Dwelling Place of God*. New Studies in Biblical Theology 17. Downers Grove, IL: InterVarsity, 2004.

Beale, G. K. and Mitchell Kim. *God Dwells among Us: Expanding Eden to the Ends of the Earth*. Downers Grove, IL: InterVarsity, 2014.

Bird, Michael F. *Evangelical Theology: A Biblical and Systematic Introduction*. Grand Rapids: Zondervan, 2013.

Blackburn, W. Ross. *The God Who Makes Himself Known: The Missionary Heart of the Book of Exodus*. New Studies in Biblical Theology 28. Downers Grove, IL: InterVarsity, 2012.

Botterweck, G. J., H. Ringgren, and H.-J. Fabry, eds. *Theological Dictionary of the Old Testament*. Translated by John T. Willis. 15 vols. Grand Rapids: Eerdmans, 1977–2012.

Braulik, Georg. "The Sequence of the Laws in Deuteronomy 12–26 and the Decalogue." Pages 313–35 in *A Song of Power and the Power of Song: Essays in the Book of Deuteronomy*. Sources for

Biblical and Theological Study Old Testament Series 2. Edited by Duane L. Christensen. Winona Lake, IN: Eisenbrauns, 1993.

Bruggeman, Walter. "The Book of Exodus: Introduction, Commentary, and Reflections." Pages 677–981 in *General articles on the Bible, General articles on the Old Testament, Genesis, Exodus, Leviticus.* Vol. 1 of *New Interpreter's Bible.* Edited by Leander E. Keck. Nashville: Abingdon, 1994.

Bucur, Bogdan Gabriel. *Scripture Re-envisioned: Christophanic Exegesis and the Making of a Christian Bible.* Bible in Ancient Christianity 13. Leiden: Brill, 2019.

Calvin, John. *Institutes of the Christian Religion.* Philadelphia: Presbyterian Board of Christian Education, 1936.

Campbell, Alexander. "Sermon on the Law." *Millennial Harbinger* 3.9 (1846): 492–521.

Capes, David B. *Old Testament Yahweh Texts in Paul's Christology.* Tübingen: Mohr, 1992; repr., Waco, TX: Baylor University Press, 2017.

Carasik, Michael. *The Commentators' Bible: The JPS Miqra'ot Gedolot, Exodus.* Philadelphia: Jewish Publication Society, 2005.

Childs, Brevard S. *The Book of Exodus: A Critical, Theological Commentary.* Philadelphia: Westminster, 1974.

Clement of Alexandria. *Stromateis: Books One to Three.* The Fathers of the Church 85. Translated by John Ferguson. Washington, DC: Catholic University of America Press, 1991.

Cohen, Shaye J. D. "Was Timothy Jewish (Acts 16:1–3)? Patristic Exegesis, Rabbinic Law, and Matrilineal Descent." *Journal of Biblical Literature* 105 (1986): 251–68.

Crossley, James G. *The New Testament and Jewish Law: A Guide for the Perplexed.* T & T Clark's Guides for the Perplexed. London: T&T Clark, 2010.

Davies, John A. *A Royal Priesthood: Literary and Intertextual Perspectives on an Image of Israel in Exodus 19.6.* The Library of Hebrew Bible/Old Testament Studies 395. London: T&T Clark, 2004.

Day, John. "Whatever Happened to the Ark of the Covenant?" Pages 250–70 in *Temple and Worship in Biblical Israel: Proceedings of the Oxford Old Testament Seminar.* Library of Hebrew Bible/Old Testament Studies 422. Edited by John Day. New York: T&T Clark, 2007.

Dennis, J. "Death of Jesus." Pages 172–93 in *Dictionary of the Jesus and the Gospels.* 2nd ed. Edited by Joel B. Green. Downers Grove, IL: InterVarsity, 2013.

Dickson, John. "Mission-Commitment in Second Temple Judaism and the New Testament." Pages 255–63 in *Introduction to Messianic Judaism: Its Ecclesial Context and Biblical Foundations.* Edited by David Rudolph and Joel Willits. Grand Rapids: Zondervan, 2013.

Diodorus Siculus. *Library of History.* Translated by C. H. Oldfather. 11 vols. Loeb Classical Library. Cambridge: Harvard University Press, 1926–1965.

Dodd, C.H. *According to the Scriptures: The Substructure of New Testament Theology.* New York: Scribner, 1953.

Durham, John I. *Exodus.* Word Biblical Commentary 3. Waco, TX: Word, 1987.

Enns, P. "Exodus Route and Wilderness Itinerary." Pages 272–80 in *Dictionary of the Old Testament: Pentateuch.* Edited by T. Desmond Alexander and David W. Baker. Downers Grove, IL: InterVarsity, 2003.

Erasmus, Desiderius and Martin Luther. *Erasmus-Luther: Discourse on Free Will.* Translated by Ernst F. Winter. New York: Ungar, 1961.

Feldman, Louis H. *Flavius Joseph: Judean Antiquities 1–4.* Leiden: Brill, 2000.

———. *Josesphus' Interpretation of the Bible.* Berkeley: University of California Press, 1998.

———. *Philo's Portrayal of Moses in the Context of Ancient Judaism.* Notre Dame, IN: University of Notre Dame Press, 2007.

Feldmeier, Reinhard and Hermann Spieckermann. *God of the Living: A Biblical Theology.* Waco, TX: Baylor University Press, 2011.

Ferguson, Everett. "Alexander Campbell's 'Sermon on the Law': A Historical and Theological Examination." *Restoration Quarterly* 29 (1987): 71–85.

Fretheim, Terence E. "'Because the Whole Earth is Mine': Theme and Narrative in Exodus." *Interpretation* 50 (1996): 229–39.

———. "Exodus, Book of." Pages 249–58 in *Dictionary of the Old Testament: Pentateuch.* Edited by T. Desmond Alexander and David W. Baker. Downers Grove, IL: InterVarsity, 2003.

———. "The Reclamation of Creation: Redemption and Law in Exodus." *Interpretation* 45 (1991) 354–65.

Friedman, Richard Elliott. *The Exodus: How It Happened and Why It Matters.* New York: HarperOne, 2017.

———. "Tabernacle." Pages 292–300 in vol. 6 of *Anchor Bible Dictionary.* 6 vols. Edited by David Noel Freedman. New York: Doubleday, 1992.

———. "The Tabernacle in the Temple." *Biblical Archaeologist* 43 (1980): 241–48.

———. *Who Wrote the Bible?* New York: Simon and Schuster, 1987.

Gager, John G. *Moses in Greco-Roman Paganism.* Nashville: Abingdon, 1972.

Geller, Stephen A. "Manna and Sabbath: A Literary-Theological Reading of Exodus 16." *Interpretation* 59 (2005): 5–16.

Gesenius, Friedrich W. *Gesenius' Hebrew Grammar.* Oxford: Oxford University Press, 1910.

Goldstein, Jonathan A. *2 Maccabees: A New Translation with Introduction and Commentary.* Anchor Bible 41A. New York: Doubleday, 1983.

Greenwood, Kyle R. "Old Testament Reverberations of Genesis 1–2." Pages 1–22 in *Since the Beginning: Interpreting Genesis 1 and 2 through the Ages.* Edited by Kyle R. Greenwood. Grand Rapids: Baker, 2018.

Grossfeld, Bernard, translator. *The Targum Onqelos to Leviticus and The Targum Onqelos to Numbers.* Aramaic Bible 8. Wilmington, DE: Michael Glazier, 1988.

Haran, Menahem. *Temples and Temple Service in Ancient Israel.* Oxford: Oxford University Press, 1978.

———. "The Shining of Moses' Face: A Case Study in Biblical and Ancient Near Eastern Iconography." Pages 159–73 in *In the Shelter of Elyon: Essays on Ancient Palestinian Life and Literature in Honor of G. W. Ahlström.* Journal for the Study of the Old Testament Supplement 31. Edited by W. Boyd Barrick and John R. Spencer. Sheffield: JSOT Press, 1984.

Hartley, John E. "Holy and Holiness, Clean and Unclean." Pages 420–31 in *Dictionary of the Old Testament: Pentateuch.* Edited by T. Desmond Alexander and David W. Baker. Downers Grove, IL: InterVarsity, 2003.

Hays, Christopher B. *Hidden Riches: A Sourcebook for the Comparative Study of the Hebrew Bible and Ancient Near East.* Louisville: Westminster John Knox, 2014.

Hays, Richard B. "A Letter from Christ." Pages 122–53 in *Echoes of Scripture in the Gospels.* Waco, TX: Baylor University Press, 2016.

———. *Echoes of Scripture in the Gospels.* Waco, TX: Baylor University Press, 2016.

———. *The Conversion of the Imagination: Paul as Interpreter of Israel's Scripture.* Grand Rapids: Eerdmans, 2005.

Heine, Ronald E. *Reading the Old Testament with the Ancient Church: Exploring the Formation of Early Christian Thought.* Grand Rapids: Baker, 2007.

Heiser, Michael S. *The Unseen Realm: Recovering the Spiritual Worldview of the Bible.* Bellingham, WA: Lexham, 2015.

Hoehner, H. W. and J. K. Brown. "Chronology." Pages 134–38 in *Dictionary of Jesus and the Gospels.* 2nd ed. Edited by Joel S. Green. Downers Grove, IL: InterVarsity, 2013.

Hoffmeier, James K. *Ancient Israel in Sinai: The Evidence for the Authenticity of the Wilderness Tradition.* Oxford: Oxford University Press, 2005.

Holladay, Carl R. *Historians.* Vol. 1 of *Fragments from Hellenistic Jewish Authors.* Chico, CA: Scholars Press, 1983.

Hong, Koog P. "The Euphemism for the Ineffable Name of God and Its Early Evidence in Chronicles." *Journal for the Study of the Old Testament* 37 (2013): 473–84.

Hultgren, Stephen. "Hilastērion (Rom. 3:25) and the Union of Divine Justice and Mercy. Part I: The Convergence of Temple and Martyrdom Theologies." *Journal of Theological Studies* 70 (2019): 69–101.

Hurowitz, Victor Avigdor. "The Form and Fate of the Tabernacle: Reflections on a Recent Proposal." *Jewish Quarterly Review* 86 (1995): 127–51.

Hurtado, Larry W. *God in New Testament Theology.* Library of Biblical Theology. Nashville: Abingdon, 2010.

Irenaeus. *Proof of the Apostolic Preaching.* Ancient Christian Writers 16. New York: Paulist Press 1952.

Isaac, E. "1 Enoch." Pages 5–89 in vol. 1 of *The Old Testament Pseudepigrapha.* 2 vols. Edited by James H. Charlesworth. Garden City, NY: Doubleday, 1983–1985.

Jacobson, Howard, trans. "Pseudo-Philo, Book of Biblical Antiquities." Pages 470–613 in vol. 1 of *Outside the Bible: Ancient Jewish Writings Related to Scriptures.* 3 vols. Edited by Louis H. Feldman, James L. Kugel, and Lawrence H. Schiffman. Philadelphia: Jewish Publication Society, 2013.

Jerome. *Commentaries on the Twelve Prophets.* 2 vols. Edited by Thomas P. Scheck. Ancient Christian Texts. Downers Grove, IL: InterVarsity, 2016–2017.

———. *St. Jerome: Commentary on Ezekiel.* Translated by Thomas P. Scheck. Ancient Christian Writers 71. New York: Newman, 2017.

———. *Homilies of Saint Jerome.* Fathers of the Church 48 and 57. Edited by Ludwig Schopp. Washington, DC: Catholic University of America Press, 1964.

Johansson, Daniel "*Kyrios* in the Gospel of Mark." *Journal for the Study of The New Testament* 33 (2010): 101–24.

Josephus. Translated by Henry St. J. Thackerary et al. 10 vols. Loeb Classical Library. Cambridge: Harvard University Press, 1926–1965.

Justin. *Saint Justin Martyr: The First Apology, the Second Apology, Dialogue with Trypho, Exhortation to the Greeks, Discourse to the Greeks, the Monarchy, or the Rule of God.* Fathers of the Church 6. Translated by Thomas B. Fall. New York: Christian Heritage: 1948.

Klijn, A. F. J. "2 Baruch." Pages 615–52 in vol. 1 of *The Old Testament Pseudepigrapha.* 2 vols. Edited by James H. Charlesworth. Garden City, NY: Doubleday, 1983–1985.

Kugel, James L. *How to Read the Bible: A Guide to Scripture, Then and Now.* New York: Free Press, 2007.

———. *The Bible as It Was.* Cambridge, MA: Harvard University Press, 1997.

Land, Christopher D. "It's Not Like Moses Veiled So that the Israelites Didn't Stare: A Hypothesis Regarding Paul's Understanding of Exodus 34." Pages 263–302 in *Paul and Scripture.* Edited by Stanley E. Porter and Christopher D. Land. Leiden: Brill, 2019.

Lee, Chee-Chiew. "Once Again: The Niphal and the Hithpael in the Abrahamic Blessing for the Nations." *Journal for the Study of the Old Testament* 36 (2102): 279–96.

Levering, Matthew. *Predestination: Biblical and Theological Paths.* Oxford: Oxford University Press, 2012.

Lewis, C. S. *Mere Christianity.* New York: Macmillan, 1943.

Longman, Tremper. *How to Read Exodus.* Downers Grove, IL: InterVarsity, 2009.

Luther, Martin. *Lectures on Hebrews.* Translated by Walter A. Hansen. Luther's Works 29. Saint Louis: Concordia, 1968.

Manguno, John M., Jr. "Accident or Acronymy: The Tetragrammonaton in the Masoretic Text of Esther." *Bibliotheca Sacra.* 171 (2014): 440–51.

Melito. "On Pascha, 67–68." *Melito of Sardis: On Pascha and Fragments.* Translated by Stuart G. Hall. Oxford: Oxford University Press, 1979.

Mellinkoff, Ruth. *The Horned Moses in Medieval Art and Thought.* California Studies in the History of Art, 14. Berkeley: University of California Press, 1970.

Milgrom, *Leviticus 1–16.* Anchor Bible 3. New York: Doubleday, 1991.

Mishnah, tractate *Pesahim* 10.3. *The Mishnah.* Translated by Herbert Danby. Oxford: Oxford University Press, 1933.

Moberly, R. W. L. *At the Mountain of God: Story and Theology in Exodus 32–34.* Journal for the Study of the Old Testament Supplement 22. Sheffield: JSOT Press, 1983.

———. *Old Testament Theology: Reading the Hebrew Bible as Christian Scripture.* Grand Rapids: Baker, 2013.

———. *The Old Testament of the Old Testament: Patriarchal Narratives and Mosaic Yahwism.* Minneapolis: Fortress, 1992.

———. *The Theology of the Book of Genesis.* Old Testament Theology. Cambridge: Cambridge University Press, 2009.

Moore, Carey A. *Tobit: A New Translation with Introduction and Commentary.* Anchor Bible 40A. New York: Doubleday, 1996.

Nicholson, Ernest W. *God and His People: Covenant and Theology in the Old Testament.* Oxford: Oxford University Press, 1986.

Noegel, Scott B. "The Egyptian Origin of the Ark of the Covenant." Pages 223–42 in *Israel's Exodus in Transdisciplinary Perspective: Text, Archaeology, Culture, and Geoscience.* New York: Springer, 2015.

Olson, Roger E. *Against Calvinism.* Grand Rapids: Zondervan, 2011.

Origen. *Origen: On First Principles.* Edited and translated by John Behr. Oxford: Oxford University Press, 2017.

Pearce, Sarah Judith. "On the Decalogue." Pages 989–1032 in vol. 1 of *Outside the Bible: Ancient Jewish Writings Related to Scriptures.* 3 vols. Edited by Louis H. Feldman, James L. Kugel and Lawrence H. Schiffman. Philadelphia: Jewish Publication Society, 2013.

Perrin, N. "Last Supper." Pages 492–501 in *Dictionary of Jesus and the Gospels.* 2nd ed. Edited by Joel S. Green. Downers Grove, IL: InterVarsity, 2013.

Philo. Translated by F. H. Colson and G. H. Whitaker. 12 vols. Loeb Classical Library. Cambridge: Harvard University Press, 1926–1965.

Pitre, Brant. *Jesus and the Last Supper.* Grand Rapids: Eerdmans. 2015.

Porten, Bezalel. *The Elephantine Papyri in English: Three Millennia of Cross-Cultural Continuity and Change.* Leiden: Brill, 1996.

Propp, William H. C. *Exodus 1-18.* Anchor Bible 2. New York: Doubleday, 1998.

———. *Exodus 19-40.* Anchor Bible 2A. New York: Doubleday, 2006.

Pseudo-Philo. *Liber Antiquitatum Biblicarum.* Pages 297–377 in vol. 2 of *The Old Testament Pseudepigrapha.* 2 vols. Edited by James H. Charlesworth. Translated by D. J. Harrington. Garden City, NY: Doubleday, 1983–1985.

Rosel, Martin. "The Reading and Translation of the Divine Name in the Masoretic Tradition and the Greek Pentateuch." *Journal for the Study of the Old Testament* 31 (2007): 411–28.

Rosenblum, Jordan. "Blessings of the Breasts: Breastfeeding in Rabbinic Literature." *Hebrew Union College Annual* 87 (2016): 145–77.

Rosner, Brian S. *Paul and the Law: Keeping the Commandments of God.* Downers Grove, IL: InterVarsity, 2013.

Roth, Ann Macy. "Work Force." Pages 519–24 in vol. 3 of *The Oxford Encyclopedia of Ancient Egypt.* 3 vols. Edited by Donald B. Redford. New York: Oxford University Press, 2001.

Rowe, C. Kavin. *Early Narrative Christology: The Lord in the Gospel of Luke.* Berlin: de Gruyter, 2006.

Royse, James R. "Philo, ΚΥΡΙΟΣ, and the Tetragrammaton." *Studia Philonica Annual* 3 (1991): 167–83.

"The Rule of the Community (1QS) 9.10–11." *The Dead Sea Scrolls: A New Translation.* Rev. ed. Translated by Michael Wise, Martin Abegg, Jr., and Edward Cook. San Francisco: HarperSanFrancisco, 2005.

Rüpke, Jörg. "Week." Columns 612–14 in vol. 15 of *Brill's New Pauly*. Edited by Hubert Cancik and Helmuth Schneider. Leiden: Brill, 2010.

Schuller, Eileen et al. *Qumran Cave 4. XXVIII: Miscellanea, Part 2*. Discoveries in the Judaean Desert 28. Oxford: Clarendon, 2001.

Shaw, Frank. *The Earliest Non-Mystical Jewish Use of Iaw*. Contributions to Biblical Exegesis and Theology 70. Leuven: Peeters, 2014.

Skehan, Patrick W. "The Divine Name at Qumran, in the Masada Scroll, and the Septuagint." *Bulletin of the International Organization for Septuagint and Cognate Studies* 13 (1980): 14–44.

Sommer. Benjamin D. *The Bodies of God and the World of Ancient Israel*. Cambridge: Cambridge University Press, 2009.

Stewart, Stanley. "In Search of the Real Queen of Sheba." *National Geographic* 234.6 (2018).

Stith, D. Matthew. "Red Sea, Reed Sea." Pages 750–51 in vol. 4 of *The New Interpreter's Dictionary of the Bible*. 5 vols. Edited by Katharine Doob Sakenfeld. Nashville: Abingdon, 2007.

Tacitus. *The Histories*. Translated by Clifford H. Moore. 2 vols. Loeb Classical Library. Cambridge, MA: Harvard University Press, 1925–1931.

"Targum Pseudo-Jonathan." Translated in *Targum Neofiti 1: Exodus and Targum Pseudo-Jonathan: Exodus*. Translated by Martin McNamara and Michael Maher. Aramaic Bible 2. Collegeville, MN: Liturgical Press, 1994.

Testament of Levi. Translated by James L. Kugel. Page 1742 in vol. 2 of *Outside the Bible: Ancient Jewish Writings Related to Scriptures*. 3 vols. Edited by Louis H. Feldman, James L. Kugel and Lawrence H. Schiffman. Philadelphia: Jewish Publication Society, 2013.

Theodoret of Cyrus. *The Questions on the Octateuch*, vol. 1: *On Genesis and Exodus*. Translated by Robert C. Hill. Library of Early Christianity. Washington, DC: Catholic University of America Press, 2007.

Thompson, James W. *Moral Formation According to Paul: The Context and Coherence of Pauline Ethics*. Grand Rapids: Baker, 2011.

"Tosefta Sukka 3.11." *The Tosefta: Translated from the Hebrew with a New Introduction*. Translated by Jacob Neusner. 2 vols. Peabody, MA: Hendrickson, 2002.

Vail, William H. "The Five Points of Calvinism Historically Considered." *The Outlook* 104 (1913): 394–95.

The Voice Bible. Nashville: Thomas Nelson, 2012.

Waal, Willemijn. "The Greek Alphabet: Older Than You May Think?" *The Ancient Near East Today* 7.3 (March 2018).

Wagner, Andreas. *God's Body: The Anthropomorphic God in the Old Testament*. London: T&T Clark, 2019.

Ware, Timothy. *The Orthodox Church: An Introduction to Eastern Christianity*. 3rd ed. London: Penguin, 2015.

Warren, Tish Harrison. *Liturgy of the Ordinary: Sacred Practices in Everyday Life*. Downers Grove, IL: InterVarsity, 2016.

Waterfield, Robin. *The First Philosophers: Presocratics and Sophists*. Oxford World's Classics. Oxford: Oxford University Press, 2000.

Williamson, Paul R. "Covenant." Pages 139–55 in *Dictionary of the Old Testament: Pentateuch*. Edited by T. Desmond Alexander and David W. Baker. Downers Grove, IL: InterVarsity, 2003.

Wintermute, O.S. *Jubilees*. Pages 35–142 in vol. 2 of *The Old Testament Pseudepigrapha*. 2 vols. Edited by James H. Charlesworth. Garden City, NY: Doubleday, 1983–1985.

Winton, David. *Wisdom of Solomon: A New Translation with Introduction and Commentary*. Anchor Bible 43. Garden City, NY: Doubleday, 1979.

Wright, Christopher J. H. *Old Testament Ethics for the People of God*. Downers Grove, IL: InterVarsity, 2006.

———. *The Mission of God: Unlocking the Bible's Grand Narrative*. Downers Grove, IL: InterVarsity, 2006.

Wright, N.T. *Jesus and the Victory of God*. Christian Origins and the Question of God 2. Minneapolis: Fortress, 1996.

———. *Paul and the Faithfulness of God.* 2 vols. Christian Origins and the Question of God 4. Minneapolis: Fortress, 2013.

———. "Reflected Glory: 2 Corinthians 3." Pages 175–92 in *The Climax of Covenant: Christ and the Law in Pauline Theology.* London: T&T Clark, 1991.

———. "Romans 2.17–3.9: A Hidden Clue to the Meaning of Romans?" Pages 489–509 in *Pauline Perspectives: Essays on Paul, 1978–2013.* Minneapolis: Fortress, 2013.

———. *The New Testament and the People of God.* Christian Origins and the Question of God 1. Minneapolis: Fortress, 1992.

Yoo, Philip Y. "Once Again: The Yam Sûp of the Exodus." *Journal of Biblical Literature* 137 (2018): 581–97.

SUBJECT INDEX

Aaron 55, 60–61, 65, 88–89, 129–130, 154, 159, 198, 201, 204, 207, 215, 221, 223, 241–242, 259, 263, 281, 283, 285, 290–291
Abihu 198, 285
Abraham xvi, 4, 6, 12, 26–27, 29–31, 47, 89, 140, 150–153, 155–156, 175, 200, 202–203, 278, 286, 305, 322
Adam 74, 186, 191, 225, 278
Adams, John 3
Adonai xv, 36–41, 44, 288, 297, 311
Agrippa, King 298
Aleppo Codex 34–36
America 3–4, 23, 50, 79, 108, 122, 181–182, 193, 249, 277
American Restoration Mvt. 193
Amorite(s) 66, 286
Amram 7
Angel(s) 19–20, 23, 26, 48, 103, 200, 238, 260, 281–282, 284–286, 302
Aquila 265–266
Aquinas, Thomas xiii, 190, 315

Ark of the Covenant 166, 217, 294, 308, 317, 323
Arminius, Jacob 72–73
Atonement 74, 99, 173, 183, 210, 229, 233–235, 244–248, 255, 293, 308, 314
Augustine 52, 76, 79, 315–316
Axum 250
Baal (Canaanite god) 23, 29, 278
Baale-judah 226, 239
Babylonian(s) 29, 113, 248–249, 252, 254, 291, 294, 312, 316
Balaam 147
Bale, Christian 9, 25
Beth-shemesh 226
Beth Yeshimon 133
Bezalel 216, 218, 234
Blood of the Covenant 195, 197, 200, 202, 206, 209, 211–212, 307
Book of the Covenant 167–169, 172–174, 184, 198–199, 202
Burning bush 18, 24–25, 53–54, 262, 280, 302, 313
Calvin, John xiii, 51, 72–73, 75, 78–79, 190, 317

Calvinism xvii, 52, 59, 70–77, 79–81, 323, 326
Campbell, Alexander 193, 317–318
Canaan, 66, 112, 128, 165, 175, 243, 291
Canaanites 23, 66, 172, 185, 202, 286
Ceremonial law 189–191
Cheevy, Miniver 108
Cherubim 221, 224, 233, 236–241, 244–245, 247–248
Church of Our Lady Mary of Zion 250
Circumcision 15, 19, 158, 162, 179, 181–184, 189
Creation 71, 113, 141, 149, 154, 165, 213, 224, 278, 295, 319
Crucifixion 85, 96–98, 100, 136, 210–211, 303, 316
Curtain(s) 216, 220–221, 224, 237, 240, 246–248, 250, 307
Damascus 298
David 36, 201, 207, 226, 239, 243, 250, 258
Day of Atonement 99, 233, 235, 245, 247–248, 255, 293, 308, 314
Dead Sea 16, 311
Dead Sea Scrolls 16, 33, 39, 41–43, 207, 311–312, 315, 324
Diodorus Siculus 39
Dwelling x, 15, 146, 219, 231, 239, 253, 292, 295, 299, 307–308, 313, 316
Easter 95, 98
Eden (Garden of) 213, 225
Edom 24, 128

Election 52, 59, 69, 72, 74, 76, 78, 80–81
Elephantine 39, 323
Eli 239, 245
Elijah 5, 21, 109, 208
Elim 106
Epimenides 29
Epistle of Barnabas 189
Esau 107
Etham 92
Ethiopia(n) 13, 250
Evangelism 79–80, 155
Exodus: Gods and Kings (2014) 9
Ezekiel 15–16, 230, 236, 248, 254, 266–267, 291–292, 321
Feast of Unleavened Bread 83, 95, 311
Firstborn 12, 62, 71, 86–87, 89, 143, 171
Founding Father(s) 3, 4, 21
Free will 52, 58, 75–77, 318
Gibeon 201, 226
Gideon 26
Gnaeus Pompey 249
Golden calf xi, 19, 217, 260–261, 269, 310
Gospels 5, 15, 47, 80, 96, 100–101, 117, 141, 192, 214, 229, 259, 295–296, 299, 316, 318, 320–321, 323–324
Hamilton, Alexander 3, 51
Heaven 15, 21, 45, 71, 103, 109–110, 112, 118–119, 146–147, 150, 164, 175, 214, 224, 227–229, 232, 239–240, 254, 278, 292, 298, 300, 304
Hell 59, 79

Holy of Holies 99, 220–223, 225–227, 229, 240, 242, 244, 247, 249, 252, 293
Holy Spirit 19, 78, 231, 294
Hophni 239, 245
Horeb 24–25, 126–128, 164, 241, 283
Hur 220
Idol(s) 19, 140, 147, 164, 168–169, 171, 173, 244, 260, 291
Impurity 16, 26, 173, 196, 230, 248
Indiana Jones 237, 242, 249, 251, 308
Irenaeus of Lyon 18, 189, 321
Isaac 27, 30, 140, 151, 155, 175, 201–202, 286
Isaiah ix, 16, 26, 33, 40, 47, 69, 145, 148, 211, 296–297
Isaiah Scroll 33
Jacob 27, 30, 69, 90, 140, 142, 145, 151, 155, 175–176, 201–202, 279, 286
James, LeBron 50
Jefferson, Thomas 3–4
Jehovah 24, 32, 37–38, 119
Jeremiah 14, 16, 26, 91, 252–253, 271
Jeroboam 261
Jerome 38–39, 265–267, 313, 321
Jerusalem 13, 83–84, 96–97, 145–146, 183, 208, 225, 248, 250–254, 298, 311–312
Jethro 18, 25, 198
Jochebed 7–8, 11, 92
John 96, 100, 117–118, 208, 229, 232, 254, 295–297, 303, 308–309, 316

Jonah 92, 147, 260, 315
Jordan 90, 175, 245
Josiah 252
Joseph 53, 152–153, 235
Josephus xiii, 7–9, 223–224, 235, 249–250, 321
Joshua 46, 198, 201, 215, 268, 286
Judah 90, 146, 207, 249, 251, 312
Judaism 35, 40, 116, 159, 166, 177, 187, 315, 318
Judicial law 189–191
Julius II, Pope 257
Justin Martyr 18, 26, 48, 189, 321
Kadesh-barnea 128–131
Kiriath-jearim 226
Kurios 41–45, 47–48
Lamb 83–84, 88, 90, 96, 98, 100–102, 211, 232, 303
Last Supper 96, 101, 116–117, 207, 209, 211, 303, 323
Latin Vulgate 235, 266–267
Law 258, 261, 270, 272, 274, 275, 306, 313, 317–319, 324, 326
Leaven 95, 98–99
Levites 155, 208, 227
Leviticus 25, 39–40, 42, 44, 165, 184, 186, 199, 219, 303, 308, 315, 317, 319, 322
Lewis, C. S. (Clive Staples) 104, 322
Lord's Supper 102, 307
Luther, Martin 52, 222, 236, 318, 322
LXX 41–44, 234–236, 311–312
Madison, James 3–4

Manna 5, 103, 106, 110–112, 114–119, 134, 136, 163, 221, 241–242, 283, 304, 319
Marah 105, 125
Marcion 189
Masoretes 34–37, 312
Massah 128, 283, 303
Melchizedek 229
Melito of Sardis 98–99, 322
Menorah 220, 223, 225
Mercy Seat 221–222, 233–237, 240–241, 244, 246–247, 254–255, 294, 308–309
Meribah 128, 130
Messiah 69, 207–208
Michelangelo 257–258, 268, 277–278, 309
Midian 12, 18, 24
Mikan, George 59
Miranda, Lin-Manuel 51
Mishnah 41, 84, 222, 312–313, 322
Moab 133, 156, 165
Moral law 190–191
Mosaic Law 161–162, 189, 193
Mount Seir 129
Mount Gerizim 250
Mount Sinai (Gebel Musa) 20, 24–25, 92, 113, 123–124, 128, 142, 153, 163, 215, 259, 262, 267, 280, 284
Nadab 198, 285
Nebat 261
Nile 7, 93, 234
Nineveh 147
Noah 12, 150, 234–235, 254
Oholiab 216, 218

Passover 12, 15, 83–85, 95–102, 163, 303, 311
Pattern 227–228, 308
Paul, the Apostle xvi, 6, 21, 29, 45–47, 51–52, 68–71, 79, 82, 98–100, 117, 134–137, 152, 157–158, 162, 179, 181–188, 190, 209, 255, 259, 269–272, 274, 298–299, 303–306, 308–309, 317, 320, 322, 324–327
Persians 249, 312
Peter, the Apostle 19, 77, 141, 159, 208, 257, 306
Philistines 226, 243, 245
Philo xiii, 7–11, 17, 44, 62–63, 94, 115, 133–134, 155, 157, 166, 222–223, 242, 321, 323–324
Phinehas 239, 245
Phoenician(s) 32–33
Pi-hahiroth 92
Plague(s) 53, 55–57, 60–65, 78, 81, 85–89, 94–95, 109, 149, 285, 302
Predestination 52, 69–71, 75–76, 80, 316, 322
Presence of God 201, 211, 214, 225, 228–229, 233, 244, 247, 279, 293–294, 313
Prince of Egypt (1998) 9
Promised Land 48, 95, 130, 225, 243, 260
Propitiation 235, 255, 308
Providence 82, 105, 111
Pseudo-Philo 62–63, 133, 321, 324
Quail 103, 109–110

SUBJECT INDEX / 333

Qumran 16, 43, 206–207, 311–312, 324–325
Rahab 12, 60, 137
Raiders of the Lost Ark (1981) 237, 243, 249, 251
Rashi 264, 266
Red Sea 6, 12, 65, 92–93, 105–106, 124, 325
Reed Sea 92–93, 325
Rehoboam 251
Rephidim 123–125, 127, 129–131
Reuel (See Jethro)
Righteous One 19–20
Rock 90, 105, 124, 126–127, 129–137, 283, 288, 304–305
Roman 6, 69, 113, 158, 249, 266, 312, 319
Sabbath 15, 110–116, 163, 165, 171, 184, 189, 202, 218, 304, 319
Samaritans 13, 38–39, 250
Sampras, Pete 59
Samuel 225
San Pietro in Vincoli 257
Sanhedrin 14, 20, 41, 96
Second Temple 35, 159, 187, 249, 294–295, 312, 318
Septuagint (See LXX) xiv, 7, 29, 40–43, 92, 152, 187, 235, 255
Shekhinah (See Dwelling) 294–295, 313
Shiloh 225–226, 239, 245
Shine(ing) 157, 257, 259, 263–266, 269, 272, 282, 298–299, 309, 319
Shishak/Shoshenq 251
Sihon 66

Sirach 40
Sistine Chapel 277
Slavery 3, 31, 85, 89, 98–99, 106–107, 139, 162, 187, 203
Solomon 15–16, 63, 65, 116, 124, 146, 236, 240–241, 250–253, 294, 312, 326
St. Peter's Basilica 257
Stephen 6–7, 13–20, 208, 210, 261, 301
Succoth 92
Synagogue of the Freedmen 13
Tabernacle x, 83, 112, 167, 197, 201, 204, 214–229, 231, 233–234, 237–238, 240, 247, 255, 288–290, 292–294, 307–308, 310, 316, 319, 321
Tacitus 249–250, 325
Temple 13–16, 19, 35, 83, 112, 146, 159, 183, 187, 213–215, 223, 225–227, 229–323, 226, 238–241, 244, 248–250, 252–254, 294,–295, 297, 308, 310, 312, 316–320
Temple Mount 252
Ten Commandments xi, 163–168, 172, 174, 184–185, 190–191, 197, 201, 304, 306
Ten Commandments (1956) 8–9, 63, 66
Tent of Meeting 6, 132, 215, 219, 227, 233, 246, 248, 285–286, 288, 291, 293
Tetragrammaton 31–32, 36–38, 40–46, 313, 322, 324
Thedoret of Cyrus 38, 325
Throne 87, 89, 94, 214, 225, 228, 233, 238, 240, 244, 294, 297

Torah 13, 15, 111, 145, 156, 162, 174, 176–177, 179, 183, 185–188, 242, 313
Transfiguration 5, 21, 269, 299
Tree of Life 149, 225
TULIP 52, 72, 74–75
Tyndale, William 236
Wadi Feiran 123–124
Washington, George 4
Wesley, John 80
Westminster Confession of Faith 190–191
Wilderness of Paran 290
Wilderness of Shur 105–106
Wilderness of Sin 106, 124–125
Wilderness of Zin 128
Wycliffe, John 235, 267
Xenophanes of Colophon 279
Yahweh 24, 32, 37–38, 41, 45–46, 203, 205, 263, 286, 288, 317
Yao 38–39
Zerubbabel 249
Zeus (Greek god) 23, 29, 278
Zipporah 18

SCRIPTURE INDEX

Genesis		12:7	11, 180	21:12	179
1	ix, xiii, xvi, 295	12:17	152	21:27	202
1–11	149, 153	14:13	202	21:32	202
1:26–27	149	15	206	22:11–18	281
2:7	180	15:5	179	22:13	264
2:15	225	15:6	179–180	22:18	151–152
2:24	180–181, 186	15:7	30	25:23	179
3	214	15:9–10	204	25:29–34	107
3:8–9	213	15:13–14	89	26:4	151–152
3:22–24	149	15:13–16	11	26:28	202
3:24	225, 237	15:16	66	26:28–31	201
5:1–2	149	15:18	206	28:3	30
6–9	234	16:7–13	281	28:14	151–152
6:5	149	17	202	30:27	152
6:8	278	17:1	30	31:44	202
8:20–21	204	17:5	179	31:44–54	201
8:21	149	18	127, 200, 278	32:24–32	279
9	202	18:8	200	35:11	30
9:6	149	18:10	179	39:2–3	153
9:20–27	150	18:14	179	39:21	153
11:4	150	18:17	200	39:23	153
12	140, 150	18:18	151–153, 180	41:57	153
12:1–2	150	18:19	150, 153	50:26	235
12:1–3	11, 305	19:1	200	**Exodus**	
12:3	151–153, 180	21:10	180	1:8	53

1–3	301	4:19–31	30	8:12–15	61
1:15–22	86	4:21	55, 57	8:15	55, 57, 61
1:22	7, 53	4:22	4, 143, 205	8:16–19	85
2	10, 18	4:23	67, 86	8:16–28	61
2:2	7, 16	4:24–26	24	8:18–19	61, 87
2:3	92, 234	4:29–31	52	8:19	56–57, 93
2:5	234	4:29	198	8:20	67
2:5–10	53	5	108	8:20–32	85
2:6	27	5:1	52, 67, 143	8:21–24	61
2:10	8	5:1–2	30	8:24	85
2:11	7, 10, 17	5:2	59–60, 149	8:25	68
2:11–12	11	5:3	30, 67	8:25–29	67
2:11–15	17	5:6–9	54	8:28	68
2:14	12, 17	5:22–23	30	8:32	56–57
2:15	12, 27, 53	6:1	30	9:1	67
2:15–22	18	6:2–3	30	9:1–7	61, 85
2:18	25	6:2–8	302	9:4	61, 87
2:21–22	24	6:3	31, 38	9:7	56–57
2:22	24	6:4–5	202	9:8–12	61, 85
2:23	53–54	6:20	7	9:11	61
2:24	202	7	85	9:12	56–57
3	4, 302	7:1–5	60–61	9:13	67
3–4	18	7:3	55, 57	9:13–35	62, 85
3:1	24–25	7:7	7, 24	9:14–16	63–64
3:2	26, 48, 281	7:8–13	61	9:16	149, 180
3:3	25	7:13	55, 57	9:17	64
3:7	143, 203	7:14	55, 57	9:20	93
3:12	25, 29, 67	7:14–24	85	9:26	62, 87
3:13	27	7:14–25	61	9:27	62
3:14–15	x, 27	7:16	67	9:27–28	62
3:14	24, 28–29, 313	7:22	55, 57	9:34	56–57, 64
		7:26–8:11	61	9:35	56–57
3:16	30, 198	8	xi	10:1	56–57
3:16–22	52	8:1	67	10:1–2	64
3:18	30, 67	8:1–15	85	10:1–20	62, 85
3:19–20	52–53	8:3	61	10:3	67
3:21–22	217	8:4	61	10:7–11	62, 67
4:18	25	8:8	67	10:8–11	68

10:16	62	12:37	91–92	16	103, 105, 110, 113, 117–119, 125, 163, 304
10:19	92	12:38	94		
10:20	56–57	12:39	95–96		
10:21–29	62, 85	12:40	89	16:1	25, 106–107
10:23	62, 85, 87	12:43–49	95	16:3	107, 125
10:24	62, 68	12:46	100	16:4	109, 111
10:24–28	67	13:4	88	16:4–5	111
10:27	56–57	13:7	95	16:6	110, 118, 304
11:1	87	13:8	95	16:7	110, 283
11:2–3	217	13:14–15	95	16:7–10	310
11:4–5	87	13:18	92	16:8	110, 118, 125
11:4–10	62	13:20	91		
11:7	87	13:21–22	282, 309	16:9–10	283, 309
11:8	87			16:10	110, 281
11:9–10	65	13:21	313	16:12	110
11:10	56–57	14	103	16:13	110
12	12, 95, 163, 303	14:2	92	16:14	110
		14:4	56–57	16:16	114
12–13	302	14:5	89	16:17–18	114
12:1–11	88	14:8	56–57	16:18	117, 180, 304
12:1–20	88	14:17	57		
12:12	86	14:17–18	65	16:19–21	118
12:12–13	62	14:19–20	282, 309	16:20	111, 115
12:13	88			16:25–26	114
12:14	88	14:21	94	16:23	113
12:15	95	14:21–22	12	16:27	111
12:17	95	14:24	94, 282	16:31	110
12:18	95	14:26–28	94	16:33–34	242, 283
12:19	95	15	85	16:35	110
12:21–28	89	15:1–18	106	17	123, 130–131, 137
12:22	88	15:1–21	94, 105		
12:23	12	15:2	106	17:1	124
12:26–27	95	15:4	92	17:1–7	104, 124, 304
12:27	95	15:22	105		
12:29–42	62	15:22–27	125	17:2	125
12:31	67	15:23–25	105	17:3	125
12:34	95–96	15:24	125	17:4	126
12:35–36	217	15:27	106	17:5–6	283

17:6 25, 126–127, 135	20–24 168	22:5 170
17:7 125, 127	20:1–19 197	22:5–15 168, 170
17:8–16 124	20:2 90, 203	22:6 170
17:8–17 198	20:4 291	22:7–8 170
18 124, 198	20:7 23, 40	22:9 170
18:1–12 25	20:8–11 113, 304	22:10–13 170
18:2–4 18	20:11 165	22:14–15 170
18:3 24	20:12 181, 185	22:16–17 168, 170
18:12 283	20:13–17 180	22:18 168, 170, 172
18:17–26 198	20:17 179	22:19 168, 171
19 105, 141–142, 305	20:18–21 163, 306	22:20 168, 171
	20:21 167, 169, 197, 284	22:21 171–172
19:1 67, 141	20:22–23 164	22:21–27 171
19:1–2 25, 124	20:22–23:33 167, 197	22:28 171
19:3 141		22:29–31 171
19:3–6 142	20:23 169	22:31 169, 171
19:5 202	20:24–26 169	23:1–3 169, 171
19:5–6 141, 203	21:2–11 168–169	23:4–6 171
19:6 154, 159, 206	21:12–14 169	23:6–8 171
	21:15 169	23:9 171
19:7 142	21:16 169	23:10–11 171
19:8 142	21:17 169	23:12 171
19:9 284	21:18–19 168–169, 172	23:13 171, 173
19:9–15 163		23:14–17 84, 171, 303
19:10 142	21:20–21 169	
19:11 25	21:22 169	23:15 311
19:16 142	21:22–25 168	23:18 169, 171
19:16–18 284	21:23–25 169	23:19 169, 171
19:16–19 163	21:26–27 169	23:20–22 284
19:18 25, 127, 142, 163, 262, 280	21:28–32 168–169, 172	23:20–23 48, 302
		23:23–33 171
	21:29 172	23:32 202
19:20 25	21:30 172	23:33 172
19:23 25	21:33–34 169	24 126, 154, 197–198, 200, 203–205, 212, 215, 307
19:25 163	21:35–36 169	
20 x, 165, 306	22:1–4 169	
20–23 168	22:3 169	

24:1 198, 200	25:21 166, 241	31:12–17 218
24:1–2 197	25:22 242, 244	31:16 202
24:3 198	25:23–30 217	31:18 25, 165–
24:3–4 167	25:30 112	166, 201, 218
24:4 199	25:31–40 217	32 xi, 164, 310
24:5 199, 203	25:40 227–228,	32–33 310
24:5–6 67	308	32–34 217
24:6 199	26 218	32:1 19
24:7 168, 198–199	26:1 224, 237	32:1–6 201, 260,
24:7–8 202	26:1–6 307	269
24:8 154, 197,	26:30 227, 308	32:6 180, 261
200, 204, 209	26:31–33 220	32:9 19
24:9–11 285	27:1–8 218	32:10 260
24:10 200	27:8 227, 308	32:14 260
24:10–11 126, 200	27:9–19 218	32:15 201, 263
24:11 211	27:18 220	32:19 260
24:12 165, 201,	27:20–21 218	32:34–35 285
215	28:1 154, 305	33:1–3 260, 286
24:12–13 201	28:1–6 218	33:3 19
24:13–14 198	28:6–14 218	33:5 19
24:14 201	28:15–30 218	33:6 25
24:16 25, 281	28:31–43 218	33:7–11 286, 309
24:16–18 215–	29:1–37 218	33:11 4, 12
216	29:12 210, 264	33:12–16 287
24:17 200, 262	29:15–21 307	33:12–17 260
24:18 167, 197,	29:19–21 154	33:14 279
201, 234, 261	29:20–21 204	33:17–23 287–288
25–31 201, 217,	29:38–46 218	33:18 260, 279
307	29:42–46 285	33:18–22 310
25–40 x	29:43 292, 310	33:19 26, 180
25:8 217–219	29:44–46 215	33:19–32 260
25:9 227, 308	30:1–10 218	33:20 12, 126, 200,
25:10 237	30:6 222	279
25:10–22 217, 234	30:7 223	33:20–23 282
25:16 166	30:11–16 218	33:22–23 126
25:16 214	30:17–21 216, 218	33:23 13, 200
25:17 235, 237	30:22–38 218	33:36–38 128
25:18 236–237	31:1–11 216–218	34 263, 269

34:1	166	39:22–31	218	16:12–13	222, 293
34:2	25	40:2	216	16:12–16	245–246
34:4	25	40:34–38	288–289, 293, 310	16:16	246, 248
34:5–7	26, 260			16:17	246
34:5–9	288	**Leviticus**		16:18–20	246
34:6	103	1–7	154	18:1–5	175
34:6–7	x, 261	1:5	199	18:5	180
34:9	19	1:9	98	18:6–8	186
34:10	202, 206, 260	1:11	199	19:17–18	177
34:12	202	1:15	199	19:18	180, 187, 189
34:14	26	3	199	20:11	186
34:15	202	3:2	199	23:4–8	95, 303
34:27	202	4	247	24:5–9	220
34:28	201–202, 261	4:6	247	24:16	40, 44
34:29	25, 262–264, 266–267	4:7	199, 210, 247	25:1	25
34:29–35	6, 259, 261, 269, 309	4:17	247	26:12	180
34:30	263–264	4:18	199, 247	26:41	183
34:32	25	4:25	199, 247	26:46	25
34:33	263	4:30	199, 247	27:34	25
34:34	263, 274	4:34	199		
34:34–35	263	5:9	199	**Numbers**	
34:35	264	7:38	25	1:1	25
35–40	217, 307	8:15	197, 199	1:19	25
36:8–38	218	8:23–24	204	2–3	215
37:1–9	217, 234	8:30	197	3:1	25
37:10–16	217	9:9	199	3:4	25
37:17–24	217	10:11	154	3:7–8	225
37:25–28	218	12	173, 197, 205	3:14	25
37:29	218	12:4	218	3:28	218
38:1–8	218	14	197, 205	4:5	222
38:9–20	218	14:1–20	205	4:7	223
39:1	218	14:7	205	4:11	223
39:2–7	218	14:14	204–205	7	216
39:8–21	218	16	99, 245, 308, 314	7:89	233
		16:2	244	8:4	227
		16:2–3	223		

SCRIPTURE INDEX / 341

9:1	25	20:10–13	129–130	4:25	291
9:5	25			4:33	280
9:15–23	289–290	20:24	130	4:36	280
10:11	141	21	131	5	165, 306
10:11–12	109	21:5	129	5:4	280
10:11–13	290	21:5–6	109	5:8	291
10:12	25	21:6	129	5:12–15	113
10:29	25	21:8	129	5:15	165
10:33	242	21:9	5	5:16	181, 185
10:34	290	21:16–18	131	5:17–21	180
10:35–36	244–245	21:16–20	132	5:21	179
11	198	21:17–18	132	5:22	165
11:4–5	125	22	147	5:22–26	280
11:5	108, 129	26:64	25	5:23–27	163
11:6	109	27:12–14	130	6:4	45
11:7–9	110	28:6	25	6:4–9	15, 313
11:10	109, 125	28:16–25	95	6:16	128
11:16–17	198	33:3	67, 107	6:22	86
11:20	109	33:4	86	6:20–25	178
11:25	290	33:15	25	7:2	202
11:31–32	110	33:16	25	7:6–9	139
11:33	109			7:18	60
12:5	290	**Deuteronomy**		8:3	112
12:5–8	4	1:2	25, 129	8:10	112
12:8	291	1:6	25	8:15	123, 127, 135–136
14:2–3	129	1:9–18	198		
14:4	129	1:19	25	8:16	112
14:14	291	2:30	66	9:3	280
14:44	243	4:5–6	156	9:4	180
16:5	46, 181	4:6	175–176	9:4–6	139
16:13	108, 129	4:9–13	164	9:6	140
16:42	291	4:10	25	9:8	25
17:1–11	242	4:12	280, 291	9:10	166
20	128, 130, 135	4:13	201	10:2	166, 241
20:1	128	4:15	25, 280, 291	10:4	201
20:1–13	305	4:16	291	10:5	166
20:4–5	129	4:23	291	10:14–16	139
20:8	130	4:24	280	10:16	19, 183

12:5	183, 215	33:8	130	7:14	46
16:1–8	95, 303	33:10	154	22:3	264
16:6	83	34:7	7	22:10	278
16:9–12	311				
16:16	84	**Joshua**		**1 Kings**	
17:7	180, 186	2:9–11	60	1:25	201
18	209	2:10	90	6:23	240
18:15	19, 206	2:18	137	8	250
18:16	25	3:13	245	8:4	227
18:18	118	4:23	90	8:8	251
18:18–19	207	5:12	110	8:9	25, 166, 241
19:15	180	6	243	8:10–11	294, 310
21:23	180	9:11–15	201	8:27	15
22:6	177	18:1	225	8:41–43	146–147
22:8	177	24:15	77	12:28	261
25:4	180–181, 186			14:25–27	251
		Judges		17:4–6	109
27:26	180	4:11	25	18:31–32	199
29:1	25	5:5	25	19:8	25
29:4	180	6	26		
30:12–14	180			**2 Kings**	
30:15–20	174–175	**Ruth**		12:9–10	235
		4:11–12	151	24:13	252
30:19	77			25	252
32	136	**1 Samuel**		25:9	294
32:4	136	4	226, 243	25:13–17	252
32:13	136	4:3–4	245		
32:15	136	4:4	239	**1 Chronicles**	
32:17	136	4:8	60	16:39	226
32:18	136	6	226	17	36
32:21	136, 180			21:29	226
32:30	136	**2 Samuel**		28:2	239
32:31	136	3:20–21	201	28:19	228
32:35	180	6	226, 250	1:1–5	226
32:37	136	6:2	239	5:10	25, 241
32:43	180	6:17	226, 250	24:6	227
32:50–51	130	7	36	29:3–7	227
33:2	25	7:6	226	36:10	252

Scripture Index / 343

36:18	252	78:43	90	10:22–23	46
		78:43–51	62	11:1	145
Ezra		81:7	130	11:10	145
1:1–4	312	81:11	90	11:16	90
1:7–11	252	83:18	38	12:2	38, 106
6:13–15	312	94:11	46	13–23	148
6:14–15	249	95:8–11	128	19:19	145, 148
6:14–16	294	99:1	240	25:6–8	145
		99:5	240	26:4	38
Nehemiah		104:2	262	40:3	47
9:10	86	104:4	26	40:13	46
9:13	25	105:23–38	90	42:6	148
9:15	127	105:24–38	86	43:15–19	207
9:20	112	105:27–36	62	45:22	47
		105:41	103	45:22–23	145
Esther		106:7	90	45:23	46
5:4	32	106:19	25, 261	48:21	127
		106:32	130	49:6	148
Job		114	90	53:7	211
4:16	291	114:8	127	53:12	211
		117:1	46	56	145
Psalms		119	176–177	59:17	278
1:2	176	132:7–8	239	59:20–21	69
17:15	291	147:19–20	176	60:11	145
19:7–11	176	150	161	66	16
22:21	264	150:3	161	66:1	214, 240
24:1	46			66:1–2	14
32:1–2	46	**Song of Songs**		66:19–23	145
33:6	295	**(Solomon)**			
57:11	281	8:6	32	**Jeremiah**	
67:2–3	147			1:6	26
68:8	25	**Isaiah**		2:6	91
68:17	25	1:4	40	3:16	252
78	62	1:9	46	4:4	184
78:12	90	2:2–4	144–145	6:10	19
78:20	127	6:2–5	297	7:12–15	14, 226
78:24	112, 118	6:5	26	7:22	91
78:24–25	103	6:9–10	296–297	7:25	91

9:24	46	**Hosea**		**Malachi**	
9:25–26	184	2:14–15	207	2:6–7	154
11:4	91	2:17	90	4:4	25
11:7	91	4:1–9	154		
16:14–15	91	11:1	4, 90	**Matthew**	
18:6	278	12:9	90	1:23	ix
18:18	154	12:13	90	4:4	117
23:5–8	207–208	13:4	91	5	173
23:7	91			5:14–16	153
31	210	**Joel**		5:16	141
31:31	210	2:13	261	5:17	ix
31:31–34	271	2:32	46	5:21–48	186
31:32	91	3:10	148	6:11	117
32:20–21	86, 91			8:4	5
34:13	91	**Amos**		14:13–21	117
46–51	148	2:10	90	15:32–39	117
52:17–23	252	3:1	90	17:1–8	269
		6:13	265	17:2	299
Lamentations		9:7	90, 147	17:3	5
2:1	254			17:3–4	5
		Jonah		19:7–8	5
Ezekiel		1:16	147	22:24	5
1:1	291–292	2:5	92	23:2	5
1:4–11	236	3:5–10	147	23:15	158
1:27–28	262, 292	4:2	261	24:2	14
8	248			26:28	209
8–11	248	**Micah**		26:61	14
10	15, 248	4:1–3	144–145	27:26	210
11:22–23	248	6:4	90	28:19	141
20:5–10	90	7:15	90, 207		
25–32	148			**Mark**	
28:14–16	237	**Haggai**		1:44	5
33:11	77	2:5	90	2:23–3:6	113
40–48	254			6:30–44	117
40:5–13	267	**Zechariah**		7	181
44:3	201	2:10–12	146	7:10	5
47:1–2	230	8:21–23	146	7:19	183
		14:7–8	230	8:1–10	117

8:15	99	13:15	47	6:22–59	304
9:2–8	269	16:29	5	6:23	47
9:4–5	5	16:31	5	6:31	112, 118
9:7	21	17:5–6	47	6:32	5
10:3–4	5	18:6	47	6:35	119
11:1–11	96	18:19–20	166–167	6:44	76
12:12	96	18:21	173	6:49	118
12:19	5	19:8	47	6:54	119
12:26	5	20:28	5	7:18	296
14	303	20:37	5	7:19	5
14:12–15	101	22:1	83	7:22–23	5
14:22–25	102, 307	22:20	209	7:37–38	230
14:24	209	22:61	47	7:40	118, 208
14:26	85	24:3	47	8:5	5
14:58	14	24:27	ix, 5	8:50	296
15:15	210	24:44	5	8:54	296
				8:58	302
Luke		**John**		8:58–59	47
1:6	173	1:1–18	310	9:24	296
1:52–53	94	1:9	296	9:28–29	5
2:22	5	1:14	229, 296	11:2	47
4:4	117	1:17	5	11:55	96
4:21	ix	1:18	296	12:1	96
5:14	5	1:19–21	208	12:12–16	96
7:13	47	1:29	303	12:39–41	296
7:19	47	1:45	5	13:1	96
9:10–17	117	2:13–17	229	13:2	101
9:23	120	2:19	14, 230	14:3	214
9:28–36	269	2:21	14, 230, 308	15:16	76
9:30	5	3:14	5	18:6	47
9:32	299	3:16	78	18:28	96
9:33	5	4:14	136	19:1	210
10:1	47	4:24	126	19:16–37	303
10:39	47	5:44	296	19:31	96
10:41	47	5:45–46	5	19:32–36	100
11:3	117	5:46	4	19:34	210
11:39	47	6:1–15	117	20:20	47
12:42	47	6:14	118, 208		

Acts		15	181	5:13	188
2:38	77–78	15:1	5, 15	5:14	5
3:22	5	15:5	5	5:20	188
3:22–23	19, 208	15:21	5	6:14	162, 188
6	13	16:3	182	7:5	188
6:5	13	17:28	29, 77	7:6–8:4	272
6:9	13	20:28	210	7:7	179
6:11	5, 13	21:8	13	7:9–13	188
6:13	13–14	21:21	5	7:12	162
6:14	5, 13	21:26	15	7:14	162
7	6, 15	22:1–21	298	8:3–4	188
7:17–44	301	22:6–9	298	8:4	188
7:20	5, 7, 16	22:11	298	8:28–30	71
7:22	5	22:20	210	9	69
7:23	7, 17	26:1–23	298	9–11	69, 162
7:23–29	17	26:13	298	9:6	70
7:25	17	26:22	5	9:7	179
7:27–28	17	28:23	5	9:9	179
7:29	5			9:12	179
7:30	18, 25	**Romans**		9:14–18	68
7:31–32	5	2:26–29	183	9:15	5, 180
7:35	5, 18–19	3:1–2	157–158,	9:17	180
7:37	5, 19, 208		179	9:27–29	46
7:38	19–20, 25	3:20	188	10:5	5, 180
7:39	19	3:21–26	254–255	10:6	180
7:39–41	261	3:25	100, 210, 248,	10:6–8	180
7:40	5		255, 308	10:13	46
7:40–41	19	4	6, 81, 181	10:17	81
7:44	5, 228	4:3	179	10:19	5, 180
7:44–50	16	4:7–8	46	11:7	69
7:49–50	14	4:9	179	11:8	180
7:53	20	4:9–12	184	11:11	70
8	13	4:15	188	11:26	69
9:3–4	298	4:17	179	11:33	69
9:8	298	4:18	179	11:34	46
11:2–3	15	4:22	179	12:1	159
13:29	5	5:9	210	12:1–2	184
13:48	76	5:12	149	12:19	180

13:9	180, 187	10:11	136, 187	3:6	180
13:10	306	10:20	136	3:8	180
14:1–6	183	10:22	136	3:10	180
14:11	46	10:26	46	3:12	180
14:14	182	11:25	209	3:13	180
14:14–18	183	11:26	211	3:16	152, 180
14:23	182	14:34	185	3:19	20
15:4	ix	15:10	51	3:19–22	188
15:10	180	15:45	180	3:19–26	306
15:11	46			3:23–26	188, 194
15:16	184	**2 Corinthians**		3:29	152
		3	270	4:24–25	25
1 Corinthians		3:1–3	271	4:30	180
1:31	46	3:3	271	5:1	187
2:16	46	3:4–6	271	5:1–4	162
3:17	231	3:6	271	5:2	181
3:20	46	3:7	272–273	5:4	182
4:7	81	3:7–11	271, 309	5:13–14	189
5	186	3:7–18	6, 21	5:14	180, 187
5:7	98	3:11	272	5:19–21	187
5:13	180, 186	3:12–18	273, 309	5:22–26	187
6:15–17	186	3:13	5, 272–273	6:2	187
6:16	180, 186	3:14	272		
6:18–19	231	3:15	5	**Ephesians**	
7:19	162	3:16	274	1:3–5	71
8:5–6	45	3:18	274, 300	1:7	210
8:15	117	4:4–6	299	1:11–12	71
9:9	5, 180, 186	5:20	141	2:13	210
9:20	182	6:16	180	2:19–22	231
10	187	6:18	46	2:21–22	308
10:1	136, 187	8:15	180, 304	5:2	98
10:1–4	135	10:17	46	6:1–3	162, 185
10:1–11	102	11:5	270		
10:1–13	305	13:1	180	**Philippians**	
10:2	5–6			2:3–5	105
10:4	305	**Galatians**		2:9	46, 302
10:6	136	2:3	182	2:10–11	47
10:7	180, 261	3	6, 152	3:2–8	184

3:20–21	300	5:3	99	12:29	280
		7:14	5	13:12	210
Colossians		7:27	98	13:15	159, 184
1:20	210	8:1–6	308	13:20	210, 212
2:11–12	184	8:5	5, 228		
2:16	183	8:11	55	**1 Peter**	
2:17	190	8:15	56	1:1	72
		8:28	56	1:2	211–212
2 Thessalonians		9:1–5	221	1:19	211
2:11–12	66	9:3–4	240–241	2:4–5	231
		9:3–5	254	2:4–9	306
1 Timothy		9:4	166, 221	2:5	159
1:13	51	9:6–12	99	2:5–9	141
1:15	51	9:7	223	2:9	159
2:4	65, 78–79, 303	9:12	210		
		9:14	210	**2 Peter**	
4:3	183	9:18–22	195	3:16	270
		9:19	5		
2 Timothy		9:22	196–197	**1 John**	
2:19	46	9:23–24	228	1:5	262
3:8	5–6	9:26	98	1:7	210, 255
3:16	194, 306	10:12	98	4:8	78, 213
		10:19	210		
Titus		10:28	5	**Jude**	
1:1	72	10:29	210, 212	9	5
		11	6–7, 16		
Hebrews		11:23	7, 12	**Revelation**	
1:3–4	23	11:23–24	5	1:5	210
1:7	26	11:23–29	6, 301	2:17	117
2:2	20	11:24–25	9–10	5:9	211
3:1–6	21	11:26	11	11:19	254, 309
3:2–3	5	11:27	11–12	15:3	5
3:5	5	12:2	13	21:3	214
3:16	5	12:21	5	21:22	232
4	128	12:24	210, 212		

www.ingramcontent.com/pod-product-compliance
Lightning Source LLC
Chambersburg PA
CBHW020350080526
44584CB00014B/965